THE RISE
— OF THE —
MATILDAS

Inside the Women's World Cup Campaign

FIONA CRAWFORD

MELBOURNE
UNIVERSITY
PRESS

Melbourne University Publishing acknowledges the traditional owners of the unceded land on which we work, learn and live: the Wurundjeri Woiwurrung peoples of the Kulin Nation. We pay respect to elders past, present and future, and acknowledge the importance of Indigenous knowledge.

MELBOURNE UNIVERSITY PRESS
An imprint of Melbourne University Publishing Limited
Level 1, 715 Swanston Street, Carlton, Victoria 3053, Australia
mup-contact@unimelb.edu.au
www.mup.com.au

First published 2024
Text © Fiona Crawford, 2024
Design and typography © Melbourne University Publishing Limited, 2024

This book is copyright. Apart from any use permitted under the *Copyright Act 1968* and subsequent amendments, no part may be reproduced, stored in a retrieval system or transmitted by any means or process whatsoever without the prior written permission of the publishers.

Every attempt has been made to locate the copyright holders for material quoted in this book. Any person or organisation that may have been overlooked or misattributed may contact the publisher.

Cover design by Philip Campbell Design
Typeset by Sonya Murphy, Adala Studio
Cover image by Rachel Bach/By the White Line
Printed in Australia by McPherson's Printing Group

A catalogue record for this book is available from the National Library of Australia

9780522880779 (paperback)
9780522880786 (ebook)

MIX
Paper | Supporting responsible forestry
FSC® C001695

For the girls and women who didn't get to play football or who did so against the odds, and the girls and women who will never know a time when they didn't get to play football

That is one of the main reasons for my writing: to prevent the erosion of time, so that memories will not be blown by the wind.

– Isabel Allende

CONTENTS

KEY TERMS, ACRONYMS AND INITIALISMS

A-League Men's	Australian men's football league 2021/22–present
A-League Women's	Australian women's football league 2021/22–present
AFC	Asian Football Confederation
AFL	Australian Football League (Australian Rules)
AIS	Australian Institute of Sport
FIFA	Fédération Internationale de Football Association
FIFPRO	Fédération Internationale des Associations de Footballeurs Professionnels
Football Ferns	New Zealand national women's football team
IWD	International Women's Day
Matildas	Australian national women's football team
MCG	Melbourne Cricket Ground
NRL	National Rugby League (Australia)
NWSL	National Women's Soccer League (US women's football league 2012–present)

PFA	Professional Footballers Australia
Soccer Australia	Australia's governing body 1995–2003/04
Socceroos	Australian national men's football team
State of Origin	rugby league competition between Queensland and New South Wales
USWNT	US Women's National Team
VAR	video assistant referee
W-League	Australian women's football league 2008–2021
WSL	Women's Super League (English women's football league 2010–present)

PREFACE

LAUNCHING BACKWARDS INTO the water, locking his hands into a 'V' and breathlessly propelling himself with an underwater dolphin kick, in the 1980s Harvard swimmer David Berkoff pioneered the 'Berkoff Blastoff' backstroke technique.[1]

Through the technique, which minimises drag, Berkoff avoided expending energy splashing on the surface trying to compete with taller, stronger swimmers. Breath held, heart pounding in his ears, crowd and swimmer noise muffled through the water refractions, he quietly focused on his dolphin kick before surfacing body lengths ahead of his competitors. In doing so, he reimagined backstroke, gave himself a competitive advantage, and forever changed the sport.

What the Matildas and the 2023 Women's World Cup organisers achieved is equivalent to the game-changing Berkoff Blastoff. Playing the long game and overcoming decades of underfunding, indifference, omission and inertia, they immersed themselves in their development work and processes, held their breath, blocked out background noise and concentrated on their drag-minimising technique before emerging body lengths ahead.

From the longest penalty shootout in World Cup history to the most-watched television event since Australian records began, the 2023 Women's World Cup was as transformative as it was gripping. Across the tournament and beyond, each match, each match result and each viewership eclipsed the previous, with sell-out crowd being surpassed by sell-out crowd, and sold-out jerseys demonstrating clamouring, unabating feverish goodwill and interest.

It was the tournament's ninth official iteration, but its sophistication and impact leapfrogged that innocuous single digit. By its end, it would record firsts beyond the ones that had long been touted: the first time there were thirty-two teams (up from twenty-four), and the first time it was co-hosted in the Southern Hemisphere and by representatives of two different confederations. The tournament's contribution was so watershed that advertising and media purveyor B&T would later put it in the same culturally significant category as September 11, Princess Diana's death, and the #MeToo movement.[2] Indeed, through its prodigious lighthouse efforts that comprehensively fulfilled the tournament aspiration of going 'beyond greatness', the team not only reshaped how women's sport can be done but left an indelible imprint on football and the wider sporting, social and cultural landscape.

But while it's clear the Matildas and the Women's World Cup have already had significant social, cultural and sporting impacts, we are at the early stages of understanding that influence. So much happened, with such intensity and across so many planes and platforms, that we haven't yet woven the independently and collectively important fragments into a cohesive, depth-filled narrative. Likewise, such was the volume and attendant inability for us to process and catalogue the events of July and August 2023 in the moment that even now, a little more than a year on at the time of writing, the remarkable event is becoming a highlights reel—that penalty shootout, that Sam Kerr goal—which does not do justice to the tournament's or the team's seismic influence. (For example, no one—and I mean no one—interviewed for this book in any way referenced the Denmark game. Sorry, Denmark.)

That's relevant not just because the stories are enthralling as we seek, against bleak world events, escapism and something to celebrate, but because we know from past experience that women's stories are not traditionally valued; their history is often not well preserved. We also know that without documenting or analysing said stories, we can't learn from or build on them. And we most definitely need to learn from and build on the transformative events of, and the Matilda Effect stemming from, July and August 2023.

So this book is a bid to document a small segment of the ephemeral details—some big, some small, some comprehensive, some fragmented and fleeting, all contributing to the bricolage of history—of the what and when and who and how of that sport- and society-shifting time before they disappear into the ether or are consolidated through the accordion of memory. It's one person's humble effort to lay down a broad-brush foundation that will hopefully soon be built on by many others.

It is, in the paraphrased words of Isabel Allende, an initial, imperfect attempt to write what should not be forgotten.[3]

1

INTRODUCTION: SOMETHING'S SHIFTED

A WEEK BEFORE THE 2023 FIFA Women's World Cup kicked off in capital cities around Australia and Aotearoa New Zealand, vibrant orange and pink tournament branding appeared overnight at key locations, adorning everything from temporary football pitches to baggage carousels to freeway lampposts.

Individual athlete sponsors concurrently unfurled their own campaigns. Apparel and activewear company adidas opted to go big, literally, by wrapping skyscraper-sized action shots of sponsored players Mary Fowler and Caitlin Foord around central business district buildings. The giant images were something of a surprise to the general public generally and the women's football fanbase specifically—neither was used to sponsors playing such a gambit around the women's game.

The images were also a surprise to the photographer who took them. 'I thought I was just coming in to shoot Rachel Daly, who is one of the Lionesses,' UK-based Madeleine Penfold says, elaborating on how a polite one-time conversation turned into her being invited to shoot first one player, then tens more: 'Before I knew it, they'd booked me to photograph maybe thirty female athletes who were taking part in the World Cup.'

Penfold started her photography career in the men's-football space, aged twenty-three. Photographing footballers was a thrilling work opportunity, but apart from the fact that she was often the only woman in the room, something was missing. *Where are the women footballers*? Penfold wondered. She also quickly noticed that the resourcing and energy expended in providing professional coverage were skewed towards the men. Throwing in much of her own time, energy and resourcing, Penfold set about trying to rectify that, shooting girls and women from the elite to the grassroots and thereby raising both the quantity and quality of coverage. As she put it, 'My whole thing was if I can just do a little bit now to shift it, and try and do everything I can so that this younger generation of girls can see these female athletes who are outstanding, then that's worth putting everything I have into it.'

Seeing the adidas skyscraper images in Sydney in real life was a slightly incomprehensible moment for Penfold. She actually first saw them second-hand. 'After that campaign was shot and done, that was kind of it,' she says of the adidas shoot. As is characteristic of photography gigs, she delivered the images and turned her attention to the next job. Fast forward to July 2023, when Penfold arrived in Sydney a few days in to the tournament. She had taken a small detour to shoot for *National Geographic*, a job too good to turn down. In the interim, she followed her friends' adventures via social media. 'I see on one friend's story they're on this motorway flyover, and they're going past this billboard. And I'm like, *Oh my god. That's my picture*,' Penfold explains. 'I messaged them—and I never get too excited [about where my work appears]—and was like, "Oh my god. That's my pic." They were like, "This is your picture?! We can't believe it! This is the iconic image that is pride of place in Sydney right now!"'

Towards the end of the Women's World Cup, Penfold finally made it down to see the image in person and at scale. She posted a meta moment of her seeing it, her in the foreground, the storeys-high image towering in the background. That moment was special—in fact, the entire tournament was like stepping into 'a real-life immersive exhibition of why you do what you do and what you love,' she says.

> Because, to go back to why I was doing what I was doing, and what I was working towards, this was exactly it. I wanted to see female footballers—because they're *so* incredible at what they do—projected and displayed in a way that captures even a glimpse of how amazing they are so everyone can see it. I remember looking at it and being like, *God, I really set out to do this. This was my intention seven years ago, and it's taken that long to get here. But we're here, and what an amazing journey it's been, for me and for them* … It was just like, *Yeah, we're here, we're here.*

★ ★ ★

Further west from Penfold's images, halfway between the CBD and Sydney's premier tournament venue, Stadium Australia, seven long-time Matildas fans set about staging some experiential, tournament-hyping events. Part of a loosely assembled group they call the Croissants, the women commenced by hanging a giant ''Til It's Done' banner outside a cafe operated by one of their number. The poster, which had vertically stacked text, referenced the campaign Football Australia had launched leading into the tournament. People soon stood examining the poster, trying to decipher its meaning. 'We probably had maybe a dozen people on the first day being, like, "What is that banner?" and standing there reading this thing going: "What is Ma/Til/Das?" By the end of [the tournament], we had people being, like, "Why aren't you showing the games?"' the Croissants laugh.

The Croissants opened the Australian leg of the tournament in their trusty Steve Irwin costumes—the iconic khaki King Gees made famous by the crocodile hunter, and platinum-blonde wigs. Prior to the tournament, they had donated one of those iconic costumes to the FIFA Museum. The Croissants had received an email request from the museum's Switzerland-based curator. 'We all thought it was a joke. We were just, like, "This cannot be real." I've been to the museum … It's got the best-of-the-best relics in there—and they say they want one of these dirty Steve things that we've Sharpied on, and this crocodile that we dragged through the streets of France. We were like, "There is no chance they'd want to display this",' Croissant Lucy Gilfedder explains. Actually, yes chance. 'We ended up sending [the costume] to Switzerland. Then it came back to Australia [for the tournament], and we didn't know it was going to be here.' FIFA set up a pop-up museum next to Sydney Harbour for the tournament, but it took the Croissants a while to make it there to see their artefacts in person.[1] They headed down one night after their own football training. It was winter, the queue to enter the museum was massive, and the Croissants' sweaty post-training discomfort was starting to kick in. The irreverent women remembered they had the curator's phone number and thought, *Why not try it?* He answered and not only allowed them to jump the queue but provided them with a VIP tour.

Months before that museum moment, the Croissants were planning their opening-match event and outfits. 'I had this vision of a sea of Steves,' Croissant and primary costume designer Gilfedder says, explaining that the Croissants wanted to host an opening-match party where they would gift 100 or more people khaki shirts and wigs and then converge on the stadium for the Matildas game. The problem was that procuring the khaki shirts in bulk was prohibitively expensive. 'I could not work out for the life of me how to do it [affordably]. I explored all my options, sent countless emails ...' Then one of the Croissants, Maddy Bart, mentioned that her mum knew someone who knew Terri Irwin. Gilfedder explains:

> I said, 'What?! Why have you not brought this to my attention?' She goes, 'No, don't use that contact.' I said, 'Give me that number.' So we got on to Terri Irwin, and she was so goddamn lovely—everything we expected, pretty much—and she loved the idea.

Irwin provided the Croissants with 100 khaki shirts from Australia Zoo and the Croissants put on pizzas and bestowed wigs and shirts on their guests. (They invited Irwin to the party, but she couldn't attend because she had a crocodile seminar on, and it was also her birthday.) 'We didn't know whether people would get into it or whether it'd be weird, standoffish,' the Croissants explain of the outfit distribution.

It was a non-issue. 'We had 100 outfits and probably about 120 people coming. They were fighting over those wigs and shirts.'

The Croissants had hired two buses to transport everyone to the game. 'Watching Steves from probably twelve years old—our youngest—to Bob at ninety-one in his wig and khaki shirt climbing onto this bus to get out to Homebush to support the Tillies [Matildas] was the most incredible thing ever,' they explain. Mission accomplished. A sea of Steves converged on Stadium Australia to see the team take on Ireland in the Matildas' 2023 Women's World Cup opening match.

* * *

The Tuesday before the Matildas' sold-out pre-tournament France friendly, and weeks before we'd see fans packed shoulder to shoulder in Naarm/Melbourne's Federation Square breathlessly following a history-making semi-final and busting out of their skins celebrating a Sam Kerr goal, 3500 people packed into that public space for an event of a different kind.

It was standing room only in a crowd awash with green and yellow scarves, beanies and jerseys seemingly impervious to the wintry conditions and the exposed landscape. Young girls held aloft handcrafted decorated signs indicative of what we were to see throughout the tournament, thrusting the signs forward in an effort to signal their fandom and to gain players' attention. One young fan, sporting a cast, had a sign that explained she'd broken her wrist trying to be a Matilda.

Then, in front of fellow fans pressing against the barricades separating them from the team that would represent the country on home soil, twenty-three girls of various ages made their way onto the stage one by one. All named Matilda, they were there to play a role in an intergenerational presentation ceremony where girls named Matilda presented jerseys to the 2023 Women's World Cup Matildas squad.

The namesake presentation was the brainchild of a Football Australia marketing-and-communications team that included marketing manager Arith Ranasinghe and media and public relations manager Ann Odong. (The latter is a longstanding women's football advocate who has been quietly providing coverage for the team for close to twenty years, as well as mentoring the next generation of women's football media; Danielle Warby, a fellow great of preserving the history of the game, describes Odong as 'the Yoda of women's football in Australia' in our interview.)

Ranasinghe, Odong and their colleagues had consulted with senior Matildas players late in 2022 as they set about developing and articulating a comprehensive 2023 Women's World Cup communications and public relations plan. They asked the players what they wanted the world to know about the team by 21 August 2023, the day after the tournament's completion. Synthesised, the team's goals were to leave a legacy, to unite the nation, and to transform how women and girls see their participation in the game and in sport. It was through the second pillar—unite the nation—that Odong and her peers felt the team could connect strongly with its fans. Enter the Matildas for the Matildas jersey presentation.

Having been steadily increasing in popularity for some years, the name 'Matilda', whose Germanic original meaning is the appropriate 'mighty in battle', was ranked the seventh most popular girl's baby name in Australia for 2023.[2] Whether or not Ranasinghe was aware of that growing popularity and, therefore, population when he initially floated the concept of reaching out to grassroots generations of Matildas is unclear, but the concept was well received and Football Australia ran a competition to seek out said-named Matildas. The barrier to entry was low: tell us why you love the Matildas in twenty-five words or less. By design, that competition criterion, which invited heartfelt entries, helped the team determine which participants would find being involved really meaningful.

The Matilda namesakes selected to present the jerseys to their heroes in front of thousands of eager fellow fans were certainly chuffed, and in some cases even a little bit teary, as they entered stage right, jersey in hand. The relevant fan-Matilda and player-Matilda then stood together facing the crowd, each holding one side of the jersey and bridging fan–athlete, current–future-generation divides.

★ ★ ★

On the first match day of the Women's World Cup, and for the Matildas, hundreds of women aged between approximately thirty and sixty converged on Sydney's Central Station. From a demographic that doesn't normally take up space or garner enormous amounts of attention, the women, clad in green hoodies and wearing an assemblage of matching green-and-gold beanies and scarves, took over the escalators, lifts and train platforms.

They may not have known who the women were, but members of the general public navigating that transport hub certainly noticed the group moving with purpose. Slowing down from their hurried commutes, they instinctively paused to pay attention and make way for the women traversing the concourse.

Some of the women in that collective knew each other well. Others knew each other only by name or reputation. But, united by a common thread of having helped build the foundations of women's football in Australia, the women, all former Matildas, moved as one towards the designated train platform and then piled onto the awaiting Stadium Australia–bound train.

★ ★ ★

Less than twenty-eight days later, hurtling through the air, unusually punctuating that space–time continuum that is international travel, everyone aboard an Emirates flight had their in-flight entertainment tuned to a single live-streamed channel. Well, everyone except one person, who was watching *The Lord of the Rings*.

At the ground, everyone in the at-capacity Brisbane Stadium, as well as millions of people outside it crowded around screens in homes and at public venues, was laser-focused on the twenty-two on-pitch players steeling themselves for what became the longest penalty shootout in World Cup history—women's or men's.

That match and its tense, definitive, nation-stopping moments were as gripping, seismic and culturally unifying as another unforgettable sporting moment: Cathy Freeman's winning 400-metre run at the 2000 Sydney Olympics. The match's 120 minutes of deadlocked, end-to-end football and twenty excruciating penalties imprinted on the entire nation a collective where-were-you experience.

2

100 DAYS, 25 DAYS, 20 PENALTIES

THROUGHOUT THE 2023 Women's World Cup, which had and continues to have an outsized effect for its modest investment, big moments were surpassed by bigger moments; records set one day were blown away by successively more impressive records the next. Indeed, the sensation that was the 2023 tournament not only made history, it nudged—if not seriously rotated—the dial to advance women's sport and gender equality.

But 100 days before the tournament started, that success was not guaranteed, and relationships with the women who had established the foundations of the Australian national women's football team were even a little shaky.

Australia and Aotearoa New Zealand had been named tournament co-hosts during the depths of COVID lockdowns, a bleak time when football had been halted worldwide. Securing the 2023 Women's World Cup hosting rights, and the funding influx accompanying them, helped Football Australia 'keep the lights on' after having had to stand down 70 per cent of its workforce.[1]

Throwing all its weight behind the Women's World Cup campaign, Football Australia shifted its business model to lead with the Matildas.[2] With the benefit of hindsight, and with players, match tickets and merchandise continuing to be in high demand, it's now easy to say it was the right decision. But at the time it could have been written off as too commercially risky, not least by the 'No one watches women's sports' camp.

Despite Football Australia's forefronting of women's football, the tournament's 100-days-to-go countdown celebrations were noticeably absent Matildas Alumni,[3] the women on whose shoulders contemporary Australian women's football was standing. 'Nobody knew,' former Matilda Renaye Iserief says. 'I came home from work and sat down for dinner, and here's all the celebrations and the release of the chant [on the news]. I'm like, *Isn't this stuff that we should be included in?*' It was especially piercing because, as former Matilda Janine McPhee explains, the alumni had completed a questionnaire nominating when and how they could make themselves available for such events.

The alumni were still also awaiting match-ticket allocations. They'd been told the tickets were coming, but the allocations were taking so long that many alumni, understandably nervous about missing out, had purchased tickets and booked their accommodation individually. (Iserief, who would go on to forge such an integral facilitation role that she would be nicknamed the Alumni CEO and bestowed with spoof business cards, equates the feeling of seeking tickets to the Golden Ticket hunt in *Willy Wonka & the Chocolate Factory*.)

The alumni felt blindsided, undervalued, excluded.

At the time, the national body would have been incredibly busy with its legacy program and wider team tournament preparation. No doubt it was intending to get to the alumni inclusion once some of the more urgent external elements had been bedded down, but the signal its radio silence sent, however unintentional, was wounding.

The exclusion came to light after journalist Tracey Holmes asked questions about the alumni's absence from the 100-days-to-go media event. She knew that at least one former Matilda was supposed to be there but was a last-minute scratching due to food poisoning. The only other former Matilda was Sarah Walsh, but her attendance was assured through her capacity overseeing Football Australia's women's football and tournament legacy program.

Contacting a few alumni, Holmes received the same answer from all: they hadn't known about it, hadn't been invited. As Holmes puts it, Iserief's response was 'No, we never knew about it—because of course we would have made every effort to get there.'

Holmes leveraged her media skills and platform to draw attention to the omission. Unsurprisingly, the information she uncovered garnered concern. Was this a blip, or was it indicative of how the long-term omission and devaluing of women footballers' contributions would continue throughout Australia's co-hosting of the largest women's sporting event in the world? Fortunately, it proved the former. Football Australia stepped up to ensure former players were appropriately involved. (It's worth noting that Holmes not only gave Football Australia the opportunity to correct the issue, but fairly credited them once they had. 'I think what I've always tried to do is not be critical without there being an avenue for something to be made better' is how she explains her approach.)

With the inclusion misstep starting to be addressed, Football Australia could return its focus to preparing the current Matildas for the tournament itself.

The lead-up to the tournament had involved an audacious plan: have the Matildas play more Top 10 teams, and specifically more European ones. Analysis had shown that the Matildas were comfortable with Asian teams' playing styles. (Geographical proximity and a budget that barely stretched for flights to Asia had fostered that familiarity.) The team invariably came up, and unstuck, against European teams in major competitions such as the Women's World Cup. Sweden, as would be relevant in the 2023 tournament, had bundled the Matildas out of the 2011 iteration; Norway had done the same on penalties in 2019.

More pressing was that European nations had invested heavily in football in recent years, evidenced by the Netherlands' remarkable 2017 Euros win and 2019 Women's World Cup runners-up finish, not to mention the undoing the Dutch had delivered the Matildas in a pre-2019 tournament friendly. England, too, was investing heavily in its Women's Super League (WSL), attracting talent including Australia's Sam Kerr and Steph Catley to cashed-up clubs such as Chelsea and Arsenal, respectively.

Additionally troubling was that Australia's squad depth was much shallower than other teams', and that Australia's top players were all playing huge numbers of minutes across the national and their club teams.[4] That was further compounded by their enduring some of the longest travel distances of any national team players in the world. The need to mitigate those issues meant head coach Tony Gustavsson urgently had to not just introduce but embed some future-generation talent.

The plan, designed both to blood new players specifically and to expose the team more widely to top European teams and higher-ranked oppostition, had to be executed within a compressed timeframe. It was certain to result in some early losses in the hope of making future gains. Still, it was hard going and hard to witness—no one likes to lose, and no one likes to watch their beloved team lose. Both Gustavsson, who was early in his tenure, and Football Australia had to hold their nerve.

Walsh has since spoken about how the lowest points of this pressure-cooker strategy played out while the team was also being filmed for an unscripted, fly-on-the-wall documentary. But then the Matildas beat England, a team that had seemed invincible and infallible on a tear that included winning the 2022 Euros. And they did it in England, far from home and without a supportive crowd.

Jump to the Matildas' send-off friendly against France, played at a packed Docklands Stadium in Melbourne. It was at the time a record crowd for an Australian women's football match—50,629. Little did anyone know that figure would be so comprehensively and so frequently surpassed in subsequent weeks that it would be all but forgotten. That electric, inimitable match finished 1–0 to Australia, a result that would hold new meaning and foster fortitude as the team progressed deep into the knockout rounds of the Women's World Cup. The match in fact acted as a partial preview of what was about to captivate and consume our collective memory—it was as though someone flipped a switch. (Former

Matilda Jane Oakley puts it well: 'France gave us some early insight that something *big* was about to happen.')

It also marked a turning point in the alumni's involvement. In an effort to redress their previous exclusion and to perhaps provide the current players with some intergenerational fortitude, Football Australia invited the Matildas alumni to enact an on-pitch ceremonial guard as the team ran out for the game. Carol Vinson terms it 'an absolute honour' to provide that support and send-off. 'As far as I know, that was the first time it had been done, and we all had a ball!' (Tangentially, it marked the important inclusion of the National Indigenous Advisory Group members, including inaugural Aboriginal Matilda Karen Menzies.[5] The group was granted permission to perform the Welcome to Country when the traditional custodian elder of the Naarm/Melbourne land on which the match played out was unexpectedly unavailable due to some Sorry Business.)

The alumni had started the day at the Professional Footballers Australia (PFA) office in Melbourne, undertaking free health screenings provided to former players as part of the PFA Past Players Program. PFA Head of Player Development Rita Mankowska says of the atmosphere:

> They were in such a jovial mood. World Cup fever had taken hold, and you could see how the former players felt deeply connected to it. They replayed matches from the 2019 World Cup on the TVs, and at one point [the women] linked arms to sing the Australian national anthem together. This was about eight hours before the France game kicked off.

Former Matilda Sue Monteath says:

> It was really exciting, because we got out there a little bit early and the players were coming off their warm-up. I was pretty much in awe, thinking, *Oh, there goes all these players from the warm-up*. Someone said Sam Kerr couldn't find the way back to the dressing room—because we were all coming and going, I suppose … So it was really special to be out there. But especially when they ran out to play the game. What a result, as well.

Football Australia and the PFA staged alumni-specific events throughout the remainder of the tournament, something Alicia Ferguson describes as making the former Matildas 'feel really respected, valued'. The national body provided two nights' accommodation for alumni who travelled from interstate for the opening game, and the alumni were also gifted hoodies and other merchandise. They proudly wore the hoodies—it wasn't, Ferguson confirms, a case of being too cool to wear the shirt of the band. It felt like new-kit day for Ellen Beaumont: 'It was a nice touch … we all looked again like teammates representing our country!'

Remarkably, the pre-match event at the Australia v Ireland game was the first time all Matildas generations had been in a room together. 'They took photos in decade groups,' Monteath says. 'They had a whole Matildas one, and then they had the 70s, 80s, 90s, and so on. So that was pretty cool. It gave you a little bit more understanding to see who was who, and try and put names to faces.'

Ferguson agrees: 'It was also really nice to reconnect with the players you played with, meet players you'd maybe heard of, but never met.' Just all-round positivity, she says. 'We're not just connected by playing for Australia—we're connected by being Matildas.'

The intergenerational appreciation was mutual, as McPhee explains:

> You bumped into players you knew were selected after you, but who you didn't really know, and heard their stories and their challenges and the fun they had and the success they had. They'd actually be saying, 'Thank you so much for paving the way.' It was just a whole lot of respect. I guess there's only 200 to 230-odd alumni, and the respect within the group, and the friendships made [with] those you didn't even know about, was fantastic.

★ ★ ★

Concurrent to alumni gathering and getting to know each other, fans were getting to better know and understand the team. Released ahead of the tournament was *Matildas: The World at Our Feet*, a Disney+ documentary designed to humanise the players and help build the tournament hype. A good strategy to garner and cement a following with fans, the documentary provided content when it wasn't competing for airtime with other football content, and took the pressure off having a film crew in the inner sanctum throughout the tournament itself.

'It was more about showcasing the diversity of our team, the amazing personalities, and just what it actually takes to be a professional women's footballer now,' explains Ferguson. Having been a Matilda and transitioned to media after her playing career, she was uniquely positioned to balance the requirements of both a production and a high-performance environment. She was also uniquely placed to help the production go beyond surface-level stories. So for the documentary, as she was for the tournament itself, she was appointed a conduit between the players and the production team.

But while Ferguson might have understood the environment better than most, even she found the experience valuable:

> I think for me, having been retired for so long and having lived in London, I found the connection back to what it actually means to be a Matilda and how important it is to the players across every single generation. Yes, it's representing the country, it's putting on the green and gold. But actually … being a Matilda is more than a brand. It actually made me go, *How good is this?*

Their budget was smaller, but an adept and nimble all-women production team was filming another documentary in parallel. ('It's very much by design,' they tell me of the single-gender production-team composition: it's a deliberate contrast to the traditionally male-dominated sports media space.) Maggie Miles and Maggie Eudes, who go by Maggie M and Maggie E but have been nicknamed 'a Maggie sandwich', navigated COVID, border closures and lockdowns to film their *Trailblazers* documentary. The film's guiding principle was that 'the team should be celebrated, even before a game [had] been played at the World Cup', explains Miles. Acknowledging that while good on-pitch results are always helpful, the results were incidental: the film's higher purpose was to underscore the team's gender equality success. In fact, it is an educational tool. Its release was accompanied by an impact campaign that has seen it shown in sporting clubs, boardrooms and schools, with lesson plans created for the latter.

The Matildas' is a precious and important story for which to act as a sort of storytelling midwife. Eudes' greatest fear was that she wouldn't do the tale justice, that the alumni wouldn't recognise themselves when they saw it on screen. She needn't have worried. The alumni who attended the preview loved it. McPhee notes an additional touch that made it special: the documentary makers asked the alumni in the room to stand up in acknowledgement of the history and their powerful contribution to it. 'Those sorts of things are starting to happen more and more regularly, where alumni are being recognised at events.'

That distinguishment sometimes comes in unexpected but entertaining forms. 'There was a group of young boys [at the preview], and they were *so* excited to meet us, which was fantastic in itself,' number 2 cap Matilda Shona Bass recalls. She and inaugural Matildas captain Julie Dolan,[6] whom Bass terms 'the real famous one', were introduced to the audience that night and the boys and their mothers came up to speak to them afterwards. 'The boys were just so excited. Then, there was a pause and they said, "Wow, we can't believe you're still alive."'

* * *

Hundred-days-to-go celebrations aside, the tournament lead-up involved some nervy times. FIFA issued verbal smackdowns and refused lowball offers after international broadcasters undervalued the broadcast rights.[7] (Fans rightly pointed out that it didn't sit well that such moral high ground was being taken by the governing body that had traditionally lowballed women's football as a whole.) That meant some jurisdictions—including Japan, a country whose team had won the 2011 Women's World Cup—were in danger of not being able to watch the tournament at all. It didn't bode well for growing the audience and market for women's football.

Then, in a kind of corporate blanding in order to head off the kinds of human-rights advocacy so often entwined with women's football, FIFA issued a ban on player activism during the tournament other than wearing armbands that generically supported addressing various issues such as racism and homophobia.[8] (This was antithetical to the history of the women's game. Speaking in early 2024, Megan Rapinoe incisively observed, as others had before her, that sport is a site for inspiring social change. Women's sports, particularly, are 'on steroids' for that, she said, something that the sports and the people in and around them should lean into and that players such as her had traditionally done.[9])

Players were threatened with penalties should they subvert the armbands and go all out on protests, but New Zealand's Ali Riley subtly skirted the rule by painting each of her nails a different colour to represent the LGBTQIA+ rainbow pride flag. (The gesture had immediate impact: it reportedly provided solidarity and fortitude for a young patient who had been admitted to a mental health ward.)[10] Signalling it was not messing about, the Brazilian team arrived in a 787 Dreamliner emblazoned with images of Iranian activists Mahsa Amini and Amir Nasr Azadani and the words: 'No women should be forced to cover her head' and 'No man should be hanged for saying this'.[11] More subtly, and more related to climate change—a crisis on which football is generally silent—forty-four players, spearheaded by Denmark's Sofie Junge Pedersen, donated money to a climate-resilience, carbon-offsetting and climate-adaptation initiative. The action was designed to counter the carbon-footprint-intensive flights taken to and from Australia and Aotearoa New Zealand for the tournament.[12]

Closer to home, Puma engaged in ambush marketing by leveraging the messiness of recognition for the women from a NSW club team who attended the 1975 Women's Asian Cup.[13] There is a deep divide over whether or not they officially represented Australia. (Since then, the players involved have been offered unnumbered caps and recently, controversially, named the First Matildas.[14]) But that was about as extreme as it got—the rest of the tournament's activism was fairly muted.

'We had players come to us proactively wanting to do something around the armbands, and we thought it was great because this was something that FIFA and the players could work on together,' says Sarah Gregorius, a former Football Fern and former FIFPRO women's player union turned NWSL advocate. The thinking was that players could nominate the causes they wanted to champion and FIFA would support them to find ways to facilitate armband design and implementation in accordance with its regulations. So, win-win. 'We also had players who were like, "Oh, this would be amazing, we could auction them off for charity and that could also go towards the cause." I'm always blown away by the ideas that the players have,' Gregorius says, acknowledging that many of the issues feel personal because many of the players are members of the marginalised communities affected by the issues they wanted to highlight on the proposed armbands.

But FIFA did what FIFA does. 'They just sanitised it. They got ahead of it in a way, because I think they didn't want their stage to be one where there was activism or protest or any attention they couldn't control. So I can understand from FIFA's perspective why they did it. Of course, it frustrates me,' Gregorius says, adding that although you can't argue with the causes, such as uniting against poverty or hunger, switching armbands and causes each game dulled the armbands' impact. 'You can't pay attention to any of them, because you only wear it for one round,' she explains. There wasn't an option to concentrate on and amplify just one issue. 'So I think it just ended up being really watered down. There was never going to be the type of activism I think we were all hoping for.'

* * *

On Sunday 25 June 2023, 4000 people collectively walked across a closed Sydney Harbour Bridge to celebrate twenty-five days until the tournament kicked off. It was a made-for-TV scene set against the backdrop of the soaring bridge structure, high above the breathtakingly blue harbour. Offsetting the imagery was the iconic Opera House that had hosted the images of Julie Dolan and Sam Kerr on the bid-winning night. That was night. This was day.

That Harbour Bridge walk was when the momentous occasion started to feel real and its specialness realised. Thousands of people had got up early to participate on a particularly nippy winter weekend morning. Leading the group, having first gathered at Observatory Hill where they were gifted alumni jackets and then ferried in a kind of VIP bus-and-golf-cart convoy, were some of the previous generations of Matildas players. 'I don't know if they thought we were invalids or if there was a time constraint, but they put us in minibuses and carted us halfway across the bridge to where they had the start. Then we walked back along the way we'd been carted,' Monteath recalls. (Tellingly, her thoughts don't go to the fact that the ever-humble alumni might have been ferried out because they were VIPs.)

There was always a plan to bring the alumni central to the tournament, and it all came together that day on the bridge. Football Australia worked closely with FIFA on recognising the players as the living history of the game: 'They built it, and so we're going to make them central to this very big moment on what is an iconic piece of infrastructure in Australia and across the globe.' The idea for closing the bridge had come from co-chief operating officer (co-COO) Jane Fernandez, tournament head of marketing Kim Anderson explains:

> She's an operations person that I like to call a part-time creative director, because she's definitely got a left and right brain going on. As far back as the bid, when we were doing those big things like lighting up the [Opera House] sails and getting that PR impact, she was like, 'Wouldn't it be great if we closed down the bridge?'

Fernandez laughs when she hears Anderson's comment:

> I do have a bit of a creative side, even though my title's operations. I like the colour and the movement. I find that really exciting. At the end of the day, my job is all about the experience. Operations is really about experience, and it's about setting the experience

> for people to make sure it's a great one from when they leave home to come to the games, to when they return to their home. So that's the nuts and bolts. That's ensuring the experience is unbelievable. But the other side of the experience is how they're feeling. What are they seeing? What are they hearing? What are the emotions attached to it? I really love diving into that.

Closing the Harbour Bridge was no small mission for FIFA—the last time Walsh recalled the bridge being closed for football was for Football Australia's 2022 Men's World Cup bid. That's the aspect that stood out to Dolan: 'The enormity of a *women's* sporting team closing the Harbour Bridge. I just couldn't get over that.' Of the 2023 shutdown, Anderson says:

> That did take some convincing of the government. There's various councils involved, there's so many logistical things to get in place to make sure these things happen. But that was a great example where we said, 'Wouldn't it be great if we gave the former Matildas a moment and asked them to come in or walk and be at the front of the queue?'

She explains the thinking:

> For that generation who had to, as Julie Dolan would say, do bake sales and all of that sort of stuff, to start to experience what the current generation gets to experience—all of this has been built on the shoulders of the giants before—it was really nice for them to have that moment and feel that excitement twenty-five days out and get really pumped up about it.

In the same vein, Anderson then says something that sums up not just the sentiment of the Harbour Bridge moment and the alumni involved but what the tournament itself would become: 'This is not just about the Sam Kerrs of the world. This is about all of the Matildas.'

3

THE CALF THAT STOPPED THE NATION

Australia v Republic of Ireland, Sydney, 20 July 2023

TENS OF THOUSANDS of people heard the news that Matildas captain, lead goalscorer, team talisman and point-person Sam Kerr had been ruled out of the Matildas' opening match when they were just minutes away from watching Australia open their years-anticipated 2023 Women's World Cup account.

The news of Kerr's calf-muscle injury (it ended up being two injuries—she hurt her other calf against Sweden but didn't realise it at the time; we're not yet at that part of the story) ripped through the crowd in contagious, disbelieving, wildfire whispers. You could see it unfolding in real time: those who knew, those who didn't, and the moment the mood-tempering information spread. (Journalist Samantha Lewis recalls seeing her phone blowing up with notifications when she was on the outskirts of the stadium: 'My first reaction was absolute panic.')

Fans had spent the journey to Stadium Australia singing and engaging in good-natured cross-cultural banter until Kerr's calf injury news started to spread. Brows furrowed, fingers swiped and anxious impatience flashed across faces as Australian fans waited for facial recognition to enliven their phones and allow them to feverishly, repeatedly, check and refresh news websites and social media.

The hope was that the platforms would provide insight and, better yet, reassurance that this wasn't happening.

But Kerr was most definitely injured. Not only was she not starting, her omission from the team sheet meant she wasn't even a possible substitute. It was the worst-case scenario, and it ratcheted up the nervous tension. It also meant we were about to find out the answer to a question many of us had privately contemplated: *What would it mean for the Matildas if Kerr got injured?*

Truth be told, I'd been anxious but not daring to speak aloud the fear that she or another integral player would sustain a major injury such as a ruptured ACL *before* the tournament. The odds were not in their favour. We'd seen many top women's footballers experience exactly that in the preceding six to nine months—for example, England's Leah Williamson and Beth Mead, the Netherlands' Vivianne Miedema, Denmark's Nadia Nadim, the USA's Catarina Macario and Christen Press, Canada's Janine Beckie ... Still, it felt as though this injury, on the tournament precipice, was cruelly ripping the bandaid off.

(Compounding it was the anxiety-inducing phone app commanding ticket sales. Ticket activation only occurring approximately ninety minutes before the game, and the dynamic QR code functionality designed to prevent screenshots and other system-subverting measures, meant fans could not opt for old-school ticket printouts. This prompted a constant low-level will-it-won't-it-activate frustration that would play out tournament-long. Further to that was the high-level frustration that you couldn't transfer a single ticket—an anti-scalping measure that was not communicated pre-tournament and that would have changed the way many of us divided up ticket-buying responsibilities. Nor could you upgrade or buy unaccompanied kids' tickets once those tickets were on the resale platform.)

It would be dubbed 'the calf that stopped the nation', and accompanied by a fervour that marked how much the game and Kerr's brand had grown. No doubt it also stopped the hearts of sponsors and companies whose KPIs hinged on Kerr's marketability. With children's books and major advertising campaigns built around her, she wasn't just a high-profile player: she was, through sheer volume and spend, the face of the national team and the tournament.

Putting aside the fact that it's a marvel the injury information hadn't leaked, the interest level was unparalleled. 'I've never experienced something like that about a woman footballer before,' Lewis says, noting that such a level of attention would normally attend someone like David Beckham, Lionel Messi or Harry Kewell. 'This was really the first time that so much attention had been focused on this one player, and this one player's particular muscle.' She says that it felt intensified due to how much emphasis had been placed on the Matildas starting the tournament strongly. For their lead goalscorer to suddenly be unavailable? 'What's that feeling when you get winded? It just sucked all the air out of the country.'

Hopes had been high leading into the tournament—perhaps unreasonably so, given that the Matildas were not at the time in the world's Top 10—with the team's opening match selling so strongly and so quickly that organisers had moved it to the much larger but still quickly sold-out 75,000-seat Stadium Australia, up from the 42,500-capacity Sydney Football Stadium for which it was originally slated.

The Homebush-based Stadium Australia, as it was badged neutrally under FIFA regulations, was the 2000 Olympics' primary site. Most notably, it was where Cathy Freeman had stopped the nation with her striding, gliding, pride-swelling 400-metre track-final win. That run is widely known to have inspired more than a few of the current crop of Matildas, and Football Australia had secretly arranged for Freeman to meet with the team prior to the tournament. 'It was really a touching moment for some of those players, because Cathy had taught them to believe,' Football Australia head of marketing Peter Filopoulos explains.

Digital lead Liana Buratti provides some more background on the Freeman moment:

> We worked really hard behind the scenes to bring Cathy into camp. I mean, we had to make sure all the stars aligned at exactly

> the right moment without the players knowing! It was a massive surprise—they had absolutely no idea.
>
> We worked with Tony [Gustavsson] and he essentially brought all the players together under the guise of a team meeting. The lights were all turned off and an inspirational video was played. While they were all distracted, we snuck Cathy through the back door.
>
> The lights were turned on and the players saw their hero standing before them. The looks on their faces will be etched in my memory forever. The way they were completely captivated, it was almost like they had become kids again, the way they were hanging on every word Cathy said. They were asking questions, sharing stories, asking for advice …
>
> I feel like working with this team, we'd got so used to seeing the players do this for others—being the hero, being the inspiration. To see those roles reversed and see them receive guidance and mentorship from someone they look up to was really special.
>
> We did end up protecting a lot of that content and only releasing a small snippet because of how personal it was. Some things are meant to be kept sacred, and this was one of them.

What was discussed in that room remains secret (the Football Australia team also provided the players with some protected time where it was just them and Freeman), but what is known is that Freeman is probably one of the only people in the country who truly understands the weight and intensity of expectation and the life-changing celebrity the Matildas experienced over the tournament's subsequent days and weeks. My guess is she was probably thinking, *Welcome to the club*.

Regardless, broken-calf news having broken, we all settled in, some of us in that record 75,784-person crowd perched in vertigo-invoking nosebleed seats closer to the stadium roof than the pitch, stress-sipping our soft drinks and stress-snacking on hot chips, trying to quell our nerves that the Matildas' prospects of a good showing on home soil at the world's biggest women's sports tournament might be over before they'd begun.

★★★

There's a saying that sometimes you have to win ugly. That 'sometimes' is especially true in opening Women's World Cup matches where you're trying to shake off intense tournament nerves and the heavy expectation that comes with being the national team of the tournament's co-host nation. Oh, and you've suddenly had to pivot your playing style because your captain and go-to striker is out with injury. Winning ugly against Ireland was unlikely to have been the game plan, but getting through however they needed to is what the Matildas did. At times they looked as rattled and as at a loss as the crowd as to how to operate without Kerr making runs, improbably rising—almost hovering—high above defenders, employing precision timing to head in goals. Ireland, bringing both technical skills and physicality and perhaps sensing the Matildas' vulnerability, pushed them to the wall.

It wasn't that the Matildas weren't giving it everything they had. Katrina Gorry, a commanding midfielder who had returned to the squad an even more commanding midfielder after giving birth to a daughter, Harper, in August 2021, covered so much ground that match that she inspired memes about how the world is covered by 70 per cent water and the rest by her.[1] (Commentator David Basheer copped flak for his observation that motherhood hadn't 'blunted' Gorry's instincts.[2] It was a poorly phrased statement that would fail the Finkbeiner test.[3] Although Basheer would have done well to check his patriarchal biases, that isn't perhaps the most interesting element here. Apart from the fact that people quickly and rightly pointed out that mothers are extremely capable of achieving anything they put their minds to, the improved conditions within the high-performance environment and the collective bargaining agreement that underpinned them had allowed Gorry to return and excel. That's unlike many of her predecessors, including former Matildas Heather Garriock and Melissa Barbieri, who experienced the definitive motherhood penalty in the kerbing of their football careers.)

Ultimately, with the Matildas unable to create real chances in open play—so many balls floated in to where Kerr would normally be rising like a salmon or lurking to slot a goal in—it was a penalty that saved them. Deputised captain Steph Catley, who herself had only recently returned from a hamstring injury, stepped up without the pressure of defenders but with all the weight of the nation's hopes and dreams to hit the ball sweetly into the back of the net. That second-half penalty, which came after more than forty-five agonising minutes of the Matildas looking rather toothless, was the match's sole goal and Catley's first for a Women's World Cup: 1–0.

Australian fans exited the match more relieved than happy. For his part, fan and Matildas Active Support member Teddy Bryant explained that he'd never felt more relief at a penalty hitting the back of the net, and likewise at the final whistle, which signalled that that single penalty had secured the Matildas the win.

Things were a little more euphoric across the Tasman as co-host nation Aotearoa New Zealand opened their campaign with their inaugural Women's World Cup win, defeating former champions Norway. It was the inverse anticipated result—Australia had been expected to win while New Zealand hadn't necessarily—but a win was a win for both host-nation teams.

Former Matilda Ash Sykes commentated that opening New Zealand match for Optus Sport. 'It was definitely more fun watching that game than Australia's first game,' she says. 'Thankfully, I wasn't on the Australia games until later in the tournament. I think the games you're invested in emotionally are way harder to do.' That match provided enough interested-observer distance for her to be happy for the Football Ferns as well as their coach, Jitka Klimková, who had previously coached Sykes at Canberra United. Also: 'I think that set the tone for the tournament: anything could happen.'

A record crowd turned out for that New Zealand match: 42,137, a massive figure by any stretch and especially for a team with few runs on the board and, with no national league and most players having to be journeywomen in the Kiwi diaspora, a small domestic footprint. (Even more curious and now heartening, although likely stressful at the time, was that the New Zealand team was almost late to its opening match because traffic heading towards the stadium logjammed the bus.[4] It was reminiscent of what happened to the US Women's National Team (USWNT) in the breakout US-held tournament in 1999.)

Knowing what we know now, those strong opening-match ticket sales, combined with the more than 1.4 million tickets sold tournament-wide before the first ball had been kicked,[5] were a preview of what was in store. Record sales figures were certainly not a host-nation, hometown-favourite irregularity. But at the time, ticket sales were the last things on most fans' minds—or, at least, only in the sense that they were likely to plummet if the Matildas tanked their opening match.

Regardless, with those two match results, Australia and New Zealand were off the starting blocks and fans were strapped in for what would turn out to be an utterly game-changing, society-changing whirlwind of a tournament.

4

THE SECOND ACT

Australia v Nigeria, Brisbane, 27 July 2023

WERE YOU TO script the Matildas' home Women's World Cup journey as a Hollywood blockbuster—for it did, in the end, contain all the makings of one—the second group-stage match was Act II, the lowest ebb in the Matildas' hero's journey narrative arc. Concussions sustained by Mary Fowler and Aivi Luik in training, Kerr's ongoing calf complaint, and Kyah Simon making up striker numbers but not actually available for selection due to undisclosed knee rehabilitation setbacks meant players to field were thin on the ground, particularly at the goalscoring end.

Although traditionally one of Africa's strongest teams, albeit one hampered by the underfunding and lack of professional opportunities that have permeated the women's game worldwide, opponents the Nigerian Super Falcons were on paper (but not in reality) comparatively slightly more beatable than the Irish and Canadian teams the Matildas would meet either side. Canada were largely expected to top the group—they were the highest ranked, they were reigning Olympic champions, and they had the mental advantage, having most recently and comprehensively beaten the Matildas twice on home ground. The Matildas were relying on the other two group-stage matches to secure a solid second-place finish to progress to the next round—hence the importance of the Nigeria game.

While you'd never be looking for a team to enter a match under a disadvantage to garner a head start, it wasn't remiss of people to wonder if off-field distractions would potentially hamper the Super Falcons' game. Nigeria, like Canada, were one of a number of teams having to fight for fair conditions and pay while simultaneously having to perform on the pitch to continually prove their 'worth' and garner any chance of bargaining leverage. The Matildas understood the fight intimately, having been in the same position in 2015, to the point where the then-off-contract team had had to strike to draw attention to the issues and force administrators to do better.

Nigeria's was one of the more visible fights, spilling messily into public view, but plenty more simmered away less visibly. In truth, and as we'd see later in the tournament with teams such as Spain, it would be easier to point to countries that weren't fighting, or hadn't previously had to fight, their federations over subpar standards and recompense. As former-US-player-turned-commentator Sam Mewis, whose career ended prematurely through injury, observes, women's football is unfailingly stuck in a cycle of women footballers outperforming their conditions and pay and administrators using that to justify a further lack of investment: if they're performing without it, why change anything? It's no-win either way.[1]

Nigeria entered the match in that rock-and-a-hard-place quandary: perform well and the federation won't be motivated to change anything; underperform and they'll use that to further stultify you. As all women's teams do, they went with the former. (Across the board, and even when things are broken, 'Stuff it, I'll still hit it' sums up women's sports can-do approach.[2])

Uncle Shannon Ruska provided a memorable Welcome to Country at the Meanjin/Brisbane game, conveying the welcome with a passport analogy, a rendition of 'Waltzing Matilda'—we sang in English while he sang it in Yagera language—and a rousing 'Aussie, Aussie, Aussie' chant. But his efforts weren't enough to buoy the Matildas. If it seemed as though the game against Ireland had tested their limits, the second game of the tournament pushed past those limits.

Nigeria were a team Australia knew little about, and that the Matildas had even less experience playing against. Such unknown teams can often be the undoing in ways a more familiar opponent isn't. Nigeria indeed proved a bogey team as the Matildas struggled with formation and timing, having not yet found a replacement for Kerr, or new rhythm or style to adjust to her absence.

Nigeria clinically capitalised on some of the Matildas' inconsistencies and the natural lull that follows the expenditure of a high-stakes performance such as the Australians had had with the opening game. That dip, Sykes notes, and as would become even more apparent for the Matildas later in the tournament, is when you can lose games.

True to Sykes' statement, Nigeria prevailed 2–1. The Australian crowd and team were stunned. Cameras kept cutting to Nigerian fans dancing in the stands, perhaps in part because those fans were joyfully surprised and because the muted Australian crowd wouldn't have made for nearly as good television. The Nigerian celebration extended beyond the stadium. Journalist Pokuah Frimpong and her team produced a well-timed story around the people at, and the experiences around, a local Nigerian restaurant that was hosting a watch party.

The Matildas' loss was a shock not because Australia had underestimated Nigeria or because the Super Falcons didn't deserve the win (they absolutely did), but because hosting a major tournament comes with attendant hopes that the host-nation team's run through said tournament will resolve neatly and happily as if a modern fairytale. This was not how the story was supposed to go.

★ ★ ★

There's a strategy of letting a team grind it out when things aren't working: make substitutes too soon and you further disrupt the rhythm and prevent that beautiful moment where things finally click. But Tony Gustavsson's lack of substitutions throughout the match—and, later, the tournament—was questioned. He seemed to wait too long and inject substitute players too late for them to have any real impact. Gustavsson would later say that the data shows the most successful teams are the ones who have the fewest substitutions and achieve the most consistency.[3] That's valid, but arguably doesn't apply when the player you most consistently field in a position is absent due to injury and the team hasn't been able to adequately adjust. It's an impossible situation, though. Had he made substitutions sooner and the 2–1 result been the same, punters would have said he'd panicked instead of letting the team work its way through. Who'd want to be a head coach?

'To be honest? I don't think I would say that I enjoyed it,' former and longest-serving Matildas coach Tom Sermanni says some months later of the tournament as a whole. His time coaching the Matildas might be over, but such was the attentiveness and longevity with which he cared for the national team that he naturally continues to wish the best for it, which also made it challenging for him to sit back and enjoy the tournament as a neutral fan. He is also the person in and around the tournament who perhaps best understood the machinations and weightiness of every decision Gustavsson had to make. Ever respectful, he understands people have opinions about substitutions. But, as he also acknowledges, 'It's easy to make the decisions when you don't need to make the decisions.'

So, at the conclusion of Act II and just the Matildas' second game, Australia were in real danger of being abruptly bundled out of their own tournament. Against the odds, the less-resourced Nigeria had relegated them to underdog status instead of home-country favourites. Weirdly, Nigeria might have done the Matildas a favour: underdog is Australians' preferred status.

5

THE COMEBACK

Canada v Australia, Melbourne, 31 July 2023

JUST TWO GAMES into the tournament, and despite having been expected to finish in the top two in the group, both the Matildas' and Canada's Women's World Cup prospects were teetering on a knife edge. Neither team's group stage had gone to plan after Nigeria, as well as defeating Australia, had held Canada to a scoreless draw in their opening match. Consequently, both teams needed to win their third game to progress. One team's World Cup campaign was about to abruptly end, and far sooner and more cruelly than anyone had expected.

Prior to 2023, never in Women's World Cup history had a host country not made it out of the group. New Zealand had sadly broken that record and were already out; Australia were in danger of making that two for two. Whether or not the Matildas were ruminating on the statistic is unclear, but no doubt Football Australia was nervous—it had staked a lot on this.

Around the time of the Matildas' Round of 16 game, but illustrative of how high the tournament stakes were as a whole, a helicopter hired by an unidentified media outlet at one stage hovered over the team's training ground to circumvent security and capture footage of the injured Kerr.[1] That experience fell into the

'There isn't a guidebook for this' category. The team had to quickly determine the helicopter's tail number and acquaint itself with the Australian Civil Aviation Safety Authority registration system to determine the helicopter's origins. Its detective work traced the chartering back to the *Daily Telegraph* and determined, via FIFA, that there was not a no-fly zone implemented above the training ground. Although the footage it captured risked exposing World Cup–jeopardising team tactics, said helicopter could legally—albeit disconcertingly—be there.

That conservative major media outlets—previously the exemplars of non-existent women's sports coverage—would go to such lengths to gain exclusive team footage illustrates the wildly changed landscape in which the Matildas were operating. It marked the evolution of a team that had rapidly gone from scarcity, precarity and relative anonymity to equal pay, national treasure and celebrity-papped status.[2] (Across the tournament, some of the country's highest-profile and most conservative newspapers even rebadged themselves. The *Daily Tillygraph* featured the front-page headlines 'Tills and Thrills', 'Heartbreakerr', and 'Who Run the World?', and the *Kerr-ier Mail* and other News Limited outfits variously released full-page colour sections that enabled fans to assemble a Sam Kerr image over five days.[3]) Tony Gustavsson tried to shrug off the 'spying' tactic with a dad joke about interest in the team being 'sky high'.[4] Media manager Ann Odong remarks now that had the helicopter scenario happened to any other team she'd have marvelled at the magnitude of interest spurring on the women's game. But as the media officer for whose team it happened and one of the people at the eye of the storm of additional work and pressure it entailed, not so much.

Irrespective of the fact that conservative media themselves had gone to great expense to snare exclusive, newspaper-selling footage of the injured Kerr, you could almost sense them preparing to feign outrage about the taxpayer money injected into staging the tournament: 'We gave you a home base, bean bag, and a barista. We expect some return on investment.' This faux fury would have been intensified by the fact that, just days before the tournament kicked off, the Victorian state government had pulled the pin on hosting the 2026 Commonwealth Games.[5] So the Matildas were on the one hand contending with the uncharted aspect of major media hiring helicopters to spy on their training, and on the other knowing said scorpion-like media would be swift to sting them.

★ ★ ★

The last time the Matildas had met Canada in an iconic Women's World Cup crunch match was 2007. That match, which was also to determine who progressed past the group stage, had taken two attempts to play due to the interference of a typhoon.[6]

In 2023, the interference was the absence of available tickets. Crowd numbers were capped by stadium size, not interest. The match was being played at the 30,000-seat Melbourne Rectangular Stadium despite demand being strong enough to sell at least twice that many tickets. (Yes, 'Melbourne Rectangular Stadium' is the sponsor-stripped name of the venue. No, I won't be using it again.)

It's not certain why Melbourne officials elected to host so few games and in a stadium that fit so few people. But, alongside an insouciance from the state government about injecting funding, the lengthy FIFA bump-in, bump-out times that prevent stadiums from being used for other sports and events would have been a significant factor.[7] I'd also hazard a guess that certain very powerful men's sporting codes operating in the state either didn't recognise the potential enormity of the event or refused to budge many, if any, of the domestic men's sports league fixtures for, gee, the largest women's sporting event in the world. Regardless, at the time when the Matildas most needed a groundswell of hometown support, just 30,000 fans could turn out in person.

Compounding the ticket-scarcity frustration, fans were slightly exasperated that while the focus had been on certain players and their injury status, other players not under an injury cloud remained on the bench. These included fan favourite Alex Chidiac, which prompted one supporter to turn up with a painted cardboard sign hung around their neck with string and featuring two words: 'Play Chids'. (Another read, slightly more cryptically, 'Go Matildas / Give 'em a moosing'.)

As it turned out, unlike the 2007 match that would determine the Matildas' first-ever progression to the Women's World Cup knockout rounds, this match would be played at first attempt, and the Matildas played it as though it was their last. They came out firing, propelled forward as if, having been dragged backwards by the Nigeria game, they'd been slingshot. Canada were, quite simply, shellshocked. As Ash Sykes notes, 'Thankfully, we learned all the lessons that we needed to from that [Nigeria] game. They bounced back, and we never really saw those sorts of shaky moments again.'

Like Nigeria, Canada had entered the event having been in dispute with their federation. (Post-tournament, the Canadian Soccer Players' Association would launch a CA$40 million lawsuit alleging negligence in terms of board members' fiduciary duty.[8]) Their build-up had no doubt been subpar, the mental load and distraction uninvited. But unlike Nigeria, Canada never really fired.

Hayley Raso scored two goals in quick succession, one each either side of a Mary Fowler goal that was disallowed due to Ellie Carpenter being marginally offside. Canada made four substitutions at half-time in an effort to reset the game, but the Matildas doubled their first-half effort: one goal from Fowler that this time was allowed, another from Catley courtesy of a penalty in extra time. (Given how stressful the lead-up had been, Matildas Active Support member Teddy Bryant says of that second half, 'The last thing I expected to be was relaxed.')

'We were so close to going out in that game. Because beforehand there was this huge pressure on the team to do well. But the crowd went in there with a clear mindset that we're going to be the 12th woman,' football administrator John Didulica says. Indeed, while the stadium was too small for the occasion, it did in retrospect afford a certain intimacy and connection to the players—the spectators were an extension of the team. Stepping out at one stage to take a throw-in, Carpenter broke the fourth wall, throwing her arms up to hype the crowd. It was as though she'd sent an electric current through it, and the crowd responded with an energising roar.

Kerr had her boots on throughout the match—whether it was a mind game or whether she'd actually be called on, the will-she-won't-she continued the entire ninety minutes. In the end, the Matildas' win was so comprehensive that Gustavsson was able to allow Kerr more much-needed recovery time. The rest of us were equal parts knee-bucklingly relieved and giddy.

Australian fans celebrated the emphatic 4–0 win as though the team had won the final. In some ways they had—the pressure release was palpable. The Matildas had arguably at best been hoping to finish second in the group. Instead, they overshot it and finished first. That prompted some hurried rebooking of flights and tickets for the team and fans alike. It was almost inconceivable, given the near-disaster that had threatened.

Media professional David Davutovic says:

> I think that's what made that game so unique and so special and so memorable—the fact that it was purely down to the sporting occasion and everything that was at stake on the night. The players sensed that, and really stepped up to the occasion. I felt like they took responsibility for that game and that performance. [The game against] Nigeria wasn't great. It didn't look cohesive. It almost felt like whatever the tactics were [for the Canada game], the players just went out and said, 'You know what, we're taking absolute responsibility for this, and there's no way we're getting eliminated tonight.'

Didulica agrees:

> It was such an overwhelming experience. If I were to look at a single game that touches on those two points around the way we play and the way we support, there's never been a better event in Australian football. Because they played so well. The actual way they played was so distinctly Australian, or what I think we want from national teams: really aggressive and fast and exciting and just edge-of-your-seat stuff from start to finish.

As we would come to know over subsequent weeks, the do-or-die match ended up being about a lot more than making it out of the group: it set us up for some of the greatest moments in Australian women's football to date.

Journalist, lawyer and academic Kieran Pender spent a lot of the tournament considering how the thinnest of margins make big differences. 'It was, from a performance perspective, such a mixed tournament,' he recalls. The Ireland and Nigeria games weren't convincing; the England semi-final and Sweden third-place play-off to come wouldn't be, either. Drawing on wider experience covering sports such as cycling, Pender notes how through the millimetre and microsecond differences that govern elite sport, you 'live and die' by results: 'That means that on one iteration you win, the other iteration you lose, and the difference actually isn't that much.' In this instance we narrowly escaped disaster, but the line is so thin that a reality in which Australia didn't make it out of the group is not just plausible, it's almost tangible.

'I think the thing a lot of people also forget is how bad it was going into Game 3, when we were heading in to Canada,' journalist Isobel Cootes agrees. She notes that everyone has a story about the quarter-final penalty shootout that would come after it, but knowing how badly it could have gone had we not won the do-or-die Canada group-stage game is anxiety-inducing, even retrospectively. 'Everyone remembers Cortnee Vine scoring the penalty [in the quarter-final] and then Sam Kerr's goal against England [in the semi-final].' In short, 'It's actually insane to think about how much hinged on that [Canada] game. Obviously more so than elimination, we now know. How much the game could have been stunted.'

Academic Hunter Fujak, who studies the business of sports, has mused that it would be interesting to see what would have happened had the Matildas gone out at the group stage.[9] Davutovic, too, considers the hypothetical now that we're safely on the other side of it:

> If they'd been eliminated, it would have been a sporting disaster. Clearly, you wouldn't have had the Vine moment, the Mackenzie [Arnold] moment, you wouldn't have had that amazing momentum you had in the knockout phase. But it

would have been really interesting to see the reaction, the post-mortem.

He alludes to the criticism that would have hit overdrive: 'There would have been so many people under the gun, headlined by the coach.' The experience would have been a first for a team that had not experienced such scrutiny and negativity before; with great investment and media coverage comes greater return-on-investment expectation and accountability. 'It was such high stakes. There was such a fine line. It ended up being one of the greatest nights in Australian football history,' says Davutovic.

⋆ ⋆ ⋆

'How good is football?!' might have been what Australians were asking rhetorically, gripping each other in celebration, but the Matildas' win was wrenching for the Canadian team and its fans. It signalled not just the end of the team's tournament, but the end of the international career of world-leading goalscorer (irrespective of gender) and all-round great Christine Sinclair. Sinclair had debuted at the Sydney 2000 Olympics, so the Australian trip was effectively closing a loop for her. Soaking up the final few moments of her last-ever Women's World Cup game, she paused to collect a few blades of grass from the pitch.

We didn't know it then, but fellow greats Brazil's Marta and the United States' Megan Rapinoe would see their international careers end soon after Sinclair's. Rapinoe and Sinclair had actually started out together during their days at the University of Portland. The latter notably blocked the USWNT Twitter account to avoid distraction in the lead-up to a match against the traditional rivals and promptly forgot about it, an 'oops' the account riffed on when it went to wish her well in her retirement: 'Hope she unblocks us to see this', it posted, accompanied by the crossed-fingers emoji.[10]

The departures of Sinclair, Rapinoe and Marta felt reminiscent of a relay race. In some ways, as first contemporary-era runners they'd come out hard from the blocks; now they were passing the baton, fading into the background, spent, as the next athletes accelerated away. It was during this tournament that it began to seem that the sport they had carried for so long could now survive without them. Marta's Women's World Cup farewell speech—at the end of her sixth Cup—talked about how she hadn't had any women to look up to when she was young.[11] How that has changed. As former Matilda Heather Garriock, now a Football Australia board member, observed, Marta was the equivalent hero for players of Garriock's era and for all women footballers that Sam Kerr is to girls and boys today.[12]

6

MORE THAN THE MATILDAS

THE 2023 WOMEN'S World Cup wasn't, as it might have seemed, just about the Matildas. (Notably, this is where the failure to enliven anti-siphoning media laws[1] hampered engagement, as the television broadcasts of many of the non-Australian matches were behind paywalls.) Across the group stage and, as it would turn out, knockout rounds, results and occurrences kept surprising. As with every women's football experience, there were many overcoming-the-odds elements, offset by bittersweet ones.

Top teams such as two-time Women's World Cup winner and 2022 Euros finalist Germany went out unexpectedly, while first-timers and fearless bolters such as Colombia and Morocco absolutely surged. Colombia might not have won the 2023 Women's World Cup hosting rights (they finished second to Australia's and Aotearoa New Zealand's bid), but Colombian fans absolutely brought the impassioned party. Even more stunning was the story of one of the Colombian team's players, Linda Caicedo, who survived an ovarian cancer diagnosis at fifteen to record a breakout World Cup performance just three years later at age eighteen.[2]

Neutral game England v Haiti was the first game that Stephanie Messinis, a fan and Matildas Active Support member, attended in her home city of Brisbane. She was unsure what to expect and hopeful that more fans would turn out than they usually did for—for example—the A-League Men's team the Brisbane Roar. The crowd numbers and atmosphere quickly confirmed that fans of this tournament were all-in. Messinis says, 'When I arrived, I remember the hysteria, the activities and stalls outside the stadium and people everywhere. I remember thinking, *What a vibe*.' That was even more elevated in the stadium, which was absolutely brimming with fans. Hearing the theme song, seeing the mascot and experiencing the pre-tournament welcome, she rightly sensed she was part of something in her home stadium that would never be forgotten and would be talked about for years to come—something bigger, which everyone was going to want to get in on.

Julie Dolan identifies a neutral Adelaide game in the same vein: 35,000 people filling an Adelaide stadium at midday to watch two non-host-nation teams play. This large, engaged audience was the antithesis of those who attended matches throughout her career. (Dolan memorably had to create and distribute flyers to try to promote and invite fans to Australia's first A International match.[3]) Acutely aware of the importance of retaining fans and building on the tournament's success, Dolan, who now works in marketing, contacted Football Australia's general manager of World Cup Legacy Programs, Carlee Millikin. Still incredulous at the number of fans who had come out of the woodwork, Dolan asked, 'Have we got all their emails?' Millikin assured her everything was in hand.

Tournament head of marketing Kim Anderson nominates the Germany v Colombia group-stage game played in front of 40,499 fans at Sydney Football Stadium as a highlight among highlights:

> I mean, the Colombians were phenomenal in terms of atmosphere. It was a really tight game and there was all this exciting stuff happening ... it was probably at a decibel level that was close to what we felt in Brisbane [at the end of the quarter-final penalty shootout], or what we felt when Sam [Kerr] scored that goal [against England in the semi-final]. I was just like, *What is going on here?* It was a neutral game and people were going absolutely nuts.

Indeed, Germany v Colombia was one of the best group-stage games by any measure. Ash Sykes says:

> I was covering that one in the studio. It was so loud you could sense it even from the studio, let alone [in the stadium]. The Colombian fans were crying and dancing. You couldn't buy Colombian merchandise anywhere [because it was sold out]. It was the quintessential football experience. My mum's obviously been forced to watch us play football for many years but hadn't ever really appreciated it. But I think the crowds drew her in [to the Women's World Cup] and she just wanted to be a part of it. I think that's an indication of what a lot of people went through with the tournament.

That atmosphere was testament to the deliberate marketing of the Women's World Cup to Australia's diverse multicultural community. The organising team had identified local communities' cultural leaders (who were referred to as 'community champions') and ensured both that they knew about the tournament and that their community was most definitely invited. They asked them a bunch of questions: 'What does your community need? Buses to get to the stadium? Musical instruments that need to be approved? Flags?' Anderson explains.

'We did induction nights with them. It was like a party atmosphere in a room in the stadium. We're all doing limbo. It was just phenomenal to think, *Wow, this is the power of football*,' Anderson says. That groundwork perhaps explains some of the tournament ambience, one free of ructions or animosity. 'I guess when you create the expectation that it's going to be this really welcoming, inclusive atmosphere, then people come with that mindset, too.'

That vibe was further enhanced by the anthem 'Unity Beat' and its audience-participation element. The song had been launched at the 100-days-to go event.[4] 'That was probably one of the first times where my boss, CEO David Beech, said to me, "This feels like a risk,"' Anderson explains. 'I said, "I get it. But we need to be doing bold things."' Also, it was true to the ethos: they didn't want a chant that was just for one team; they wanted a chant that was for everyone. Anderson continues:

> So we launched it. Of course, it got a bit of fanfare around [the time of] that 100-days-to-go event, but the proof was going to be in the pudding. Would this last the distance and become part of the fan experience? Or would it be a laughing-stock where everyone was like, 'Oh, that funny little song that they tried to launch'?

It proved the former. During the song, fans switched on their mobile-phone torches and waved them in time with the pumping bass, tens of thousands of goosebump-inducing phone glow-worms or fairy lights illuminating the darkened stadium as if at a rock concert. The song was far and away an improvement on one of the 2019 audience-participation activities that had encouraged everyone to scream as loudly as they could. In 2023, the Unity Beat didn't get old; in 2019, the screaming very quickly did.

'For me, those moments were amazing,' Anderson says. 'I even had people text me at the semi and the final to say, "I can't believe tonight's my last Unity Beat".' So what was its hook? 'I think the beauty was in the simplicity of it,' Anderson explains. 'It was something that anyone could bop along to. There weren't lots of words [to remember]. It was really easy for everyone to get involved with, whether you could stand or not.' She's referencing the fact that you could move or not move as suited you, you could activate your mobile-phone torch or not, you could sing or not, you could simply observe and let it wash over you.

There were bangers across the board. In addition to songs such as 'Strawberry Kisses' that were being pumped out of change rooms, the in-stadium aural experience included intergenerational hits ranging from John Farnham's 'You're the Voice' to Men at Work's 'Down Under', Outkast's 'Hey Ya!' and Eminem's 'Lose Yourself'. Also featured were Shania Twain's 'Man! I Feel Like a Woman!', Vanessa Amorosi's 'Absolutely Everybody' and Bon Jovi's 'Living on a Prayer'.

When Mallrat was announced as one of the tournament's theme-song artists, she happened to mention to journalist Isobel Cootes her memory of, and the inspiration she got from, Nikki Webster descending from the sky on a swing at the 2000 Sydney Olympics opening ceremony. It was a fleeting reference, but it came full circle later in the tournament when Webster's song 'Strawberry Kisses' came up in the Australian press conference. 'We were obsessed with the music that day, because nothing else was happening,' Cootes says. She asked what music the team played in the change room to pump themselves up for games. 'Strawberry Kisses' was Catley's playlist request. 'That just became a perfect encapsulation of the tournament,' Cootes explains, including the seminal and continuing influence of the 2000 Olympics.

Energy was high across the Tasman, too. Co-host nation New Zealand had their most successful Women's World Cup to date, despite not progressing past the group stage. Football Fern Ali Riley, from a generation of players who knew just how hard-won and significant the achievement was, told media this wasn't about winning a game, it was about inspiring a country. For while most fans on the Australian side of the Tasman had been developing calf-tear-grade expertise, New Zealand had not just won their opening match, they'd recorded the first-ever win in their Women's World Cup history. This despite having woken to the news that a gunman had shot at construction workers in Auckland's CBD the first morning of the tournament.[5] They were evacuated from their hotel a few days after that—a man was later charged with arson and burglary indeterminate of whether it was tournament-related.[6] Both incidents were quickly subsumed by the event's groundswell to become mere footnotes.

'The first game feels like a bit of a blur,' former Football Fern Sarah Gregorius says. 'The last ten minutes of the match, I don't think I've ever been more stressed and then more excited in my entire life.' By virtue of her work and responsibilities as FIFPRO women's player union advocate, she was in the VIP area with fellow former Football Fern Maia Jackman and then–FIFA chief women's football officer Sarai Bareman.

> We were just in bits, crying and hugging. It was so cool. Even thinking about it now gives me such a buzz, because of the amount of times I've stood on a field at a World Cup game as a player and been absolutely distraught at the result [and now I was] deliriously happy. Even though I wasn't on the field, it was the best night of my football career.

She went to a pub near the stadium after the match to celebrate with former teammates. 'We all said the same thing: "We didn't play, but this is the best night of our footballing lives."'

The winner's high was short-lived. The mental and emotional stamina required to back it up wasn't yet there, and the Kiwis were defeated by neophytes the Philippines, another of the new teams who played out of their skin (they were steered by former Matildas coach Alen Stajcic). No matter. Progress had been made. As the Croissants put it, 'New Zealand was a vibe in general.'

The Croissants had opened their trans-Tasman leg of the tournament with sheep costumes adorned with images of Football Fern Malia Steinmetz, whom they knew, and cottonwool that shed as the day progressed. They had inadvertently chosen the same pub at which the Football Ferns' friends-and-family event was being held. 'Every family member from the New Zealand team would walk past and they just thought the sheep were the funniest thing,' the Croissants explain. The New Zealanders invited the Croissants up to the private friends-and-family event. 'We were like, "We're so embarrassed that we're dressed as sheep, but sure." So six sheep are walking up the stairs, dropping little pieces of wool, collecting them for each other, being like, "Be cool, guys, be cool, act cool."'

It made the Croissants' day, but probably also the families', as they hadn't previously seen significant support on home soil. Claudia Bunge's brothers, for example, had watched Bunge play professionally just once before because, in the absence of a strong domestic league, her career is mostly being conducted overseas. It was doubly surreal for them because Bunge was one of the faces of the billboard-sized Visa advertisements erected around town.

It wouldn't be women's football if there weren't tricky elements, too. Spain, for example, reportedly left their Palmerston North base camp early because it was 'too boring'. That prompted the local council to post tongue-in-cheek on social media that it wasn't bitter about the 'break-up' and wished Spain luck for the remainder of the tournament, saying 'You'll continue to be our second favourite team'.[7]

Spain maintained they had left only to move closer to Wellington, the location of their next game.[8] Given the players' long-running dispute with their national federation and what happened later in the tournament (spoiler alert: sexual assault), one now wonders whether there was something more going on. Unless someone from the Spanish team or federation speaks out, though, we may never know.

Continuing the theme of on-pitch results starkly contrasting with off-field challenges, Jamaica, like Nigeria, overperformed. In an astounding effort, they drew with France, defeated Panama and knocked out Brazil to make their inaugural appearance in the sudden-death rounds. This was in spite of financial and condition woes that had forced the team to crowdfund to get to the tournament.[9] These afflictions were a continuation of the ones they had long faced. Speaking about Jamaica, but in a statement perhaps more widely applicable, footballer Chinyelu Asher mentioned that she was regularly asked about what progress had been made to address the financial and conditions precarity in the four years following the last Women's World Cup. Her response indicated not much: 'We're here doing it again.'[10]

Not that it's a competition for most hard-done-by, but the Afghanistan women's football team operated on the tournament periphery. The team (most of whose players now live in Melbourne after seeking asylum in 2021) was excluded from the tournament—FIFA won't admit a team if its domestic national federation won't recognise it. In Afghanistan's case, the federation is all-male and run by the Taliban. Commentator, human-rights activist and former Socceroo Craig Foster termed the action (or inaction) 'gender apartheid'.[11]

The Afghanistan team and their supporters did a solid job of advocating and attracting media attention to spotlight the intractable issue. Both Nobel prize winner Malala Yousafzai, who famously survived a Taliban assassination attempt in 2012 at the age of fifteen, and former Afghanistan national women's football team captain Khalida Popal came to lend their support. Despite their best efforts, and despite presenting a petition containing more than 160,000 signatures, the team couldn't gain any traction. FIFA maintained radio silence.[12] 'We've heard nothing about a pathway for the [Afghanistan] women to be allowed to represent their country again. We're just getting absolutely zero,' football administrator John Didulica says. 'That's probably the frustration. I felt we did everything we could through that period, but it didn't move the dial.'

There's a reason, albeit a frustrating one, why FIFA would have been reluctant to move on this issue. FIFA is an association of associations: it recognises a single association per member country. One of the few ways a federation can be kicked out is for not being a country's monopoly. So the concept of recognising a national team not endorsed by, or operating under the monopoly of, its member federation is a bridge too far.

But there were more upsides than downsides across the tournament in general. Canada's Quinn, for example, became the first non-binary athlete to play in a World Cup.[13] Just two minutes into the game against France, Panama's captain and emerging star Marta Cox scored a highlights-reel-worthy goal (and Panama's first in a Women's World Cup) from a free kick.[14] It was perhaps an unscripted changing of the moniker's meaning and the guard as the Women's World Cup career of Brazil's Marta concurrently ended. Marking that end in the most respectful way possible, Jamaica's Khadija 'Bunny' Shaw made a beeline to Marta when Jamaica knocked Brazil out of the tournament to congratulate her on a stellar career and tell her she had been the inspiration for her own.[15] France's Wendie Renard meanwhile scored her 35th national team goal, a huge account for a centre back, but a goal we nearly never saw because she initially boycotted the tournament due to undisclosed issues relating to the team's previous coach.[16]

Ireland left the competition at the group stage, but were unlucky to do so. A lot like New Zealand, the results did not reflect how far Ireland had pushed their opponents and how close they'd come to more favourable outcomes. Irrespective of results, the Irish fans were memorably all-in. Pokuah Frimpong was part of a media team that created a story about the Irish fans. 'We literally just walked around with Google Maps open, saying, "Well, OK, this is an Irish pub, this is an Irish pub, this is an Irish pub,"' Frimpong explains. The group formulated a plan: '"Let's go here, here and here, see who we can meet, see what we can create." That was fantastic because I ended up getting pulled into an Irish dance. I had no idea what I was doing.'

A 180-degree turnaround of support that occurred throughout the tournament was when Brazil's government changed local work hours to facilitate Brazilians being able to cheer on their team. Such an accommodation would be impressive even for the men's game, but it was doubly so here, given women were banned from playing football in Brazil for almost four decades—the ban's too-recent end date was 1979.[17] (The country later also successfully bid to host the 2027 tournament, so expect the positive sentiment to kick on.)

Brazilians turned out in force here, too, and absolutely lifted the roof with their support. 'Brazilians were everywhere,' former Matilda Alicia Ferguson recalls of the France v Brazil game that took place at Brisbane Stadium. 'So much so that they took over Caxton Street. And there were about ten French fans with baguettes walking down Caxton Street ripping off and throwing chunks of baguettes.' Intercultural dance-offs ensued.

Morocco's Nouhaila Benzina became the first woman to wear a hijab in a senior Women's World Cup, in addition to helping Morocco become the first Arab or North African nation to represent on the world stage.[18] This hijab first wasn't something Benzina or the Moroccan team wanted to focus on—for them it was normal, as it should have been. Also, as former Matildas vice-captain and former FIFA Executive Committee member Moya Dodd AO notes, nearly a generation had come and gone in the years intervening the hijab safety trial[19] and the maturation at a senior level of women being allowed to play in hijab, so while Benzina was the first, she shouldn't have had to be. The moment was historic but reminds us we shouldn't ever be too patient in enacting such important changes. Perhaps what we should have been celebrating is the fact that Morocco has in recent years invested heavily in football development (some US$65 million across three years, spread across both women and men) and is one of the few countries to have two professional women's football tiers.[20]

While the tournament feel was generally buoyant and safe, it did cross the line a few times. In one press conference, a (male) reporter asked the Moroccan captain whether there were any gay players on the team.[21] Homosexuality is banned in Morocco, so the question wasn't just intrusive, it was imperilling. While the question reflected the reporter's ignorance, journalist Eleni Psaltis says, 'I always find it interesting how sport sometimes is the stage for moral absolutes to clash … and how FIFA navigates that. Because it very effectively is the UN, at least with football.'

Mostly, though, the tournament was an all-round success. Apart from breaking broadcast records and bringing the nation to a reverential standstill, it generated US$570 million in total revenue and delivered more than A$3 billion in media value and a A$7.6 billion boost to the Australian economy.[22] That tracks with research by the Office for Women in Sport and Recreation that has identified that every dollar a corporate sponsor invests into women's sport visibility yields, on average, $7.29 return on investment.[23] 'I mean, people spent money,' Matildas Active Support member Fatima Flores says. 'That's important. It generated a lot of revenue, just looking at my own bank account with all the memorabilia I bought, the food, the drinks.'

The tournament was pitched as a tournament of firsts. While that would come to be realised in ways that exceeded the imagination, among those planned firsts of home bases and world-class training environments were the tournament's first-ever fan zones.[24] (There were some small activations at the 2019 tournament, but, as Flores notes, they were underwhelming and a missed opportunity. Sports historian Jean Williams agrees that France as a whole gave the tournament a giant 'Gallic shrug'.) Overall, the nine sites were magnetic. They provided an atmospheric introduction to the game for people not otherwise familiar with it, and a 'second-best' venue for hundreds of thousands of people to watch games to which they hadn't been able to secure a ticket. As we would see during the knockout phases, they would also yield erupting mass celebrations.

The site visitors weren't confined to fans. Attendees included former Matildas coach Tom Sermanni, who had been working for Canada in a technical advisory capacity periodically since 2015. (Something worth noting, now that we're distanced from that intensely stressful situation, is that Sermanni, *the* former Matildas coach who launched the national-team careers of many of the current generation of Matildas, was the person tasked with helping Canada determine the best strategies for defeating them. That's definitely one to chalk up to being glad not to know about ahead of the Canada v Australia group-stage game.) Regardless, fans who attended those sites at the same time as Sermanni were probably oblivious to the history-making Matildas coach just beside them.

First-capped Matilda Julie Dolan also traversed the space and appreciated its broadening of fan engagement. She considers how it contextualised the Matildas' skill at, and relative position in, the world game:

> I saw a goal scored by the Japanese team [while watching from a fan zone]. I don't think I've seen a better goal scored. I was amazed at the level of skill that was on show. At the time, I was so happy because the public got to see how good women footballers were. This hasn't been seen before. There's still very little women's football on TV.

Fan-zone attendees also included FIFA employees at the heart of delivering the tournament. They quietly gravitated to the zones as they immersed themselves in and sought to process some of the tournament's greatest moments. One such moment was after the Australia v France quarter-final. Having survived the penalty shootout, marketing lead Kim Anderson and her peers went to the Brisbane fan zone to watch the England v Colombia game scheduled immediately after it. It was in many ways exactly the space to be, because it made sense to want to keep the party going, but in other ways Anderson and co. were physically and emotionally spent and were content to allow the Colombian fans' excitement to wash over them. Anderson says, 'We were all sitting there drinking lemonade. It was like we didn't have any energy left. We'd expended it all in that moment and were just sort of dumbfounded at making the semis and the way it had all gone.'

7

A MILLIMETRE MATTERS

THE ROUND OF 16 passed rather uneventfully for the Matildas. Truth be told, with the exception of the moment when the newly returned Sam Kerr slipped on the pitch and the entire nation collectively gasped in fear that she was reinjured,[1] there's a sizeable blank spot in my memory of that match. Perhaps it was because it was wedged between such memory-cementing matches as the Canada do-or-die group-stage game and the sudden-death penalty-shootout France quarter-final. Perhaps it was because my brain was so overwhelmed and exhausted it went on the fritz. (Sorry, Denmark. It's me; I'm the problem.) Either way, despite the match being the first knockout one of the Matildas' run, which ramped up the stakes considerably, they dispatched Denmark 2–0 fairly clinically. They and we then focused on what was to come.

The round was not so uneventful for the US team, which recorded its earliest-ever and perhaps most bewilderingly heartbreaking Women's World Cup exit. The team had scraped into the Round of 16 thanks to the shot-saving heroics of an Eden Park goalpost. The post had denied Portugal's Ana Capeta's stoppage-time shot in front of a record New Zealand crowd of 42,958. A millimetre different and the US team, which had only needed a draw to progress and was expected to make it through relatively untroubled, would not have made it out of the group. As it was, the Americans had not looked at all convincing. They entered the Round of 16 off the back of their least-successful-ever group-stage effort and the first time they had not topped their group. (Later, their world ranking would be downgraded to their lowest-ever position: fifth.[2])

Still, things had started lightly enough. The USWNT social media account posted that the team was 'under the lights in "Melby"', having flown across the ditch. The nickname did not fly with locals and the US team copped a roasting. (Even opponents Sweden joined in, posting that the team was 'under the sun in Melbs'.)[3] But that was the least of the US team's concerns. In the match, things quickly turned more serious. Goalkeeping by goalkeepers and goalposts alike meant the match against Sweden finished at 0–0 for the first time ever and subsequently went to penalties.

The shootout seesawed. Or, rather, sawed as Sweden missed, but then, unexpectedly, so did the US team's Megan Rapinoe, the kind of experienced penalty taker whose penalty you'd almost consider a sure thing. Goalkeeper Alyssa Naeher saved Sweden's next attempt. The United States' Sophia Smith missed. That marked four consecutive misses (if you include one save). The rest was a blur. Naeher took the kick when the teams were tied at 3–3. She scored to put the Americans back into the lead, then stepped into the goalmouth to defend. Soon after, Kelley O'Hara, a player as similarly experienced and steady as Rapinoe, hit the post and missed.

Then, Kristie Mewis excelled in a pressure moment you couldn't script: having been substituted on shortly before the end of extra time, her literal first touch of the ball was when she took her penalty. She scored when it would have been entirely understandable had she not. But all of that was nullified courtesy of the penalty with the millimetre that will haunt the United States forever: Sweden's Lina Hurtig's shot hit the crossbar and bounced down and then—as the video assistant referee (VAR) showed down to an infinitesimal degree—in.

To the naked eye, Naeher seemed to get a hand to save Hurtig's penalty, but it was referred to VAR for final determination. There, through replaying the shot in slow motion and from a variety of angles, VAR deemed the whole ball to have crossed the line. (A still image shows its curve abutting just a sliver the right side of the line in a kind of visual challenge that messes with you.) Naeher and the rest of the USWNT were in utter disbelief, shaking heads and fingers, futilely imploring the referee to overturn the decision. Naeher later said that she has a screenshot of the VAR of the ball crossing the line on her phone and has reviewed it 'an unhealthy' number of times.[4])

So, in stunned silence as they processed the gravity of the situation and understandably dove into denial, the US team left the match and the tournament: they'd lost the penalty shootout 4–5. ABBA music was played over the loudspeakers post-penalties—a stark cheeriness bouncing around the stadium's hard surfaces and sure to have put the US team off the Swedish greats. This moment in Melbourne, which played out in a stadium that was proving the downfall for teams other than the Matildas, marked a brutal end to Rapinoe's otherwise limelit career. Given that fellow greats Sinclair's and Marta's World Cup careers also ended there, more than a few media and fans asked if Melbourne was a burial ground for World Cup legends' careers.

It wasn't just occupations. Costumes also fell foul of Melbourne's curse. The Croissants don't take themselves too seriously, approaching everything and everyone with openness and enthusiasm. 'We often talk about that as a very Croissants thing. We call it "the 180". People [at first] either don't understand what we're trying to do or don't like us, and then we manage to swing their opinions pretty quickly,' they explain. Unfortunately, the 180 didn't work on one particular stadium security team. The Croissants have a history of creating ambitious costumes that tend to come on to security's radar as they scan for ambush marketing. Their inflatable crocodile was almost involuntarily admitted to the cloakroom in France in 2019;[5] their Victoria Bitter (VB) costumes (because the game was played in Victoria) suffered that precise fate in Melbourne in 2023. 'We knew there was no marketing allowed [other than that of official sponsors],' the Croissants explain. The plan had been to flip the outfits with the VB motif inside out until they were safely inside the stadium. 'Then the night got away from us, and we got too cocky,' they shrug. (Read: they had a few too many VBs at the pub.) A security guard zeroed in on the costumes and refused them entry in those costumes.

Characteristic of Melbourne meteorology, it was fairly chilly that night. The Croissants had been relying on the costumes to provide them some top-layer warmth. No dice. On social media they subsequently wished everyone except the Door A security team well, after those guys left them 'naked', shivering and 'afraid'.[6] (The Croissants had thin and lightweight Matildas' jerseys on underneath—coverage that offered modesty but not warmth.)

But back to Melbourne's ejection of some greats of women's football. 'That was extraordinary,' David Davutovic says, acknowledging that although Melbourne didn't host a lot of games, it did host games that provided plot twists. He says of the disbelief that accompanied the USWNT's departure, 'USA, the big dogs. It's almost like, surely they can't be knocked out. It's not meant to be; they haven't read the script.'

Rapinoe issued a wry, grief-stricken smile as she traversed the post-match media mixed zone: the ejection's enormity was beginning to sink in. (Equally bad was to come—she would rupture her Achilles minutes into her final National Women's Soccer League (NWSL) match a few months later, two outcomes not befitting the send-off such a game-changer on and off the pitch deserved. As she said afterwards of her Achilles, 'I rode it until the wheels came right off.'[7])

The recriminations about what went wrong began amid a bunch of discussions about goalposts, given the United States had improbably made it in to the Round of 16 after a defensive save by a post and went out via missed penalties that included hitting a post. Coach Vlatko Andonovski departed soon after, but he was arguably the fall guy for what was probably a combination of two main factors. Primarily, before 2023 the previously dominant team had had what sports academic Hunter Fujak explains is 'first-mover advantage'.[8] It was a lead achieved by virtue of investing in the space ahead of the curve and probably as a result of the Title IX legislation, enacted in 1972, that prohibits gender discrimination in education or federally funded activities such as sport.[9] Now that other nations had finally started investing in developing their women's football programs, the United States had been caught up to. (Incidentally, Fujak thinks what we're experiencing now is the Matildas' peak, and that similar first-mover challenges are in the Matildas' future.[10])

Eleni Psaltis notes that even with first-mover advantage, the United States has also seen a number of its women's football leagues fold through lack of investment, so the lead the team had on the world was still relative compared with men's sport. But to Fujak's second point, with some players on the verge of retirement and younger players not yet experienced enough to fill their shoes, as well as too little cohesion gelling the two, the US team was undergoing transition. It happens to every team at some stage, and it's never not excruciating.

8

17 MINUTES UNDER SATURDAY NIGHT LIGHTS

Australia v France, Brisbane, 12 August 2023

THE CALF THAT stopped a nation was surpassed only by the match that stopped the nation: the Matildas' quarter-final against France. It was 0–0 at the end of 120 tense minutes of box-to-box football that included an almost-certain Mary Fowler goal that was saved on the line by the defensive heroics—and specifically the quad—of Élisa De Almeida, who was absolutely outstanding for France and troublesome for the Matildas all match. So the quarter-final headed to the cruellest, most heartrate-elevating of deciders: penalties.

France attempted to do a 'Grey Wiggle' (that is, substitute the match-day goalkeeper with a penalty-saving specialist, as the Socceroos had successfully done with grey-kit-clad Andrew Redmayne in their 2022 Men's World Cup qualifier[1]), injecting Solène Durand into the game shortly before the final whistle. Australia made no such change, electing to stay with its first-choice goalkeeper, Mackenzie Arnold.

As is customary, the penalty-taking order was determined by the flip of a coin. France was to go first. Those of us aware that the team that kicks first tends to win tried not to think of that statistic; we tried instead to recall that the Matildas had defeated France in a friendly in what now seemed like a very long few weeks ago. Heaping on more mental-game pressure was the knowledge that we'd gut-wrenchingly lost on penalties before, most recently against Norway in the 2019 Women's World Cup quarter-final, but also against Brazil at the 2016 Rio Olympics.

So, as the teams stood together in clusters in front of their benches in the minutes before lining up for the penalty kicks, taking in last-minute coaching instructions and pep talks while sipping on electrolyte-replacing drinks, we fans were doing mental arithmetic and our stomachs were doing somersaults. Then, both alone with their thoughts and under the expectant gaze of tens of thousands of people—millions, if you include everyone at home, in pubs, and in fan zones—players from each team steeled themselves and focused on the penalty spot, the ball, and the goal.

What followed that coin flip bent time and changed history.

Watched intently by a stadium full of fans who were not hostile but who were certainly wearing an intimidatingly greater amount of yellow and green than blue, Selma Bacha stepped up to open the penalty-shootout account for France. Connecting solidly, she put her shot left and low, but Arnold correctly anticipated the direction and dove right and saved it. No goal. Australia was off to a good start.

Caitlin Foord was the first penalty taker for Australia. She too went left and low. But unlike Bacha, she buried hers into the bottom corner: Australia took a one-penalty lead, and the mental disadvantage of going second briefly seemed to be overcome. It was nullified almost immediately as Kadidiatou Diani put hers past Arnold to equalise: 1–1.

Stand-in captain Steph Catley, who had successfully taken the penalty in the opening game against Ireland, was next. She put her shot on target but within the keeper's range. Durand parried: Australia's advantage eroded, the score remained 1–1.

French captain Wendie Renard, who had almost boycotted the tournament, scored to edge France ahead: 2–1.

Then Sam Kerr, a usually assured penalty taker but no doubt feeling a little less than in peak form given she had only briefly been on the pitch and by no means invulnerable to pressure, stepped up. By this stage of the tournament, her on-pitch appearance was a steadying presence, but the team had demonstrated that her absence was no longer disastrous. Still, while we were bolstered by the fact she was there, Kerr would have been acutely aware of the 2019 Women's World Cup quarter-final penalties against Norway that were rough and didn't go our way; on that fateful occasion even she, normally assured, sprayed hers. Here, she made it—not by a lot, but by enough: 2–2.

The relief was brief. Eugénie Le Sommer, the leading French national team goalscorer of any gender, assuredly put France ahead again: 3–2.

As if almost oblivious to the pressure, sending the keeper right, Mary Fowler went left. She connected sweetly, putting the ball into the netting with a satisfying thunk: 3–3.

Ève Périsset's penalty hit the post, the tinny 'ding' ringing out. Australia tensed further in anticipation: the shootout had tipped in our favour.

As if she hadn't had enough to do between the posts, Arnold, still gloved and having walked not from the team huddle on the halfway line but from the spot to the right of the uprights where she had been waiting during the alternative penalties, stepped up to shoot. If she scored, Australia was through to the semi-final for the first time in Australian women's or men's footballing history. The headlines were almost writing themselves as she steadied herself to kick. But Arnold's shot, as with Périsset's, rebounded off the post with a deeply dissatisfying and hollow metal ring.

In that moment, Arnold could have dropped her head. Instead, she demonstrated resilience few could muster and managed to get a hand to the next French penalty, that by Grace Geyoro. Arnold didn't quite save the shot, but her tip gave her and us some hope that all was not lost. Australia had one more chance to stay in it.

All eyes turned then to Katrina Gorry as she completed the interminably long walk to the spot. Somehow, she defied her legs of jelly to sink her penalty. It was especially impressive given that she did so just two days after her partner's father had passed away and years after missing a penalty in the 2016 Rio Olympics that had shattered her confidence—a spiral from which she had only in the past few years emerged.

Australia's nerves remained shot, but its hope was never more alive. At various stages in and around this pressure-cooker situation, Arnold threw her arms up, redolent of an orchestra conductor, inviting adulation and guiding our cheers to a crescendo to fuel her next save.

Anticipation ratcheted up yet another notch. Sakina Karchaoui powered her penalty in via a ricochet off the crossbar and with a strength that could easily have sunk the Matildas mentally. But Tameka Yallop, a utility player and veteran of three Women's World Cups, put hers to the right to draw the Matildas level: 5–5.

Maëlle Lakrar made it 6–5. France edged ahead again.

Ellie Carpenter, who had been walking off the line to congratulate or commiserate with each player as they completed the long walk back from taking their shot, stepped up. She hit the post but had her physics right. The shot bounced in: 6–6.

Kenza Dali was next, but Arnold picked the penalty's trajectory and dove to deflect it near the post. Impervious to the fact that fans could scarcely take much more stress, VAR deemed Arnold off her line. The referee ordered a retake. Dali went the same direction in the do-over. Arnold, composed, wasn't wrongfooted and again saved it: VAR this time deemed Arnold's footwork legitimate.

Clare Hunt, a relative newbie but with poise belying her recency to the team, put her penalty straight down the middle. She was banking on Durand diving left or right. But Durand read the course and stayed central and on her feet. She saved the shot: 6–6.

No one, especially not the fans, could take much more of this. Smart watches were sending warnings to their wearers about their dangerously elevated heart rates. (Cheek Media summed up the armchair athlete experience: 'My watch telling me I'm going into cardiac arrest but I'm actually sitting in a chair eating hot chippies watching a group of women fight for their lives on the field.'[2]) Some fans, too stressed to watch, turned their backs to the pitch and experienced the action refracted back at them through the myriad tensed bodies and pained facial expressions.

Taking the 19th penalty, Vicki Bècho hit the post. It was the third post denial of the shootout. Still 6–6.

Then Cortnee Vine, Australia's 10th penalty taker, the 20th penalty taker of the shootout, and someone whom no one thought would have been taking a penalty at this time, stepped up to potentially win it. An eerily oppressive silence and stillness fell upon the 50,000 fans in the stands. It was as though the entire stadium—even its physical structure—was holding its breath.

Without fanfare and with even less hint of the nerves that must have been coursing through her, putting her shot right and out of Durand's reach, win it Vine absolutely did: 7–6.

Australia was through to its inaugural World Cup semi-final.

The stadium—nay, the country—nearly burst with pride and excitement. The roar emitted from the Brisbane Stadium crowd was, for fear of sounding hyperbolic, almost an out-of-body experience. Decibel testing would later reveal the noise and reverberation had broken the stadium's sound record.[3] But in the moment, time slowed down. Jumping, celebrating, bodies moved in slow motion. Overwhelmed senses couldn't comprehend the onslaught of images and sentiment. It felt as though the ground physically shifted. (Cheek Media summed up the organic forcefulness as being able to 'power the city if we had a Monsters Inc electrification setup'.[4] Sydney Water, Australia's largest water utility, later released a graph showing that toilet usage dropped dramatically during the penalty shootout because no one was leaving their couch.[5])

The appreciation for what the team had achieved and the mythology around the penalty shootout grew in subsequent hours, days and weeks. John Aloisi, long lauded as the player who secured the Socceroos' 2006 World Cup berth with an equally diamonds-creating penalty, was happily relegated to being the country's second-best penalty taker.[6] Arnold's penalty-saving heroics spawned 'Brick Wall' nicknames, 'Minister of Defence' memes, and a spoof that included the federal defence minister, Richard Marles, flagging that he was temporarily stepping down for Arnold to take over.[7] As former Matilda Jo Powell terms it, that penalty shootout was 'the making of Mackenzie Arnold'.

It was the making of Vine, too. Befitting how the Matildas' tournament played out, it wasn't their highest-paid, highest-profile player who took the ultimate match-winning, semi-final-berth-cementing penalty. It was the homegrown, domestically based talent Vine, a player who would have been somewhere between the 20th- and 23rd-selected squad member. With the greatest respect, David Davutovic says, 'I reckon if people had fifteen or twenty guesses, I'm not sure they would have picked Cortnee Vine to be the shootout hero.' So life-changing was her effort that Davutovic now refers to the epochs as 'before penalty–after penalty: BP–AP.' It was, Teddy Bryant says, the 'ultimate version of Vine Time',[8] the chant domestic fans had long done in appreciation of Vine and her game-changing, goalscoring prowess.

Almost everyone on the pitch had taken a penalty. Normally, five or so is the upper limit; no way would Vine have expected to be in the mix. Apart from forever changing the way penalties are practised across the country, with everyone further down the list now taking them a little more seriously and assuming they may well have to take one, almost unfathomably this all came after Vine had gone from starting the first two games to being benched, something that can chip your confidence. The mental grit to go from being an observer to a game-changer was next level. Even more incredibly, Vine had never scored a match-winning penalty before. She later said Arnold saving the penalty immediately before her lessened the pressure slightly.[9] I think everyone else witnessing that penalty shootout would beg to differ. 'Penalty shootouts are never good for your health,' Davutovic agrees.

But these were thoughts that would come later. In the moment, we were celebrating what Bryant terms 'the exorcism of Nice', a reversal of the 2019 France quarter-final penalties that proved the team's tournament unravelling. Matildas Active Support member Fatima Flores was so pumped she broke the drum she was tasked with playing: 'I just let loose on that drum and completely punctured a hole through the thing.' (Fortunately, they had back-ups in case of such spirited displays, fellow Matildas Active Support organiser Majella Card explains. They had bought a bunch of second-hand drums from Facebook Marketplace and strategically stationed a few in each state for ease of transport.)

The moments following that penalty-shootout win were ultimately rapturous, proud, awe-filled. But they were laden with a bittersweet sense that we could and should have been here sooner. For so long, a *century* or more, we'd been told ad nauseam that there was no market for women's football, that nobody wanted to watch it. The quarter-final and its pressure-cooker penalty shootout didn't just prove that wrong—it put it in the bin. The men who had blocked and in some cases actually managed to ban women's football over the past century for fear it would outperform and outsell the men's game? Their fears had finally been realised. They would have been absolutely rolling in their graves. It was reminiscent of sentiment-equivalent social media posts that declared it a brutal day for the 'Nobody cares about women's sports' crew.

What had just happened was absolutely seismic. In stark contrast to all the times when the Matildas had been on the cusp of a breakthrough only to have their support fall away and apart, this not only felt different, but everyone instinctively, definitively *knew* it was different. That's what made it so powerful. There is now an identifiable, point-at-able moment in women's football, and in Australian culture more widely, that is before that penalty shootout and after it. Nothing and no one can undermine it. ('Not just a game-changer—a society changer,' former Matildas manager and head of competition for the tournament Jo Fernandes wrote on social media the day after the quarter-final. 'I mean, we're not doing things by halves,' Danielle Warby told me.)

Suffice to say, Caxton Street popped off that night.

Also, there were tears. Lots of tears. After initially almost levitating through euphoria at the Matildas' win, I stood very still and very silent, ugly-crying, almost out of my own body, amid 50,000-odd fans pinballing around the stadium in relief and delight. I thought my emotional outpouring was an anomaly, but over subsequent hours and days I discovered that a number of other women in and around the game had had similar experiences. These included journalist Sam Squiers, who posted an emotionally raw video of herself sitting at her TV news desk. She says:

I was just exhausted, overwhelmed. I felt like every ounce of emotion had been drained out of me in that shootout. I was at work and took myself off to the production room to watch. Unbeknownst to me my colleague took a video of me just after we won, sobbing uncontrollably, an ugly cry in the room by myself. This match was more than just Australia winning. To me it was about the bigger picture, it was about the nation—the world, even—finally investing financially and emotionally in women's sport. The country had taken this unprecedented passion and interest in the team winning this match, getting to the stage no Australian team had ever been before, and sealing victory now in this shootout after all this emotional investment would unleash a euphoria, an excitement, a collective elation like we'd never seen before. [If we lost] now, I felt faith would be lost, it would feel like a collective false hope. So when Cortnee Vine made that glorious penalty, it all came crashing down on me.

I had to go straight on air and, minutes beforehand, as I was touching up my makeup and fixing my hair on air, I was overcome again and buried my head in my hands on the desk, tears flowing again. I had seconds to clean myself up until I was on air. I thought I did well, but people later said they were themselves overcome with emotion seeing my tear-filled eyes during that bulletin on Fox Sports News.

It was the most magical, professional, fulfilling and validating month of my career. I felt like I was constantly living in the future, the future we knew was always possible but were constantly fighting to convince everyone else. Images of the Matildas projected high on the city's skyscrapers, billboards with their faces, walking to school and hearing dads, mums, girls and boys all talking Matildas tactics and excitement, then the ratings, the live sites, the viewing figures we'd never seen before—astronomical figures we never thought were possible to reach in this age of entertainment options, distractions and social media. Our Matildas transcended what was possible.

> Standing outside Stadium Australia for the Matildas' semi-final, I took a moment to watch [75,000] people flooding through the gates and reflected on the fact that less than a decade before I was writing articles and questioning the hierarchy [about] why the Matildas games were being played behind closed doors and questioning their response that they couldn't fill a stadium. They could. They hadn't changed—they were champions then, most of the players now were the Matildas playing then—but finally everyone else had caught up, had realised how incredible they were and were loving every part of their journey too. Sport would never be the same again.

Former Matilda turned commentator Grace Gill was also among the women who registered the enormity of it all: 'When it went to the sixth, seventh kicker, I think one of the most impressive things was the players kicking not to win the game but to stay in the game. To me, that pressure was palpable. And terrifying and exciting.' Like the players, Gill couldn't allow the emotion to consume her; moment by moment, she focused on the job she had to do. After Vine scored the winning penalty, she and co-commentator David Basheer provided an initial explanation of the result. Then they deliberately went silent to allow the moment to breathe, to allow the television audience to absorb the emanating crowd noise and the historic enormity. 'After we let that nice moment of pause play out, I came in to do my part as expert commentator, and my sentence … my voice just broke,' Gill tells me.[10]

That heart-in-throat emotion played out with Ash Sykes, who was commentating the match with journalist Niav Owens and footballer Chloe Logarzo. The latter had narrowly missed being selected for the tournament itself. In the seconds following Vine's penalty, Sykes and Logarzo, both of whom have experience of playing in, losing out from or missing out on Women's World Cups, understandably struggled to speak. 'Niav, because she's such a pro, kept the show going for us,' Sykes explains of the crucial filled airtime Owens bought them to regroup.

★ ★ ★

It was a twenty-penalty shootout that marked the longest penalty shootout in World Cup history—Women's or Men's—and that played out across seventeen excruciating minutes. (It took 49.11 seconds for Cathy Freeman to change Australia forever; seventeen minutes is how long it took for the Matildas to do the same.)

In the post-match press conference, French coach Hervé Renard commended his team 'for playing so well against an entire nation'.[11] He wasn't wrong. Brisbane Stadium and beyond had been a cauldron of support. That match and specifically that penalty shootout spawned nationwide where-were-you moments.[12]

Comedian and football fan Mel Buttle watched those penalties from the stands, linking arms with strangers. She likens the anticipation level to the knockout phases of reality TV shows:

> 'The person leaving us tonight is ...' We were all holding each other. The bar at the venue had closed. There was nowhere else to be. Everyone was watching in silence and then roaring or going 'Ohhh'. I had my fingers crossed. I had my legs crossed. I had my arms looped around people. We were turning to each other, almost praying.

Documentary-maker Maggie Miles was working away on another project while the Women's World Cup played out, so she lived vicariously through co-director Maggie Eudes' adventures and broadcasts. 'I was actually quite remote, moving between places and desperately trying to get an internet connection so I could watch each of the games. A couple of them I had to watch on my phone because it was such crappy reception,' Miles explains. She recalls checking in to some fairly humble Cairns accommodation the afternoon of the France quarter-final:

> There was an older woman behind the reception. She said, 'You watching the game tonight?' That was it. No precursor. No 'Which game?' I said, 'You bet I am.' She knew nothing about me, and just that exchange, I thought, *Wow, that means more than: Are you watching the game tonight?*

Eudes was in the stadium for the match, and it feels appropriate now perhaps to mention that Miles originally hails from England and Eudes from France. Eudes had a friend who knew a player from the French team. That player's family and friends hadn't travelled out for the tournament, so Eudes and her partner were fortunate recipients of the player's complimentary tickets. 'But that meant we were in the friends-and-family section,' Eudes says. 'I was going for the Matildas,' she says, despite her French origins, 'and my partner was in full Matildas gear.'

Football fan and football mum Sharon Meitner and her husband had been sharing parenting responsibilities and match attendance all tournament, with one of their daughters volunteering as a flag-bearer. (That daughter had the quintessential woman footballer experience, with the only kit available comically oversized and absolutely swimming on her; it better fits her dad.) Meitner had drawn the short parental-duties straw on quarter-final night and had taken one of her daughters to a dance eisteddfod that inadvertently coincided with the match. She and the other parents in the audience weren't channelling any kind of stage-parent facade, though: while their children danced, they furtively kept an eye on the penalties on their phones, including receiving updates from their partners who were watching live or at home.

Avid fan Bryan Crawford and his wife Emma,[13] who had taken their six- and four-year-old daughters Audrey and Ivy to the game, delayed longer-term pain for short-term gain by stoking their tired but wired daughters with sugar-filled lollies as the extra time and penalties extended the match well past the girls' bedtime. It was the first match Audrey and Ivy had attended in person, and the 50,000-strong crowd and breathtaking twenty-penalty shootout set the bar for all subsequent games inordinately but impressively high.

Karen Menzies, who was the country's first Aboriginal Matilda,[14] was watching on television at her Newcastle home. Needing to work off some of the nervous energy, she paced up and down her lounge room. 'As soon as we got to extra time, I didn't sit down for the thirty minutes,' she says. She continued pacing throughout the penalty shootout 'and became the official commentator of my house'.

Journalist Eleni Psaltis's husband is French and the couple were watching the match—and the penalties—together at home. 'He did say to me, "Eleni, whatever happens it doesn't matter." I said, "It sure fucking does,"' she laughs. 'He was gracious. I was not.'

They weren't the only ones experiencing that. Fan Lucie Curry Chéenne explains it thusly: 'Our French-Australian household felt very torn, but also a winner no matter what!'

Fan Clair Zaghini was out to dinner with her husband and friends at a tiny fine-dining restaurant in the Brisbane central business district. They were trying to wait politely until the match finished before leaving the restaurant, but weren't expecting the penalties. Caught in no-person's land, they ended up ducking across the road to watch the shootout at a packed, slightly seedy pub. Their children were watching at home and providing text updates to supplement their viewing. 'I don't usually follow sports while out at social events and was trying not to be rude at dinner,' Zaghini explains, 'but I was invested and then realised the whole restaurant was doing the same thing.'

Shona Bass witnessed the penalties firsthand in the stadium with fellow Matildas Alumni. She gained a sense of what it was like to watch from home, though, through receiving multiple texts from a CEO she knows who had never shown any prior interest in sport. During the penalty shootout, the CEO messaged, '"Oh my god, I've gone and done washing now" because she [couldn't] stand the tension,' Bass recounts. 'At the end of the penalty shootout she sent me a photo of their burnt dinner that had been in the oven and neither [she nor her partner] remembered.'

Melbourne-based fan Joanne Bee happened to be visiting family in Brisbane that weekend. Bee watched the Spain v Netherlands match at the South Bank fan zone and thought that would be as good as it would get during the trip:

> The night before the match I was half-heartedly playing the ticket resale marketplace lottery (refreshing the page over and over) and scored a single ticket! So with less than twenty-four hours' notice I ditched the family to hang out at [Brisbane]

Stadium instead. I also caught up with an old friend and made a new friend because of that match.

Self-described lifelong fan Linda Male and her family had tickets as part of their savvily pre-purchased stadium passes, not in any way anticipating that their second-row seats would be directly behind the penalty-shootout goal. The intensity of the match was a level Male had not experienced before and has not experienced since: 'After the pandemonium my granddaughter's watch went off, warning her that the noise was damaging her ears ... It was later reported that the decibel level was the highest ever recorded at [Brisbane] Stadium!'

Katherine Harris and her daughters took her mother to the game in what could now only be termed as unsurpassable timing and forward-thinking:

> She had never before been inside a sporting stadium, let alone a sold-out stadium. She started following the Matildas from her home back in New South Wales, where she lives alone, because my daughter has the goal of being in the A-League Women's. She knew all their names but had never seen them play off the screen. She brought her earplugs. Little did we know that she was really going to need them!

Perth-based Cassie Crispin and her partner had booked tickets to *The Rocky Horror Show* at Crown Perth. The two surreptitiously followed along as best they could throughout the performance. The moment the show finished, they were out of their seats and 'practically running' to the sports bar in the same venue. The West Australian–Queensland time difference worked in their favour and they were able to catch the rest of the second half as well as the extra time and penalties surrounded by hundreds of other people loudly cheering.

Jarrod Gunn was at a 1980s-themed trivia night with terrible reception and a (slightly implausible given the circumstances) ban on phones. The final round had to be delayed because his friend managed to establish a few bars of reception and get the feed to work on his phone. Another friend took photos of the crowd of people huddled around that one phone to document the historic moment.

Fan Natasha Hackett had been following all the games and realised the quarter-final would coincide with a friend's fiftieth birthday party that was due to be held at a pub close to the Brisbane Stadium precinct. Hackett and her partner elected to travel in early to watch the game on a big screen before the party started. They watched part of the first half on their phones on the train on the way in. Then, they heard the stadium crowd explode while they were walking down Caxton Street and ducked in to the Caxton Hotel to see what was happening. At half-time they continued on to the party venue, settling in in front of the big screen there and thinking they were set:

> Here we were, thinking we were so smart fitting this in before the party, but little did we know what was ahead. As the game went on, we watched more of our friends pass by and head into the function room for the fiftieth. *We can be fashionably late, right?* The game continued and then we saw the birthday girl arrive and enter the room. Crap!

Realising they couldn't delay any longer, they headed into the party but proceeded to venture out every few minutes to check the score. Increasing numbers of people joined them in doing so. 'We were all feeling bad for our friend but were desperate to see the Matildas win,' Hackett explains. They eventually decided they couldn't miss any more of the match and, gathering around the big screen to watch the penalties, were prepared to face the wrath of the birthday girl. That wasn't all that was going on in the hectic moment. 'We'd watch in anticipation on the big screen but the "real-life" screams from the crowd at [Brisbane] Stadium would resonate from outside and beat the TV coverage! So we had had a three-second preview of the result before the coverage on the screen.'

Eleven months into a sixteen-month camper-trailer trip, Sarah Wordsworth, who normally lives a four-minute drive from Brisbane

Stadium, was in Broome, Western Australia—the town that is, she says, 'about as far away as you can get from the stadium without leaving the country'. But she found a way to make it work:

> We planned ahead by phoning a local sports bar on Cable Beach to make sure they were showing the game, then had to book the dog into the local vet for overnight dog-sitting so we'd be able to sit inside the pub to see the TV. We got there as early as we could to get a good table, and plied the kids with chips and lemonade to keep them happy.

Making a day of it as it fell within Wordsworth's and her husband's birthday week (her husband was born on 10 August and she on 15 August, bookending the game, which was on 12 August), the family watched the penalties amid other Australian and French fans. 'The stress of watching that penalty shootout was unbelievable, more stress than I've ever felt actually being in one myself!'

Needing to expend some of the cortisol the penalty shootout was inducing, Isobel Cootes had been pacing back and forth around a less-busy part of the media tribune. She had her noise-cancelling headphones on and was attuned to the commentary playing through them, writing, pacing some more, tensely waiting. 'I was stressed. I remembered the losing penalty shootouts at the [2016 Rio] Olympics [and the 2019 Women's World Cup quarter-final]. I was just like, *I don't know if we're going to have learned from it. We're notoriously not great in these situations.*'

Cootes had a history of injuring her right shoulder and had even undergone a reconstruction. Her left shoulder had until that point been trouble-free. But when Vine's penalty sent the Matildas to the semi-final, Cootes instinctively leapt up in a two-handed celebratory 'Oh what a feeling, Toyota' jump. In her words: 'I've babied my right [shoulder], which is my bad one, and then just gone full throttle with my left.'

That full-throttle physical reaction dislocated her left shoulder. Given the post-penalties pandemonium unfolding in the stadium, no one around Cootes noticed. Her team were scattered at other locations, working around the stadium. Other people in the vicinity were either too busy revelling, or too busy working to convey the match result and its significance to the millions of people watching the broadcast from fan zones and from home, to notice. Also, the ever-professional Cootes had a story to file. She threw her shoulder back in ('Thankfully, I have nearly a PhD in shoulder dislocations and relocations,' she quips) and raced back to her desk to submit the piece.

Story filed, she headed down towards the mixed zone and press conference that were about to kick off. 'There was actually a very cute moment,' she recalls. Matilda Clare Hunt had had a shoulder reconstruction amid a run of injuries that had delayed her admission to the team. Cootes coincidentally crossed paths with Hunt just minutes after her own dislocation and said, 'Guess what I did?' 'She was just laughing, like, "Oh my god, are you OK?"'

The match-induced exhilaration no doubt curtailed the worst of Cootes' shoulder pain and carried her through the subsequent hours—deadlines and the desire to mark the incredible football occasion prevailed, and she didn't return to her hotel until 3 a.m.

> It was an insane day and night that if you had told me what was going to happen, I would have said we were not going to make it through the day. But thankfully, just the adrenaline and the absolute scenes in Australia made it OK. But the next day we're in the airport, and I'm like, 'I need to go get a sling.' I think [my colleagues] were very confused: 'Oh, you're being serious.' And I was like, 'Yeah, what did you think I meant?'

Pokuah Frimpong was at Federation Square in Melbourne for the penalty shootout. It was a masterclass in people watching. Frimpong explains:

> Not to say that women's football is just for women, but there were men there about whom you would typically say, 'Oh, you would *never* be interested in women's football. It's not a thing for you.' But there were so many of them, saying, 'Oh, go,

> Macca, go!' You know, saying the names of players. They had learned the nicknames of players and were going, 'Oh, Sammy, you can do it' and stuff like that. Particularly Fed Square, being there for the Men's World Cup playing Denmark [in 2022 to advance to the Round of 16 for just the second time] and then also being there for the [women's] game against France, it was actually quite a similar demographic of people who were: *Oh, OK, I'm all in. I really am invested in this, I identify with this team, this team represents me.*

Frimpong says that was heartening to see, and notes that underpinning it is an important commercial reality:

> I think it's important to continue making women feel incredibly comfortable in the space so they can come into it. But in order for the game to be more financially viable, you need to have men as well, younger children, older people, investing in the game and wanting to spend their money to buy jerseys and encouraging other people. Seeing that at Fed Square made me feel really positive about the long-term viability of the game in Australia.

(FIFA marketing professional Evie Chamberlain makes an interesting observation about that jersey uptake: 'There seems to be a bit more depth in how people will decide their favourite player.' She compares it to the previous ubiquity of, say, Messi jerseys among fans, especially young boys. 'Every single person had a Messi jersey. There was just no conversation about that. Whereas here, my impression was you saw a lot more diversity of names on the shirts. People were making informed decisions. They were watching the games, they were watching that player's social media, they were actually interested in asking, *Who is this person?*')

'I died a thousand times in that penalty shootout, like everyone. I don't think I will ever forget it,' Kim Anderson says. 'Totally emotional' is how she later describes it: 'We were crying, happy, cheering. There's crazy videos of us just sort of— I don't even know what we're doing.' She references the thought so many of us had—how long it had taken to get to that point—but also the collective experience:

> I had a little one-year-old niece who was sitting in the stadium. My brother was texting me going, 'Is this going to be over soon? Because she's probably not going to [last].' In the beginning, she's clapping. Then by the end, she's got the headphones on. The cheers were way too loud. It felt like a rock concert or something ... there's something so tangible about everyone feeling the same thing at the same time.

Fan Karleen Stevens was watching from the Adelaide live site with her brother, who was visiting from Melbourne. 'When Cortnee Vine kicked that winning penalty, we were jumping up and down like crazy people,' she says. 'It was probably the first time in more than thirty years that I had spontaneously hugged my brother!'

For Football Australia digital lead Liana Buratti, the moment was the culmination of a long road:

> When I first started in this space almost a decade ago, barely anyone was covering women's football or women's sport generally. I approached various federations and was told there was no budget to cover it, so I offered to write profiles and match reports for free. That's where I started.
>
> Fast forward to 2023 and we're hosting a FIFA Women's World Cup on home soil. We've overcome all this adversity, like the players having to go on strike to advocate for equal pay, we've had multiple changes in coaching ... Between April and September of 2021, we played twelve matches and only won two. The public and the media were absolutely brutal on social media during this time, not quite understanding the 'method behind the madness'. The criticism became less about the players being players and more about the players being women, or in some cases, being women from the LGBTQIA+ community, which was really horrible to deal with and moderate on social media.

> This is why our content strategy has always been based around something I like to call 'Come for the performance, stay for the personality'—because results aren't always guaranteed, but if you fall in love with these players for who they are, because they are great people before they are great athletes, you connect with fans and supporters in an authentic and holistic way that isn't just based on what the players do on the pitch.
>
> So, in saying that, sitting through that nailbiting penalty shootout against France and covering it for the Matildas channels was an experience that I don't think could ever be matched in my career, because of how meaningful it was in so many ways. I believe in professionalism on the ground, but these women had united the nation, they'd changed perspectives, they'd totally redefined what it meant to be a female athlete ... so once we'd done what we needed to do, I excused myself from the media box to take it all in and that's when the tears started flowing!

Lisa Duhig's family of five and her mother watched the penalties in the live site outside Stadium Australia, ahead of the England quarter-final to be played there that night. They were joined by a group of England fans—complete strangers—who lived every rollercoaster moment with them before melting back into the crowd. 'It was made more interesting by the fact there was a delay among screens and we could hear the crowd response from the next screen up!' Duhig explains. 'When Vine scored we celebrated and hugged, then we never saw [the England fans] again. We did get English flags on our faces to support [our] new friends.'

Celeste Harris and her father were at the Brisbane Showgrounds for the annual agricultural show, or the Ekka as it is known ('Ekka' is short for 'exhibition'), and sat down to eat one of the event's famed strawberry sundae ice creams. Harris pulled out her phone to watch the penalties and she and her father were joined by a few other families who came over to peer at the screen. 'It was just my dad and me and a crowd of about twenty other people. They were people I had never met before, but in that moment everyone was connected by the Matildas,' Harris explains. 'They stopped the car show in the main arena to announce that Australia had won the penalty shootout, and the crowd went crazy.'

It went wider than that. Plausibly apocryphal, pizza delivery people reported that every house they visited had the match on. Likewise, one person reportedly watched the penalty shootout with a house of strangers after wandering into the wrong party. It was such a significant moment, though, that those strangers invited them to stay. At the opposite end of the spectrum, and something that brought joy to those of us weary of his Teflon-coated buffoonery, conservative politician Barnaby Joyce inadvertently watched a replay of the previous month's friendly rather than the live quarter-final.[15]

Fan Simone Shelton's daughter Annabelle was a part of the England v Colombia quarter-final ball crew in Sydney. Given that that match was due to kick off shortly after the Australia v France game, her daughter was ensconced in the stadium while the additional time and the penalty shootout unfolded. Shelton explains:

> She was a little disappointed not to be able to watch it properly, but excited for the job ahead nonetheless. She got to watch snippets of the game in the dressing room as they waited, but the teams started warming up so the ball crew were needed in their places ready to retrieve and return balls for the players. One of the media people on the sideline was watching the game on her phone and my daughter quietly asked how it was going as she walked to her place. The woman was nice enough to stay near Annabelle so she could watch a little bit between tasks and whisper updates, but unfortunately the ball crew had to go back into the dressing rooms before the end.

Shelton witnessed it second-hand, too. She and her husband were in the Stadium Australia stands to support Annabelle. (The family have since moved from Coffs Harbour to the Illawarra region to enable Annabelle to attend the sports high school there and pursue her aspirations of becoming a Matilda.) The roar after each penalty that was emitted from the live site outside Stadium

Australia for fans to watch the Australia match before heading inside provided a kind of real-life surround-sound experience. It was so loud that Annabelle later said she could hear the cheering from inside the change rooms.

Vi Truong was out to dinner celebrating her twentieth birthday and delayed the song and cake-cutting to watch the penalties: 'Oddly enough, [it] felt like a really fitting coming-of-age moment watching the players seal the deal and leaving my teen years behind.'

'I remember going out for dinner that night with friends. I was late because, you know, I hadn't planned for penalties. I thought they'd get it done within ninety minutes,' Davutovic says. He needn't have worried. It was the only topic of discussion for anyone in and around the restaurant when he finally made it.

It was the talk of marathon training, too. Susan Franco was late to training the following morning, but spent the entire 30-kilometre session talking about and energised by that epic moment. 'My women-only running group couldn't wipe the smiles off our faces,' she says.

Em Tea's experience is, by their own reckoning, a 'much less glamorous tale—I'd ended up with two prolapsed discs after jumping around like a maniac after the Melbourne match [against] Canada, so was relegated to watching the France match horizontal on the couch—I couldn't even get up to cheer!' Tea was grateful that the painkillers they'd been prescribed for back spasms helped them remain slightly calmer during the penalties: 'There were still tears of relief and happiness by the end, but [I was probably] only 60 per cent as stressed as I might have been otherwise.'

Sixty per cent less stress wasn't what former Matilda Sue Monteath or fan and mother of aspiring Matilda Katie Zerbst experienced. While Zerbst found the whole experience so intense it triggered a migraine and left her unable to drive home, Monteath experienced the penalty shootout inside the stadium alongside Katrina Gorry's father, Peter, and stepmother, Michelle—so it was a doubly stressful experience. Acutely aware of how tricky the unsuccessful Olympics penalty had been for Gorry, Michelle couldn't watch her taking this one. 'What a relief when Mini [Gorry] coolly put her penalty away this time!' Monteath says.

Fan Ann Fraser Oldford had tickets for the England v Colombia quarter-final, and juggling travel time with watching both matches proved tricky. After watching the first half and some of the second half from their hotel, they boarded a train bound for Stadium Australia along with other fans trying to do the double:

> We were all watching the game on our phones, on which, of course, were all getting the feed at different rates. So each penalty rippled through the train car—a remarkable shared experience. Every time we went through a tunnel, we'd all lose the stream! We got off at Sydney Olympic Park just in time to catch the last couple of pens.

Streaming proved a challenge for Selina Ali Cisneros, too, as she and others attending the England match tried to watch the penalties on their phones:

> The bandwidth kept failing so we'd hear cheers and groans echoing across the grounds. We ended up huddling by one man who managed to get it running on his phone—there were like thirty of us trying to watch on one phone, stressed out by the chaos around us as different moments were happening.

Meanjin-based writer Ellen van Neerven wasn't in town for what they term the 'most important match ever on Yagera and Turrbal land' because they had prior Byron Writers Festival commitments. Trying to zig and zag between the three panels they were on, the pub showing the game, and an event featuring four Bundjalung writers, van Neerven too had not accounted for penalties. Conflicted and wanting to fulfil all commitments, they sat at the back of the theatre supporting their peers while surreptitiously studying the game's progression via the Optus Sport app. At the ultimate moment they, like a few others they encountered there, snuck out to the foyer to watch the penalties on tiny phone screens, hoping no one would notice their absence.[16]

Anna Santaguida was at her cousin's wedding with more than 600 other people. Dotted among the reception tables were people watching the penalties on their phones. 'All throughout the guests were reacting, and when the winning penalty kick was scored the place erupted and [the cheering and celebration] basically took over,' Anna explains. 'The DJ blasted "Down Under" and everyone was on the dance floor celebrating!'

Kieran Pender witnessed the match from a wedding, too. As he had done with the 2019 iteration, he was covering every match for *The Guardian*, but the quarter-final coincided with his best friend's wedding—she was the bride and he was her best man. Pender had informed his editor from the outset that he could cover every Matildas match *except* the quarter-final, if the Matildas made it. Fast-forward to game and wedding day. The match played out during the post-ceremony photos and canapés. Pender was sitting at the bridal table as it went to penalties:

> I managed to watch the first five penalties on my phone, but then the father of the bride began his speech, so I figured she would kill me if I still had my phone out, and I put it away. Which meant I missed what followed, until there were audible cheers from the back of the venue as tables that hadn't put their phones away reacted to the winning pen.

For once, Bruce McAvaney, whose narration has for so long provided the soundtrack to our most memorable sporting moments, including the Cathy Freeman one, did not attend in person. He experienced the penalty shootout as so many of us have so many great sporting moments, mediated and guided through by broadcast commentary:

> This was very weird for me. I'd been too unwell to travel to that single incredible match, so watched from home. It was unbelievable, that whole night. Surreal, because I had a sense of

> loss by not being part of it, but that was completely overshadowed by the outrageous ending to an exceptional match. The television rating figures were off the charts—not a complete surprise because of the build-up, with each match leading into that quarter-final drawing bigger and bigger numbers. Nobody who saw that match will ever forget it.

It's no small detail that McAvaney draws a direct link between the Freeman 400-metre final and the Australia v France quarter-final. 'The Freeman moment is as strong symbolically today as it was twenty-four years ago,' he tells me. 'My belief is the [2023] tournament will always be a where-were-you moment. And the centrepiece of that will be Cortnee Vine putting the ball in the back of the net, and the scenes that followed.'

'After watching all the group games and Round of 16 matches, I had to go to a sixtieth [birthday party] on the night of the quarter-final against France,' says Declan Boylan, who is the founder of Seven Consulting, the firm that sponsored the Matildas in the years when women's sports were not considered viable investments. The firm also provided paid internships for Tameka Yallop and Elise Kellond-Knight. Declan continues:

> After watching the first half with my son at home, I rushed by Uber across town, watching on my iPad and passing by dozens of packed pubs filled with green-and-gold-covered supporters. Arriving at the Northern Beaches rowing club, the attendees were all increasingly in thrall as we moved through the second half, extra time and into penalties. The speeches were all deferred continually as the man of the moment conceded to the women of the moment. Each penalty taken, scored, saved was felt throughout the room, as people took to the air, knee and each other. Having worked with Tameka in Seven Consulting over the years, I found a new level of religion as she stepped up in sudden death and scored. The ecstasy of when Cortnee Vine scored of knowing we were going to a World Cup semi-final lifted the room, and rooms across the nation.

Ell Katte and her partner didn't watch the game live as they were attending her nephew's birthday party. They decided to block out all media and watch a recording back at home afterwards. The drive home took approximately an hour and Katte and her partner glimpsed images of Mackenzie Arnold on screens at a pub they were driving past. The two tried to avert their gaze and keep their 'horse blinkers' on to preserve the blackout. The moment they entered their apartment, they could hear cheering, then pauses, then more cheering from the apartments around them. Katte rightly deduced that the game had gone to penalties but still, demonstrating superhuman willpower, they watched the game from the start. The two sat up for the next few hours and had, as she explains, 'our own little delayed review of it'.

US-based fan Laura Dabney and her family committed to overcoming the time difference. They had caught a few of the games while visiting Australia but had returned to their hometown in Indiana by the time of the quarter-final. 'We set our alarms, the kids had some of their friends over, and we watched it in the wee hours of the morning. It was so fun—everyone was so invested and shouting!'

Mikayla King was a volunteer with the Women's World Cup airport transfer team. She was on shift during the game and, as it was one of the quieter nights (perhaps ostensibly because everyone was in a stadium or at home watching the quarter-finals), the team watched the first half of the game together on site before being sent home at half-time. She says:

> I continued to watch the game the entire way home on the train. I managed to get to my car just before the penalties started, and I didn't turn on that car until it was over. I was a crying mess by the end of it. It will always be a where-were-you moment!

Journalist Samantha Lewis maintained her composure throughout the tournament, but the penalty shootout entailed a brief moment where she allowed herself to temporarily sidestep her professional objectivity. 'I literally stood up from my chair. I was like, *Fuck this, I'm filming this on my phone. I need to be part of this moment, just in case it happens. Because it's literal history.*' She still has the video of herself 'screaming and shattering the eardrums of the people in the vicinity' after Vine's penalty hit the back of the net. She continues:

> After maybe an hour of running around to all of my friends in the media box being, like, 'Did that really happen? Oh, my god, did that really happen?', I had to very consciously compartmentalise and put my own emotions aside and click into work mode. Because I had deadlines, I knew I needed to be able to somehow capture this moment and how it felt and what it meant for so many people in order to tell a cohesive and coherent story for the following day. I think I was up until four o'clock in the morning trying to put the story together.

In echoes of peer Sarah Gregorius's earlier experience, Sarah Walsh witnessed the shootout in the VIP enclave alongside former teammates. Walsh explains:

> We were, like, we want to fill this place with people who built it, so we would rotate alumni through the VIP [area]. That night the prime minister was in there, but I remember when I watched the penalty shootout with a group of us former Matildas, we were in tears together. When it finished, we were beside ourselves. It was fitting that we could all be together to watch it.

Matildas Active Support member Stephanie Messinis recalls the three-second silence that occurred when the whistle went at extra time to send Australia and France to penalties. She and best mate and fellow member Flores stood in silence for another thirty seconds with thousand-yard stares, processing the gravity of the situation. Eventually, Messinis turned to Flores and stated that this was it, make or break. Flores responded, 'I can't handle this, it's too much.' Feeling much the same sentiment but grasping for something comforting to say, the only words Messinis could think of were 'Keep the faith.' Repeating the mantra, she braced until the end of the interminably long shootout, when Vine's shot released a nationwide pressure valve.

So stoked were the Matildas Active Support group that they spent a further twenty-five minutes hugging, screaming, issuing high fives, and chanting in their dedicated supporters' zone until security politely asked them to exit the stadium—the game was over; it was time to go home. But they weren't going home. Wanting to soak up every moment and feeding off the energy of everyone around them, the crew continued chanting and marching out to the Wally Lewis statue—a kind of stadium touchstone—and then trod a reverse path up Caxton Street and partied into the night.

From attending the Australian national women's football team's first-ever A International match to travelling as far afield as Uzbekistan forty-five years later, football administrator Heather Reid AM has watched many a Matildas match in her time. (The 2023 Women's World Cup was her seventh World Cup. She was also the first Australian to obtain media accreditation for a Women's World Cup when she attended the inaugural official Women's World Cup in China in 1991.) The quarter-final was the eighth 2023 Women's World Cup game she'd attended as she journeyed with her partner up and down the east coast to support the team and tournament. But this match was a little different:

> It was the only game where I didn't leave my seat to get food or drinks or go to the loo. I was riveted for the entire 120 minutes plus injury time, plus every single one of the twenty penalties … until Vine scored the final winning goal, when all hell broke loose. It was the most tense, sickening, thrilling game I'd ever seen in over four decades of supporting women's football.

For Football Australia corporate affairs and brand chief Peter Filopoulos, the significance of the moment was demonstrated by how it reached his family, and specifically his 86-year-old mother: 'She rang me the night of the penalty shootout. She was crying, and couldn't believe how good they were—"It's amazing, and I'm so proud of you for being involved with this thing, and I didn't realise how big …"' Filopoulos was taken aback. It was a sign of how far-reaching the tournament's impact was that his mother had tuned in and watched every minute of the game and been so swept up emotionally. 'I thought, *Wow, my mum, she does not watch sport …* For her to sit there and watch all of that game and have that reaction meant *OK, we've really touched every part of [the country].*'

Football administrator John Didulica watched the match from a first Holy Communion after-party at a Croatian community hall. The room would normally have divided into three groups: men, women, kids. Except on this night, no one split off:

> There was not one person, old or young (I'm talking about demographically from eight to eighty), who wasn't around the TV cheering the Matildas on. That was quite profound for me because it was so different from what normally happened for me watching sport … I'd never seen anything like it.

'Nothing like it' is accurate. The match played out under Saturday-night lights in the prime time normally reserved for men's sport. TV news bulletins were delayed—a rare move for each station's flagship program. The Australian Chamber Orchestra's Sydney concert was also delayed as performers and audience members alike peered intently at phone screens to watch the penalty shootout in a perhaps unparalleled meeting of sports and arts culture. Coincidentally, French ambassador Jean-Pierre Thébault was in attendance at the orchestra's show.[17]

Both the Melbourne Cricket Ground (MCG) and the Sydney Cricket Ground altered Australian Football League (AFL) Men's game start times and broadcast the Matildas match in-stadium to avoid fans electing to stay home to watch the Women's World Cup as the Australian public made it abundantly clear which match/code/gender it chose. The national women's football team has only been around officially for a little over forty years, but that night it surpassed a male sporting code that has existed for more than 100.[18] There's even YouTube footage of AFL commentators veering into Matildas commentary mid-match.[19] Wheelchair tennis great and former Australian of the Year Dylan Alcott, who was at the MCG, posted a video on his social media with a caption documenting the moment the MCG crowd witnessed Vine sink her penalty: 'My god, closest I've ever been to standing up!!!'[20] Truly, the match stopped the nation *and* moved men's sport.

★★★

Even before the penalty-shootout heroics, the match had been shaping up to be epic. People were wearing jerseys and scarves in public reminiscent of the all-day affairs people normally engage in with men's sports. With fans making a day of it and converging on Caxton Street and the stadium hours before game time, the precinct was humming. Then, just before kick-off, the small but merry Matildas Active Support crew marched down the street making noise. Majella Card was leading on drums, Pied Piper style. As they approached the stadium forecourt, Card, Teddy Bryant, Messinis and Flores glanced behind them to encounter a sight that was almost visionary for the small group of fans, who were well versed in having to make sound inversely proportionate to their number: Caxton Street was enveloped by green-and-gold-clad fans folding in, packed shoulder to shoulder, following their lead, singing and chanting. Flores recalls:

> That pre-match was amazing. The Caxton pub, obviously being nice and close to the stadium, made it so awesome to walk with hundreds of people en masse to the stadium. The energy there was incredible. But then if we compared it to the penalty-shootout moment, I was sick. It was sickening. Every emotion went through me.

She unpacks that:

> It was emotional because it meant so much more than 'We won a penalty shootout for once' and we'd been pretty terrible at them historically, and the realisation of what the team had just achieved and what that meant for women's football in this country ... It wasn't relief. It was: 'Finally we have done something big.' Obviously we've won the Asian Cup. That's big.

> That's huge. But a semi-final of a World Cup? That's another level. That's, like, we're so close here to being the world's best. At the end of that match there were tears, there were hugs and kisses … there was everything, and it was just surreal to see what the future could hold for us in Australia. I obviously felt proud for the players but [I was also] proud for every women's football fan in this country—every past player, administrator, coach, fan of the game. I just felt, *We did it.* Obviously not on the field for us, but we had a role to play. That moment I'll remember forever.

Former Matilda Tal Karp, too, touches on that theme. She recently revisited an interview she conducted off the back of the penalty-shootout win. 'I was insanely euphoric,' she says of hearing the replay. Her takeaway from the match and the tournament was 'the realisation that we were finally being seen':

> Women have been playing football for generations. But suddenly, half the country was watching—and celebrating women for their skill and athleticism on the football field. And it wasn't just women and girls turning on their TVs and turning up to matches, but men and boys too—screaming, crying, going nuts over our Matildas. It was this amazing shift in public consciousness, an awakening of sorts. For me, it was about being seen.

* * *

Being seen and demonstrative support were central to the tournament. Indeed, Psaltis highlights that the first documented women's football match played in Australia, in 1921, was almost a curtain-raiser for a men's Australian Rules football match: 'When I was watching the penalty shootout, I was thinking of 1921. No longer the curtain-raiser, they *are* the event.'

With some distance and perspective, we can begin to situate the significance of the match and the venue in history. First, there is the fact that Australian Rules and Brisbane, and specifically Brisbane's two most famous sporting stadiums, have been central to two of the most iconic Australian women's football moments on home soil: the Gabba hosted the aforementioned 1921 exhibition match, and Brisbane Stadium played host to the game-changing quarter-final. Second, from the report of the 1921 match we know there was one team from the north side and one from the south, there was some mention of outfits and a player name or two, and there was a penalty—yes, there was a penalty in that game, too—but we know little about the women who played. We know immeasurably more about the women who were catapulted from relative anonymity to national celebrity through the 2023 quarter-final and its penalty shootout. That match is embedded in our national psyche and its moments have been filmed, photographed and written about in never-before-seen volumes.

We'll also know about the girls who were inspired by it. Some of the next generations' Matildas undoubtedly witnessed the match. This was their Cathy Freeman moment, and they will be inspired by women who themselves had been inspired by Freeman. Better yet, the first generations of Matildas were there, too—present players on the pitch; past and future players in the stands.

So the tournament—particularly that quarter-final—invoked greater visibility of the game and the players, but fans also went out of their way to be seen to support the women's game. Perhaps most evident in that visibility was that a goalkeeper—the position most overlooked, and the player whose jersey would traditionally be seen as the least commercially viable—became one of the most seen and sought-after players of all.

Prior to the tournament, sports-merchandise retailer Rebel had taken a punt and gone big with its merchandise order—a huge financial investment with a long lead time, akin to the long-game risk Football Australia had taken years earlier by positioning the Matildas front and centre. As the tournament approached, Rebel rolled out floor-to-ceiling posters featuring top-tier Matildas and positioned the swaths of merchandise in prime store positions. Its punt paid off: not only did Matildas kit sell well, it outsold Socceroos kit thirteenfold.[21]

The Rebel buyers wouldn't have known it at the time, but working in their midst selling the merchandise they had ordered was a staff member who was an original Matildas fan. Meshelle Ryan can't recall how long she's been supporting the Matildas, and women's football more widely. What she and I can recall is that she's been road-tripping to support the team since the time when crowds were tiny and there wasn't a broadcast or live stream.

Ryan purchased an entire box of Matildas scarves a few years ago when they first (and finally) became available. The scarves were the water-testing step the then Football Federation Australia (now Football Australia) took into the merchandise arena. 'I got a box online—we're talking a big box of scarves,' Ryan says. Like her employer, she went big early, accurately anticipating the demand. Some friends gave her money to reserve scarves from that order. She had one left over that she was able to give to former Matildas captain Melissa Barbieri, who didn't have one. (Just because you were in and around the team didn't guarantee anything.)

Rebel traditionally does the pop-up stores for Men's State of Origin rugby league games in high-traffic locations such as Brisbane's Queen Street Mall. Knowing such stores tend to go off, Ryan put her hand up to work there when they did the same for the Women's World Cup. Still, even she was surprised by the party atmosphere the store attracted. A shipping container fitted out with Rebel branding, it flew the flags of the countries that were playing each day. The team working there offered value-adds such as jersey personalisation through iron-on custom names and numbers, as well as face painting. Presumably because of their ease of wearing and the fact that it was winter when the tournament played out, scarves of the thirty-two teams were a perennial favourite. Jerseys and beanies also sold strongly. (New Zealand kit was among the most popular, which both makes and doesn't make sense: there are a lot of Kiwis residing in Australia, but the Football Ferns also didn't play here during the tournament.) Goalkeeper jerseys were the most sought after and the hardest to find.

It was a tournament for goalkeepers, as we would discover not just through the Australia v France quarter-final but throughout the event as a whole. England's Mary Earps and Australia's Arnold and Sweden's Zećira Mušović were all formidable, their defence almost impenetrable. But you couldn't buy their kits. If ever there were something that summed up how women's football simultaneously excels while being thwarted, this was it. (Comedian Jimmy Rees released a reel: 'We can buy a jersey, right? We can buy a jersey, right? What the—?! Unbelievable.'[22])

Nike later affirmed a further ten-year team sponsorship commitment, including goalkeeper jerseys. (Fascinatingly, as Arnold later told Grace Gill during a panel at Vivid in Sydney, she used to wear her jersey down the street and people would assume she was a fan.[23]) Then, in a gesture that benefited both its own pockets and fans, Nike briefly made the iconic purple jersey Arnold wore for that penalty shootout available for purchase. It may be drawing a long bow given it could well have been chosen purely for on-pitch contrast according to football protocols, but purple is a colour associated with the women's rights movement, and was the colour chosen for the shirts worn by Australia's first out lesbian women's football team, the Adelaide Armpits.[24] Colour relevance neither here nor there, the jersey sold out within minutes. (Even federal sports minister Anika Wells had multiple devices open at work as she competed in the general public mix of trying to secure one.[25])

Breakfast radio host and self-described 'mother of a keeper' Libbi Gorr also endeavoured to obtain one of the limited-release jerseys. Fittingly, she spoke to me while watching her daughter play at the Victorian State Football Centre, the official 'Home of the Matildas'. Shortly after telling me that 'we [goalkeeping families] love a good penalty shootout', Gorr explains that she 'queued [for a jersey] like all the other goalkeepers' mums'. She initially tried buying the jersey online—no luck. So: 'I literally picked up my keys and left work' and drove to a sports retailer in the inner-north suburb of Collingwood, where staff were handing out tokens to the people in the queue, which extended well out the door, and explaining which sizes they had left. 'By the time they got to me, they only had certain sizes. I just took what I could get because I thought, *Oh well, she'll grow into it eventually*.' (Demand for tournament merchandise was similarly unreal more widely. 'I bought merch that was five sizes too big because I wanted something and the rest was sold out,' Cheek Media founder and author Hannah Ferguson says. 'It's just a general 2023 Women's World Cup shirt. I wear it to bed. I wear it around the house like a dress.')

Such strong jersey sales shouldn't have been a surprise. Doctor and cyclist Bridie O'Donnell, who is also a sports administrator and commentator, shakes her head at mention of it:

> The fact that Nike was kind of guilted into creating goalkeeper jerseys, not just for [Arnold] but for the English goalkeeper as well, that they'd [thought] they wouldn't be popular enough—I mean, did no one sit in the room and offer an alternative suggestion on that one?

(Full disclosure: I managed the Football Federation Australia women's football social media accounts from around 2010 until 2012 and would regularly receive imploring messages about where to buy jerseys that at that time didn't exist. I duly passed on the messages and tried to help demonstrate that there was a market for women's football jerseys. So, like so many others who've been in and around the game for a while, I feel heartened at the recent robust jersey sales. As a further side note, I soon saw firsthand the positive impact of the limited-edition jersey release: one of the goalkeepers in my suburban women's over-30s football league not only secured a purple jersey but is actually wearing it as her week-in-week-out kit. That's a marked improvement on the oversized men's goalkeeper jerseys with voluminous amounts of material that are often provided to female grassroots players. Those purple jerseys are not just for show.)

Women's football academic Jean Williams cautions against the commercialisation of jerseys. 'I know that I'm kind of like King Canute trying to stop the sea on that,' she says when we speak. 'People are still going to buy shirts, and I understand why.' She just wants to ensure commercialisation doesn't come at the expense of the organic, collaborative, subversive self-expression that has traditionally infused women's football. 'Femorabilia', a portmanteau of feminist and memorabilia, is the term she uses to describe the innovative fan-made, fan-led feminist shirts and ephemera that document specific historical junctures in women's football and form women's football's cultural tapestry (think recycled and repurposed materials that reject mass-market monoculture). She considers quite cynical the scarcity mindset Nike created by failing to release the goalkeeper jerseys until there was fever-pitch demand, and that by buying the relatively expensive jerseys when they do briefly become available sees us 'colluding in our own economic exploitation'.

Williams touches, too, on the perpetual challenges around the ethics of sponsors that have the money to invest and embed their products throughout a tournament but that perhaps don't lead to great health, human-rights or environmental outcomes (think sportswashing by fast-food manufacturers such as Coca-Cola and McDonald's, which are at odds with the healthy lifestyle sports otherwise promote). 'It almost feels like we're at a kind of crossroads where FIFA is going to sell women's football in ways that don't tie in with the self-made nature of women's football,' she says. Women's football is, indeed, currently wrestling with such teething pains as it tries to commercialise while retaining its soul.

Such considerations sit awkwardly with women in football, and even women societally, as we've been conditioned to consider it crass to discuss money and to be grateful for what we receive. Williams says:

> Rather than being grateful for Barclays [bank] being involved in record-breaking deals with women's football, let's have a look at why Barclays is pumping money into women's football. It's A: because it's really, really cost-effective—you get a lot of bang for your buck—and B: we had the financial crisis in the UK where the banks were all helped out by the taxpayer, so they've wanted to seem more socially responsible since then because they clearly couldn't regulate themselves and we had to bail them out. So it's a form of gendered sportswashing.

Goalkeeper jerseys were not the only things that sold out. Perhaps inadvertently reminiscent of the iconic Megan Rapinoe pixie-cut silhouette fan-art design that went viral at the 2011 Women's World Cup, designer Beck Feiner's made-to-order T-shirts filled a crucial gap in the market. They also represented a more bespoke, arguably femorabilia-adjacent jersey alternative. Inspired by what she was witnessing in the tournament, Feiner created vibrant, playful designs that encapsulated the mood. She drew one player, then another, then another, carefully studying and incorporating such accurate, relevant details as Hayley Raso's ribbon and Ellie Carpenter's pre-wrap headband.[26] The T-shirts went gangbusters.

The made-to-order approach Feiner takes is economical, but it did put her under pressure as people swept up by tournament fever wanted shirts in time for the next game. 'I make art relating to what's happening at the time. So social issues. My friends joke that they sometimes hear news from me through my breaking-illustration news,' she says. 'I always say I just a shine a spotlight on what's happening at the time.' Women's football was indeed the timely topic.

Still, the interest in Feiner's shirts took her by surprise. 'I had no idea they were going to be this successful,' she says. (In comparison, she created a shirt for Taylor Swift's Eras tour that she says sold well, but nowhere near as well as the Matildas shirts.) She muses that perhaps the surprise was widespread, as in: 'No one expected to feel like this.'

The hype has continued. Months after the tournament, Feiner was contacted to provide shirts for an Amazon delivery ad in which Arnold was appearing. It was at that point that Feiner realised Arnold would actually see her shirt—a moment equal parts thrilling and terrifying. Gathering her thoughts, she asked if she might pop in an extra shirt for Arnold herself. The answer was yes, and word has it Arnold and her partner thought the shirt was great.

Feiner explains that for her designs she tried to encapsulate 'that feeling of empowerment that was represented' throughout the Women's World Cup: 'I loved showing these strong women but in quite abstract ways.' Women recognised this and 'were able to wear these expressions of female empowerment at the games'.

Feiner has picked up on an aspect Ann Odong explicitly sought to create through the Matildas communications plan that united and connected with the country. As part of that plan, Odong worked to create an environment and coverage where the players were respected as athletes and to whom a range of people could relate. Marketing to girls alone would not bring the team the cut-through it required or deserved, nor would it link in with its audience's perceptions. Odong identifies the sentiment she feels as a grown woman: 'I'm not inspired by these players—I'm empowered by them.'

Empowerment notwithstanding, in some ways it's remarkable that Feiner created her artworks at all. 'I get really anxious watching sport,' she explains. She had to watch the Women's World Cup matches peering out from under a blanket. To which I respond, 'That was a tournament that was going to make you anxious.'

Oli Clothing's experience was similarly intense. The Perth-based company and friends of Arnold created some 'Brick Wall' T-shirts to celebrate Arnold's penalty-shootout heroics. Demand for the bespoke handprinted shirts was so high that the company made an exception to its rule of not reprinting and restocking items. It shared a behind-the-scenes photo of the stack of pre-order printouts on social media—a handspan-sized stack of paper thicker than an old-school phone book.[27] Equal parts support, superstar-meets-superstar and banter, Sam Kerr later turned up to camp wearing one of the shirts. Arnold posted a picture of Kerr in the shirt on social media with a caption telling people to get themselves a friend like this.[28]

9

WE'LL ALWAYS HAVE THAT SAM KERR GOAL

Australia v England, Sydney, 16 August 2023

HOURS BEFORE THE first ball was kicked at the semi-final that swept up the nation in feverish, diary-marking anticipation—before the players started warming up, before fans were admitted to perch anxiously on their plastic fold-down seats—Getty photographer Robert Cianflone climbed up to take his allocated position on a metal catwalk in the Stadium Australia rafters.

Cianflone was one of two agency photographers in that location, likely not far from the Aboriginal and Torres Strait Islander flags that were there for the first-ever time in Women's World Cup history thanks to the advocacy of such people as Karen Menzies, who had, through her work on the FIFA Cultural Panel, overcome decades of rigid thinking and protocol to ensure the flags' momentous display.[1]

Cianflone had had to complete a full-day working-from-heights course to be granted permission to photograph from the catwalk. He'd also been walked through the walkway's low-hanging structural elements and trip-hazard cable locations in daylight hours as part of a safety briefing ahead of the night-time shoot. Bathroom breaks were not feasible given the safety technicalities required to ascend and descend from the catwalk, regardless of nimbleness working at height, so Cianflone was well ensconced on that metal walkway by the time the crowds filtered in. There, he remained largely invisible or at least relatively unobserved, watching and waiting, snapping images as 75,000 fans and tens of elite women's footballers crisscrossed the stands and the pitch.

In the past, Cianflone and his peers had to pause, download, edit and send images at various intervals throughout matches. But with contemporary digital SLR cameras wifi-enabled or able to be connected to an ethernet cable, Cianflone's semi-final images were transmitted instantly, electronically, to Getty's picture-editing desk and published on its global feed in less than two minutes.

One of the images Cianflone shot from that precarious location—one that summed up the sentiment of the match and the tournament as a whole, and that *Australian Photography* later named as one of four images that defined 2023[2]—was of the Matildas' heart-shaped post-match team huddle. The image features players and staff leaning in in solidarity, arms around each other, listening intently to the post-match pep talk as the realisation that their Women's World Cup campaign was over was sinking in. It was an image so stunning that it would be picked up by everything from major newspapers, which ran it on their front page the next day, to the Matildas' own social media and team and staff laptop background images and screensavers.

'It was just good timing,' Cianflone says unassumingly of the image that would later win an award that was, appropriately, presented to him by former Matilda Lydia Williams (something Odong says was really appropriate given that Cianflone had long covered the team, including as far back as the 2011 Women's World Cup). It was good timing honed through hard work developing his professional craft and instinct. 'I didn't realise at the time that it was that special,' he continues. Cianflone had been shooting the England team as it celebrated its win. The exuberant celebration naturally drew your attention as it was all energy and action, while the Matildas' huddle was a quiet, contemplative moment that could easily have been overlooked, featuring a team devastated by the loss. Something made Cianflone glance over at the more subdued Matildas just as they and their support staff organically assembled in what would prove to be an accidentally heart-shaped huddle. (The huddle was an integral part of Gustavsson's approach. He'd called on the team to move in closer in the moment as they had spread out as they reeled at the result. The tightening of the circle resulted in the unanticipated heart shape.) The formation looked interesting, so Cianflone photographed it and filed the image but thought nothing more of it until his workplace contacted him the next day to tell him it was absolutely blowing up.

* * *

It's difficult to pinpoint who was most surprised that the Matildas had made it to the semi-final. Even the team itself seemed a little stunned. A flurry of flight and accommodation changes later, a bunch of Australian fans, too, were boarding planes to attend the unmissable event. The country was whipped into a frenzy, stoked by a newfound steady stream of media coverage.

'Tonight, the Matildas storyline will include a new chapter, and the entire population has packed an extra pair of pants in preparation for the stress,' Cheek Media wrote. Also: 'Today is the day, again. Where the unwashed kit from a couple of days ago becomes a measure of good luck, not a tight game turnaround with no motivation to put on an extra load of laundry.'[3]

The Matildas and the wider population weren't thinking magically that Australia could overcome England and make it to the Women's World Cup final. Aside from the fact that it felt fated—it would be Katrina Gorry's 100th national team appearance and was her daughter Harper's second birthday—they were buoyed by the rapture and momentum of the Canada/Denmark/France match trifecta and the knowledge that they'd managed to achieve all three without relying on principal goalscorer Sam Kerr. The Matildas had also previously, recently, beaten England—a team that had been on a seemingly unstoppable tear after winning the 2022 Euros. As with the France quarter-final, the Matildas had a mental edge heading in.

Still, they were in uncharted territory. Despite having made the quarter-finals consistently since 2007, they had no experience of the pressure of being in the final four. England, by contrast, had been there twice before. There was also the no small feat of having to recovery physically, mentally and emotionally from the quarter-final in the space of four days. 'Once we won that France game, which was such an intense match and the longest penalty shootout ever in Women's World Cup history, from a recovery perspective, I just knew that the team *could not* recover in four days after *such a huge output of energy*,' former Matilda turned psychologist Sue Read explains. 'So then the whole country, of course, jumps on board and watches when we were not at our best and were really struggling to play to our potential because we were so tired. So much adrenaline and energy were used up in that penalty shootout, as well as in all the commitments in the following days.' That prompts the naysaying. It's why, Read argues, 'You've got to show every single game of a tournament for people to be fully invested.' That means on free-to-air TV—but we'll discuss that further later.

Having had to return to their day jobs towards the end of the tournament, time and budget constraints meant the Croissants had planned to recycle their iconic Steve Irwin costume for the semi-final. The turnaround time between the quarter- and semi-finals was too compressed, so chief designer Lucy Gilfedder was not keen on the new costume idea that kept circulating in the group chat: brick walls. But Maddy Bart, the Croissant who had suggested it, was hell bent on the idea. 'We were just like, "All right, if one Croissant's in, we're all in,"' Gilfedder explains. 'Thank god I had a Tuesday, because that's when life gets done.' (Tuesdays were Gilfedder's day off. The game was the next day, Wednesday.) 'We knew shit would get done on a Tuesday,' Ciara O'Sullivan laughs. A flurry of group-chat messages would ensue.

Sunday afternoon was crafternoon, when the Croissants would converge on Gilfedder's house late to assemble the costumes under her guidance. Gilfedder laughs:

> We don't have the best crafters. We have enthusiastic crafters, but not the most talented. So I will have laid it out for them like Year 3 craft, and everyone will have their pair of scissors and their piece of fabric that we're going to cut out, and you'll

> have a little stencil. Then the teacher will demonstrate how we're going to cut a circle. Then they'll all go off and cut their circle and bring back a rectangle and [be] like, 'Is this good?' and you're like, 'Well, sure.' We have no mistakes. That's my one rule: no mistakes. We're not re-buying anything …

O'Sullivan concurs: 'No costume was left for the bin.'

Still, the brick-wall costume wasn't without complexity. For starters, the Matildas goalkeeper jersey wasn't available for purchase at the time. Everything the Croissants found was too expensive or there was too little time for it to ship. It was also extremely difficult to locate the precise shade of purple. Gilfedder determined that the only option was to dye everything. (She wouldn't have known it at the time, but this was not dissimilar to the approach Australia's first out lesbian women's football team, the Armpits, had taken in dyeing a range of shirts purple in the absence of having formal kit.[4]) She bought white shirts, fabric and purple dye. The rest of the Croissants were oblivious to this and were still sending ideas relating to possible purple shorts, socks, and even a fast-fashion jumpsuit.

They turned up for a crafternoon that was more like a crafter-night: it ran from 9 p.m. until 1 a.m. Either way, Gilfedder revealed the masterpiece: accurately purple-dyed shirts and shorts. The Croissants then affixed material to the jersey underarms and sides to reveal brick-wall wings when the wearers outstretched their arms. The costume was masterful and even contained a tiny ambush-marketing nod to the group (who did, this time, make it past security's watchful eye): they included a tiny croissant in the jersey design.

Suffice to say, with momentum and serious hometown support (including some whipped-up brick walls) on their side, the Matildas' semi-final tilt felt preordained. The match played out on 'Ekka Wednesday'—a public holiday for the annual Brisbane agricultural show. Interstate and absent a public holiday, people wore jerseys in offices and feigned interest in work until it was time to head to the stadium, the pub or a watch party. Hannah Ferguson sums up the reality: 'I remember at midday on the day of the England game just thinking: *No one's fucking working*.'

Celebrities, sporting greats, women's football investors and politicians converged on the game. As head of delegation, former Matilda Alicia Ferguson found herself among them. Settling in, she spotted tennis great and gender equality advocate Billie Jean King and actor Natalie Portman a few seats away. Also: 'I had [Senator] Penny Wong on one side and [federal sports minister] Anika [Wells] on the other—just boss women in politics.'

Seeking to capitalise on the national sentiment, politicians had channelled Bob Hawke's America's Cup move by dangling the prospect of a national public holiday if the Matildas won. Sadly, the offer was moot: the Matildas never came close to winning. England were in charge from the opening to the closing whistle, and the Matildas' hopes were dented by a scything tackle on national treasure Sam Kerr.

Most women's football fans would tell you they're not normally violent people, and most people who had come within metres of the tournament had marvelled at the lack of aggression and violence that imbued it. But the desire to get out of our seats and punch someone was almost palpable when Kerr, the team talisman whose calf the country wished to be protected at all costs, was deliberately targeted and felled by her own Chelsea club teammate and off-field friend Millie Bright.

The Matildas' hopes were temporarily revived by a stunning solo Kerr goal before being entirely dashed by an unfortunate mistake at the back by the otherwise outstanding Ellie Carpenter that gifted Lauren Hemp, and ultimately England, a golden opportunity to stamp victory. The score at this point was 2–1 to the Lionesses. It would finish 3–1.

Kerr kicking aside, the Matildas might have beaten the Lionesses under different circumstances, but the reality was that they didn't. It truly, simply, utterly wasn't their night. We'll spend an eternity musing that they could have won had the tactics been different, had the squad rotation been higher, had the selection been more clinical and squad-depth-minded, and had the physical, mental and emotional fatigue not been so great. None of those are wrong. But to dwell on them would be to do the Matildas' achievements a disservice—they'd given all they had and then some. Even the crowd was muted, tired, barring the roar it emitted following Kerr's goal.

Her strike was a sweetly hit hint of what she, a world-class player who stepped up to meet the occasion, was capable of. Redolent of Ellyse Perry's 2011 quarter-final goal that had looped into the top corner, Kerr's technically gifted goal briefly reignited a nation's (and former generations') hopes.

Not dissimilar to a mother channelling superhuman strength to lift a car off a child, fan Louise Corkett was so excited in the moment that she physically lifted her nine-year-old son off the ground. As she terms it, 'That goal and the atmosphere gave me strength I didn't know I had.' The alumni, too, were out of their seats. Carol Vinson says:

> When Sam scored *that* goal against England, she was running towards the goal we [alumni] were behind. When the ball left her boot we stood as one, and when it hit the back of the net we were jumping up and down and hugging one another.

Out on that elevated catwalk hung from the stadium's rafters, Cianflone had a bird's-eye view of the crowd swelling and the roaring rush of noise it emitted. 'It just felt so much louder out there, presumably bouncing back off the roof.'

In scenes that would quickly radiate out on social media, fans packed shoulder to shoulder in Melbourne's Federation Square erupted, leaping into the air, gripping, hugging, pinballing into and off strangers. Football writer Kieran Yap, who was part of that celebration, says, 'It was beyond anything I've ever seen in football in Australia—it was more than the men's broadcast. Yeah, it was more than [the Men's World Cup in] 2006.' Director of the Office for Women in Sport and Recreation Sarah Styles was in that crowd, too. 'Pretty sure I had frostbite on my toes,' she quips, before talking about the sheer and collective joy she experienced after the goal. Unsurprisingly, the footage of the unbridled celebration remains an important video-or-it-didn't-happen cultural proof touchpoint.

As Teddy Bryant points out, for the following eight minutes 'you could almost, nearly, picture the Matildas in a World Cup final'.

Around this time, the Matildas became the first Australian women's sports team to surpass 500,000 Instagram followers and recorded more than 130 per cent overall social media growth as interest and adoration surged and Australians clambered aboard the bandwagon.[5] (At the time of writing, follower numbers were sitting upwards of 785,000.) But the game soon ended in a 1–3 whimper and a nation's raw, crushed hopes. It will probably be a long time before an Australian women's football fan can hear the 'so good, so good!' chant from English celebration song 'Sweet Caroline' without wincing. (As Matildas Active Support member and fan Bryant explained, the only 'good' thing to come from the Matildas' exit was the communal grieving and attendant empathy that permeated the country.) Still, as overheard on the interminably long train ride home, and as was also stated across many social media channels, our tournament run might have been over, but 'We'll always have that Sam Kerr goal'.[6]

The semi-final was the most-watched event in Australian recorded televisual history, reaching *checks notes* 11.15 million people. ('11.15 million viewers is a terrifying thought, particularly listening to my voice,' former-Matilda-turned-commentator Grace Gill jokes.[7]) The match and its broadcast reach outperformed the Men's State of Origin and National Rugby League (NRL) and AFL finals, which had previously held record average viewership. Adjusted, given that the 11.15 million figure didn't include the paywalled Optus Sport figure or the sheer volume of bodies in pubs, fan sites and venues such as the MCG, it was probably closer to 17 million, which equated to more than half of the country's population. (By comparison, Cathy Freeman's 400-metre Sydney Olympics race attracted approximately 8.8 million viewers.) It was around the time these and other astounding figures were emerging that Sarah Walsh and her peers became acutely aware that the push model of media, which women's football had long had to engage in, had comprehensively moved to one of pull. The tournament and the hype around the Matildas had taken on lives of their own.

Such impressive broadcast figures are reminiscent of Alexis Ohanian's prescient tweet: 'Facts don't care about your feelings: people want to watch women's sports.'[8] (Ohanian is Serena Williams' husband and an Angel City Football Club co-owner. He also co-founded Reddit.) That's not to say everyone was stoked with the stats. Male keyboard warriors wanted to argue with Hannah Ferguson after she posted about the Men's NRL/AFL/State of Origin–beating figures on social media. 'Their argument was that FIFA is an international viewing audience because it's not an Australian sport,' Ferguson explains. The stats were the Australian viewership—see previously re: facts don't care about your feelings. 'I got a lot of heat from men who were threatened by the comparison.'

An additional blow beyond the Matildas' loss was the traffic chaos that followed the match. Copper-wire theft hamstrung the train-network controls and stalled all trains heading in and out of the Stadium Australia precinct. Standing cold, tired, sad and largely silent with 100,000 other people for three hours post-match on a 6°C late-winter evening was bleak. Analogous to the set-up of a bad joke meeting apocalyptic scenes, 75,000 of the people stranded were Matildas and England fans, clad in green, gold and blue jerseys accompanied by fast-dispersing glitter, skew-whiff ribbons and smudged zinc; the other 25,000 were country music fans wearing fringe, cowboy hats and cowboy boots, having just departed a nearby concert by singer Luke Combs. (The *Betoota Advocate* headline the next day spoofed that fans' heartbreak was 'soothed' by an unexpected three-hour-long catch-up with 100,000 of their closest mates.[9])

So long, so dire and so claustrophobically sardined was that wait and trip home that I may have wept a little, cutting a bowed, cold-nosed, frozen-toed figure huddled in my puffer jacket. More than a few of us said afterwards we'd never forget the voice of the employee who had the misfortune of having to periodically crank up the intercom to inform us that the trains were still, in fact, not running. My one request of Transport NSW when it is tasked with moving masses: never rely on one mode of transport. Next time, please have some back-up buses.

10

THIRD OR FOURTH IS ACTUALLY VERY GOOD

Sweden v Australia, Brisbane, 19 August 2023

THE MATILDAS AND their fans yo-yoed between Brisbane, Sydney and Brisbane again for the quarter-final, semi-final and then third-place play-off. It was a fatigue-inducing commitment to the cause. A win in that semi-final would have seen the Matildas stay in Sydney and saved them and their fans a bunch of additional travel. (Matildas team manager Gina Rees' enthusiastic celebration after Kerr's goal was explicitly related to her glimpsing the prospect that she would not have to again move the entire team, including support personnel, to another city.[1] The hurt-locker pain around this time was compounded when many of us encountered half a planeload of overexcited mid-primary-school students heading interstate on a school excursion. Those students piling themselves onto our flight prompted an exchange of slightly startled, exhausted and resigned looks from worn-out women who were counting on that flight to catch some desperately needed shut-eye. The whole scenario had echoes of a point made by fans Emily Purton and Katrina Dunn: it wasn't just the players—we, too, needed to be match fit.)

Instead, the Matildas and their entourage returned to Brisbane and the site of the history-making penalty shootout amid hopes they could channel some of that energy to finish strongly. It wasn't to be.

Brisbane Stadium was again sold out and blanketed in Australian colours as bedecked fans overtook the precinct. But Sweden, determined to come away with silverware, were commanding from the outset. For their part, the Matildas couldn't find the spark. Sam Kerr tore a second calf in the match, but wouldn't realise it until later. No matter. Whether she or we knew about it in the moment, it had little bearing on the game. Stina Blackstenius would cause the most grief: just a minute into the game, she rocketed off a shot that jolted players and fans and forced Mackenzie Arnold into a diving save. The Matildas narrowly escaped that Blackstenius moment, but halfway through the first half the ever-steady Clare Hunt, who'd had a dazzling Matildas experience that had seen her go from fan to fixture in just a handful of caps, clipped Blackstenius's heel in the box. The contact was so imperceptibly subtle you had to see replays to understand the call. Still, contact was contact. Fridolina Rolfö assuredly slotted the subsequent penalty: 1–0.

It was one goal, but finding one or even two goals felt almost insurmountable. Hinting at the on-pitch niggle and simmering frustration as the Matildas tried to dig deep for an equaliser, Katrina Gorry got in a chest-bumping face-off with Kosovare Asllani. Then Kyra Cooney-Cross's tired, mistimed slide tackle facilitated the counterattack that yielded Sweden's second, game-killing goal.

The Matildas looked spent—physically, mentally, emotionally. (We crowd members were, too, and did little to boost them, something for which I feel some responsibility.) The lack of rotation was acutely evident. The *23 for '23* adage Tony Gustavsson regularly cited (that is, it was implied that he selected twenty-three players to ensure success at the 2023 event) didn't hold as he never drew on the full squad depth.[2] Five squad members—three outfield players in Kyah Simon, Aivi Luik and Clare Wheeler, and two goalkeepers in Teagan Micah and Lydia Williams—didn't play a single minute during the tournament, and Charli Grant's and Courtney Nevin's pitch time was so brief as to almost be negligible. In stark contrast, core player and deputised captain Steph Catley ran 77.2 kilometres across the tournament; Gorry, Mary Fowler, Caitlin Foord and Ellie Carpenter weren't far behind.[3] The data revealed that this level of rotation—part of Gustavsson's focus on consistency and continuity—was the lowest in the tournament. His approach was disparate from that of his international counterparts.

Perhaps the one black mark on Gustavsson's steerage is that he kept Simon in camp when she clearly wasn't fit. He initially explained that he selected her not on her current form but on her tournament-time potential.[4] In the elite athlete arena, few—if any—other athletes are selected on such aspirational grounds. Simon later suffered injury setbacks that extinguished hopes of her involvement.[5] At best she could take a penalty, but in the end she didn't even make it on to the pitch to do that. Michelle Heyman, Emily Gielnik and Chloe Logarzo were all fit and could have sparked comebacks. We'd seen Logarzo do it through individually inspiring the Matildas' 2019 comeback against Brazil in the Miracle of Montpellier.[6] We'd see this in early 2024 after Heyman received the call-up after Sam Kerr's ACL injury.[7] To be fair, hindsight provides insight. It also would have been a brutal blow for Simon, who is ageing out of her career and has missed not one but two consecutive Women's World Cups through injury. (She was ruled out on the eve of the 2019 tournament due to a troublesome hamstring.)

David Davutovic says the will-she-won't-she speculation around whether Simon would play, whether she'd take a penalty, signalled the maturity of the women's game. It was typical of the drama and rumours that unfold in and around major men's football teams and tournaments and the fearlessness that comes with being able to criticise a sport without having to worry about damaging its reputation or ultimate success. (One of Davutovic's first actions attending men's training used to be to count the number of players on the pitch, and if the numbers were short, to use a process of elimination to determine who was injured and then to seek out the story.) As he terms it, the 2023 tournament was 'a pure footballing World Cup with so many authentic football/sporting storylines'. Hosting the tournament wasn't a feelgood-factor corporate social responsibility exercise: there was genuine scrutiny.

Davutovic's one constructive criticism is not related to player selection but, rather, coach selection. He says that although

Gustavsson absolutely delivered, it would have been fantastic to see an Australian coach with deep domestic ties steer the team through the tournament. I'd take that one step further: an Australian *woman* coach. I will concede, though, that it would have been an impossibly pressured experience for a woman to have had the top job for the 2023 tournament—perhaps too akin to installing a woman on the infamous Glass Cliff, under which women tend to be helicoptered into precarious positions of power and essentially set up to fail.[8] Still, given that the Australian Institute of Sport (AIS) has released a plan for addressing the 'leaky pipeline' to enable women to reach the pinnacles of high-performance coaching,[9] I anticipate seeing a woman coach, with the requisite support to help her succeed and grow, at the helm in coming years.

But back to the football. With that fourth-place finish, the Matildas recorded Australia's best-ever World Cup result—Women's or Men's. It was even more impressive given that the Matildas finished fourth with more teams in the tournament than ever before (thirty-two up from twenty-four). They also became just the second Women's World Cup host nation to finish in the top four (host nation the United States won the tournament in 1999, and finished third when the tournament returned there due to the SARS pandemic disrupting China's planned hosting in 2003). So the result, whichever way you slice it, was impressive.

The Matildas might have been deflated at the way their tournament, which for a moment had held such captivating promise, ended with a whimper rather than a bang. It was their second fourth-place finish in consecutive major tournaments—the previous one had been the rescheduled 2020 Olympics, and they'd been gutted by that so-close-and-yet-so-far result, too. Terming it a 'preview' rather than a 'pinnacle',[10] journalist Kieran Pender articulated the paradox: the Matildas 'overachieved' across the tournament as a whole, but 'underachieved' against Sweden in the third-place play-off.[11] Certainly, it was a flat performance ill-fitting the gritty heroism of their previous matches.

The aura had been dimmed slightly in the interceding days. Carpenter had copped social media abuse for her semi-final mistake: a turnover after misjudging a long ball, which contributed to the goal that killed off the game. Apart from the fact that mistakes happen and Carpenter very rarely makes them, what was not understood or at least forgotten was that she was just months on from returning from a knee reconstruction and was in comparatively unbelievable form after incurring such a major injury. Still, what she copped was typical of a yet-to-be-stemmed social media abuse onslaught that women, in particular, receive.

The FIFPRO tournament Social Media Protection Service Report, which analysed 5.1 million posts and comments for abusive content, similarly identified that one in five players received targeted discriminatory, abusive or threatening messaging. Homophobic, explicit and sexist abuse accounted for almost 50 per cent of those abusive messages. Worse, the abuse was gendered, with women players 29 per cent more likely to be targeted than male players when compared with the 2022 Men's World Cup.[12] This mirrors Deakin University research, which found that nine out of ten sportswomen experienced gendered online abuse in and around 2023, with one in four experiencing homophobia and one in five experiencing racism. The subpar solution the women interviewed for that study reported being presented with was to ignore or block the abuse and self-censor what they post—the same inappropriate burden women have long carried in all aspects of their lives.[13] Unsurprisingly, most players reported insufficient mental health support and preparation for the Women's World Cup.[14]

(Worth contextualising but not excusing it, this abuse is something that occurs beyond the sporting realm. It's an existing and escalating issue that needs to be addressed. So, too, is the mental load and attendant pressure that comes from the dramatic shift we've seen in players operating in relative anonymity to near-hysteria surrounding their sudden celebrity status. Physical fitness and prowess are starting to get there for players and teams, but the emotional and mental strength-and-conditioning and support networks are still playing catch-up.[15])

Regardless, concentrating on that fourth-place result is to do the team and their extraordinary efforts a disservice. Sarah Walsh didn't ever explicitly say what success in the tournament would look like, despite media desperately wanting it defined. She certainly never said it would look like making a semi-final or at the least coming away with a podium finish (and, retaining her high-performance-athlete mindset of never thinking about more than the next game at a time, she in fact banned her wife from even suggesting the Matildas would win the Women's World Cup as a whole[16]). Australia loves a winner, especially an underdog winner who topples an Olympic champion when their back is against the group-stage wall. Walsh and her peers were circumspect, though, and tried to manage expectations. Australia is but one of 210 nations that play the world game (the hint is in 'world'). Australia was, at the time of the World Cup, ranked tenth—impressive, yes, but not considered favourites to win. (They later dropped to eleventh, despite finishing fourth.)[17]

Earlier in the tournament Gustavsson had also been pressed on what failure would look like. Obviously, he said, not making it out of the group.[18] Success, he said after the France game, is when you give it everything you have, win, lose or draw.[19] It's fair to say that even had the Matildas not won the penalty shootout, it would still have been considered a success—they left absolutely everything out there.

At the end of the 3–4 play-off, Gustavsson rightly stated that the Matildas had 'achieved something bigger' than winning a medal.[20] They had certainly got the memo about performing well on home soil. Likewise, they'd got the memo that it was about more—much more—than delivering a few weeks of entertaining football. Kerr noted that the public were saying 'Thank you' rather than 'Well done', as if the Matildas had done the country a great service.[21] Which they had. The team had broken through the grass ceilings of stymied playing access, participation, conditions, media coverage and pay that had held back not only the current generation but also all the generations before them. That alone represented celebration-worthy progress. Artist Sam Leighton-Dore created a '3rd or 4th is actually very good' graphic that appropriately put the Matildas' momentous achievement in perspective. The graphic, which depicted people holding supporter signs in stadium stands, contained some additionally great statements, including 'Wait, sports is fun?', 'What is men?' and 'How good are women?'[22]

And so, the Matildas' tournament was over barring a cameo 'Strawberry Kisses' performance from Nikki Webster herself,[23] and the team being given the keys to Brisbane.[24] (Ann Odong literally obtained approval and funding to fly Webster up the day before. She called Webster at 5 p.m. and, impressively, Webster agreed to fly up at short notice. She was on a plane first thing the next morning and at the venue to complete the sound check at 9 a.m. before performing at 11 a.m. Odong says the looks on the players' faces when Webster appeared on stage to serenade them was priceless and absolutely worth the tight, hectic logistics.) Alongside the key presentation and ahead of the $200 million the federal government would announce for women's sports (albeit with all women's sports lumped in together),[25] the then Queensland premier, Anastasia Palaszczuk, announced two things: a $37 million legacy investment for girls and women in sport, and a permanent Matildas tribute in the form of a bronze statue outside Brisbane Stadium.[26] That statue, which will be a not-insignificant 6 metres wide and 2.5 metres high, is an appropriate tribute given the location of the game-changing, nation-shaping penalty shootout. It will undoubtedly become a key meeting point for future generations and an alternative to the current (male) Wally Lewis go-to.

That statue's presence, in addition to the murals painted at Sydney's Stadium Australia and on the beachside wall at Bondi,[27] will also help begin to address the wider issue of the dearth of statues and visible celebrations of women. (Not dissimilar to how racehorses have traditionally received more media coverage than women and have even won Sportswoman of the Year awards,[28] just 17 per cent of the statues erected in Australia's capital cities depict women.[29] Indeed, there's an underpinning storyline in the *Barbie* movie that was playing in cinemas alongside the tournament that relates to Ken—spoiler alert—thinking horses are fundamental to the patriarchy. In some ways, he is right: horses have long been elevated over women. There are more statues of men and animals such as horses in Australia than there are of women.[30]) Predictably, some men, including basketballer Andrew Bogut and tennis player Nick Kyrgios, thought the Brisbane bronze statue counterbalance was a little rich given the team's fourth-place finish.[31] Said athletes failed to grasp that winning sometimes looks like more than medals. Just wait until they hear that Victoria has commissioned six public art projects celebrating women and breaking through the 'brass ceiling'.[32]

Statue announcements aside, with just the final to go and the Matildas no prospect for it, for many it might have felt like the tournament was over. Little did we know there was a lot more to play out, on and off the pitch.

11

THE FINAL (STRAW)

Spain v England, Sydney, 20 August 2023

JUST AS PHOTOGRAPHER Madeleine Penfold hadn't anticipated that her images would be selected to adorn skyscrapers, she couldn't anticipate that she would find herself photographing two players on the eve of the day that would forever change their lives.

Having completed most of her work prior to the tournament, Penfold set out to attend as a fan and document the event from a purely fan perspective. But as clients and brands realised she was in Australia for the breakout tournament, they started sending work her way. One job was tentative and last-minute, with Penfold receiving intermittent updates. 'So each day, they'd be like, "It could be today", and I'd be like, "OK, well, I was going to go to Bondi today, so let me know."'

Cue the eve of the tournament final, by which time Penfold had figured this particular job wasn't going to materialise. She made plans to meet a friend who lived in Sydney and whom she hadn't seen for two years.

> As soon as I got in her car, I got a text saying, 'Can you be at the camp in half an hour?' I was like, 'Oh my god, we need to get my cameras. I need to go.' So my friend drove me to that

training ground, which weirdly enough happened to be the stadium she'd trained at as a young girl. She was like, 'I've not been here in years. This is so nostalgic.'

The shoot went well. The players were remarkably relaxed given it was the eve of the world's pinnacle women's football final, and Penfold was stoked she'd had the opportunity to photograph such impressive players and human beings. All of that would take on new significance just twenty-four hours later, when post-match events unfolded around the very two players she had worked with: Spain's Jenni Hermoso and Olga Carmona.

* * *

Just days before, Australians had temporarily dared to dream that it would be the Matildas, a team that had broken new ground at every turn throughout the tournament and in the forty-five years since its inception, who would again exceed all expectations and bring home Women's World Cup gold. In the end, it was a final played out between two colonising nations: one a country where women had been banned from playing for around half a century; the other a country in dispute with its coach and federation. There was also a sexual assault that overshadowed it all—but more about that later.

Many fans headed to the match grappling with conflicted feelings: support Australia's colonising country and traditional rivals, or a country clearly at odds with its male administrators' and coaches' treatment of the players? While one fan quipped that the determinant between which of two colonising countries to support came down to which had the better food,[1] those who opted for neutrality returned to the axiom that 'Football is the winner'.

(Compounding the complexity of those feelings was the fact that the traditional custodians in each state had been generously performing Welcome to Country ceremonies at the start of each match—the country's marginalised people welcoming sport's marginalised. Writer Ellen van Neerven documented the event for Siren Sport and was horrified to witness commentators speaking over Dharug elder Aunty Julie Jones' Welcome to Country at the

Matildas' opening match and to see the broadcast disrespectfully cut to a deodorant commercial during it.[2])

Regardless of the difficulties of who to support, what was clear was that by the end of the match a new Women's World Cup champion would be crowned for the first time since 2011. That was because former winners and usual contenders the United States, Norway, Japan and Germany had made unexpectedly early exits.[3]

Prince William, who elected not to hop on a plane to support the Lionesses on the valid grounds of environmentalism, posted a social media video of him and his daughter wishing the Lionesses luck.[4] It slightly missed the mark. This tournament wasn't just about inspiring girls—it went far, far beyond that. The video also encouraged the Lionesses to enjoy themselves, a statement that would never be said to men, who would be encouraged to win. But that misstep was comparatively mild compared with what was to come.

As with many finals, the 2023 tournament's ultimate match was in many ways anticlimactic when compared with the football that had spun teams out of the tournament in the quarter- and semi-finals. England looked as physically and mentally wiped out as the Matildas had against them, their heavy legs and their inability to put the ball into dangerous spaces a stark contrast to Spain's lithe ball movement and tiki-taka prowess. The result was 1–0, but Spain's win was never really in doubt. Carmona, one of the players with whom Penfold had worked and the player who scored the game's sole goal, found out after the final whistle that her father had passed away in the preceding days. Rightly or wrongly, depending on your perspective, she had been shielded from this news so she could concentrate.[5]

Spain were relative newcomers to the space—they had not actually competed in a senior Women's World Cup until 2015. Even more impressively, their dominance extended beyond the 2023 tournament—the country and its teams concurrently held the U-17, U-20 and senior Women's World Cup trophies. Nor were they necessarily fielding their strongest team in 2023, given that a number of their players were effectively on strike, which is scary for their opposition but sad for the players and sport as a whole. Prior to the tournament, fifteen players had signed a letter raising concerns about conditions and practices and calling for change. One well-documented detail is that players were required to leave their hotel-room doors open to allow for curfew checks. The players had also highlighted an absence of appropriate professional support to prevent injuries and to enable the team to excel.[6]

Aitana Bonmatí was one of just three of the fifteen signatories who, having withdrawn their complaint in order to be considered for selection, attended the tournament—others either continued to sit out or were not called up.[7] (Bonmatí would win just about every award possible in the months after the tournament, including becoming the first player to win the Women's World Cup Golden Ball, the UEFA Women's Player of the Year, and the Ballon d'Or.[8] To think we almost missed her talent.) Importantly, and in line with her wider efforts to provide elevating coverage to female players otherwise overlooked, Penfold later sensitively portrayed players such as Lucia Garcia who had missed the tournament because of the protest.[9]

Player revolt should never be required. But Jean Williams makes an additional relevant point in relation to Spain and other teams that hints at some—however incremental—progress: 'It says a little bit about player power that they feel they can be in open dispute.' She also picks up on a similar theme addressed by Hermoso, whom *GQ Spain* later named Woman of the Year:[10] that Spain became world champions because it was the only option for them to be heard and respected. 'It also speaks to the continuation of the gendered governance of football that you've got to win a World Cup to draw attention to the fact that your federation is systematically discriminating against you,' Williams says. The USWNT prevailed under the same conditions in 2019.[11]

Which brings us to the 'kiss'. I didn't and don't want to give too much oxygen to the sexual assault that overshadowed a tournament of legion achievements, but it wasn't just a kiss bestowed on Hermoso during the medal ceremony in overzealous excitement. Almost forgotten is that Royal Spanish Football Federation (RFEF) president Luis Rubiales also hoisted Athenea del Castillo Beivide over his shoulder and carried her around the pitch in a kind of fireman's lift; before that he had grabbed his crotch celebrating the result in the stands.[12] Journalist Annabel Crabb sarcastically summed Rubiales' preceding actions up thusly: 'Such a cool and OK response to a big moment for your all-female team of world champions.'[13] Crabb scintillatingly wrote, too, about how the players were exemplary in skill and conduct—representing greater moral and marketing value—for a fraction of the prize money but were 'overshadowed again and again by second-rate blokes'.[14]

What arguably made the assault so shocking was not just that it was so public and so unapologetic—although that alone was enough—but because it was so starkly at odds with the four weeks that had preceded it. Those four weeks had allowed women to dare to hope that the lever was moving on gender equality. Hannah Ferguson says:

> We'd just had such a brilliant experience of women's safety, of women's success, of women's empowerment as a nation and as a sporting industry. But then to see that really proves it's the regression, it's the two steps forward, one step back. But I think it's important, because it's like: How can something like that *still* be darkened by a man and his entitlement?

While the public sexual assault could never be considered necessary or excusable, without Rubiales' inappropriate actions the Spanish team's concerns would likely have continued to be diminished. Sarah Gregorius notes that while it was 'brutal, because of what those players lost in that moment, as well, in terms of the ability to celebrate and the ability to be celebrated', she believes it created solidarity and accountability, and meant we turned a corner. 'That's also important, because I think it demonstrates that it was shit but it wasn't meaningless. It *was* a catalyst for change.'

But first, it descended into an omnishambles. Rubiales' mother went on a hunger strike and locked herself in a church.[15] Rubiales himself went on broadcaster Piers Morgan's TV show and into Piers' right-wing, public-relations-friendly embrace.[16] At a subsequent RFEF extraordinary general assembly, Rubiales refused to resign his position.[17] The assault and the handling of it sparked or reignited something of a #MeToo movement. Women protested in Spanish streets and on social media worldwide. #SeAcabó ('It's over'), 'Todos somos Jenni' ('We are all Jenni') and 'Contigo Jenni' ('With you, Jenni') were emblazoned and amplified on everything from signs to shirts to handwritten tape adorning wrists.[18] Some eighty-one Spanish players signed a letter saying they would refuse call-ups unless Rubiales resigned.[19]

Under immense pressure, FIFA suspended and later removed Rubiales and banned him from football activities for three years.[20] The Union of European Football Associations (UEFA), the organisation of which Rubiales was then vice president, remained silent before accepting his reluctant resignation.[21] (At the time of writing, Rubiales was set to face a criminal trial over the assault.) Coach Jorge Vilda was eventually ousted, but he was hired as Morocco's head coach thirty-seven days later.

Montse Tomé was appointed interim coach. We on the outside wondered whether her being the first woman to hold the role was tainted by it being an example of the Glass Cliff phenomenon,[22] or a fair appointment as she'd been doing the work the entire time. Player reaction indicated they considered her complicit in the systemic conditions under which they had been operating. (Around the same time, Hermoso was implausibly left out of the squad's next training camp. The confounding reason given was that it was 'for her protection'.[23] *From what?*)

While the Spanish officials may have become the lightning rod for pushing back on things that aren't great in the operational space, the challenges aren't contained to that one federation or country. FIFA president Gianni Infantino termed the 2023 tournament 'transformational' during an otherwise tone-deaf bloviation.[24] Prefaced by the fact that he has daughters at home (that is, he can 'relate'), Infantino informed the women in the room that the doors were open. He encouraged them to 'pick their battles' and push open said doors.[25] (This is the same incumbent FIFA president who declined to open the pay-parity discussion door in the tournament lead-up with 'Now is not the time.' *If not then, when?*)

In an article entitled 'You first, Gianni Infantino',[26] sports reporter Lindsay Gibbs responded to Infantino's efforts to 'gaslight a gender' 'because apparently on this day, he was feeling sexist'. (This was a reference to his infamous 2022 statements about the day he was feeling disabled, gay … you name it.[27]) She also wrote of Infantino's audacity: 'This. Fucking. Guy.' Suffice to say, she was, like most women, feeling a little fired up. *Guardian* journalist Marina Hyde correspondingly wrote: 'Any chance YOU could get the door? After all, it is your actual job.'[28] *Athletic* writer Meg Linehan also nailed it with the following article opening: 'As the daughter of a father …'[29] In the same article, she observed that you never hear the line 'As the father of sons …'

While Infantino's actions are oftentimes infuriating, Tracey Holmes provides a measured perspective. She is critical of organisations if they warrant it, but recognises that, as the figurehead of an organisation that is for all intents and purposes equivalent to the United Nations, Infantino's diplomatic task is enormous and fraught: 'You think about the number of countries in the world … they are all ideologically or religiously or economically different and at different stages of development. Making decisions that everyone is happy with is an impossible job.'

Also, during the Women's World Cup Holmes found a way to work with rather than against Infantino. She had heard through some trusted contacts that while he was completing few if any interviews throughout the tournament, he was scheduled to tour the broadcast centre. She contacted FIFA to see if she might be able to interview him while he was there. The media team was polite, but hedged. Holmes, knowing how these things worked, anticipated they would call her minutes before Infantino was due to arrive and ask if she could pop down, saying they were so sorry about the late notice and, oh well, if she couldn't make it they were afraid they couldn't possibly find another time in his schedule. So she drove to the venue and waited in her car for hours. Sure enough, the last-minute message came through: Infantino would be there in five minutes, apologies for the late warning, was she available? Holmes texted back two words that likely almost made the FIFA media person drop their phone: 'I'm here'.

Holmes asked Infantino three rapid-fire questions as he emerged from his car. By design, they were fun and friendly—the antithesis of the combative, gotcha journalism he so regularly encounters. They were also insightful. One sought to determine whether it was likely Australia would ever host the Men's World Cup—a valid question given the success of the Women's World Cup and the humbling failed bid for the 2022 Men's World Cup that long pre-dated it. Infantino responded well to this refreshing line of questioning, and Holmes ingeniously executed her doorstop interview.[30]

That the tournament discussion still temporarily surrendered to speculation about whether to bid for the Men's World Cup did niggle a little, as if that were the endgame and this the warm-up. Why must conversation and comparison always turn towards and privilege men? Fortunately, Football Australia put discussion of a Men's World Cup bid to bed, announcing it would instead focus on bidding for the 2026 Women's Asian Cup.[31]

⋆ ⋆ ⋆

With the final now in the distant past but its repercussions still being felt, there are perhaps few better acquainted than Gregorius with the two-forward-one-back steps the tournament took. Alongside having a front-row seat to the best athleticism and advocacy in and around the women's game, she necessarily sees some of the hardest stuff: players having to fight federations over pay and conditions, the ongoing spate of ACL injuries … Did the win give her a sense of: *I can enjoy this moment for a moment, then back to the grindstone*? She responds:

> We get a massive sense of pride when players can do what they do in spite of what has happened to them. But at the same time, [there are] some very frustrating feelings because you're like, *God, what would I be watching if everyone was in an environment where their health and their safety were prioritised psychologically, physically, mentally, physiologically?* What if they had not had the, in some instances, proper trauma coming into the event, and

> hadn't had to engage in all of these fights, both public and private, with the people who should be providing them the best environment possible to compete on the world stage? I think, if you have a job like mine, you always feel a little bit of both—a hell of a lot of pride, but also a bit of, like, *One day, the shackles will be off, and then you'll really see what this game is, what it has got to give, and what players have got to give.*

Gregorius says her already-interesting job at the coalface of women's football advocacy became more interesting in the tournament's aftermath, and that there's a women-specific education piece the team is carrying out—an education piece you'd never need for the men's game:

> Sometimes we have to spend time saying to players, 'This is what you deserve, and you don't have to be grateful. You can let go of that gratitude guilt that you've carried for so long, because actually, you *are* entitled to equal conditions, and you *are* entitled to participate in the wealth that's generated off the back of your performance.'

Such conversations invariably involve equal prize money. I'm not naive, but I dared hope FIFA would be motivated by the prospect of good public relations by, off the back of the tournament's strong ticket sales and breaking even, deciding to tip in some extra money to the prize pool. As in: 'Oh look, the tournament's been so successful we found some extra cash for you.' It had been shamed into promising equal prize money for 2027 anyway,[32] so what was four years of holdout worth?

It turns out, a lot. Not only did FIFA *not* find any extra prize money to at least partly reduce the US$330 million gap between the Men's and Women's World Cup prize money, but Infantino suggested that such a thing would only be 'a symbol' and wouldn't make a difference.[33] I beg to differ. Also, it would send a very important message—a symbol, if you like—that women's sports are valuable.

Infantino is clearly not the only man who feels this way. A survey of more than 3000 fans across 120 countries revealed that less than half of male fans (48 per cent) compared with more than three quarters (83 per cent) of female fans believe prize money should be equal.[34] (And yes, questions should be asked of that remaining 17 per cent.) Still, it reminds us that the shift is not just monetary—it's attitudinal.

The fact that equal prize money is on the horizon seemed to take the wind out of the advocacy around it during the tournament. 'In a way, we should never stop until we have the equality,' Gregorius says of advocating for equal pay, stat. 'Because that's what the players deserve. They deserve to be paid the same as what the men get paid.' Also, she adds, because the prize-money figure is capricious:

> It's not linked to revenue. It's not linked to performance. It's an arbitrary number. So of course I think the players deserve equality, and there's definitely an argument for us to have kept that fight up and kept up that collective pressure. I do think, though, in the long run, the really meaningful change was the per-player distribution.[35] Certainly in conversations I've had with players of loads of different nationalities, that money has changed lives.

She cites some examples. The money made up for the six years one player went without being paid a single cent for playing football and for which they had to quit their job to train; others were able put a down a deposit on a house. Gregorius continues:

> I think guaranteeing that was the most important thing, as well as the equal conditions. There's no excuse for FIFA not providing equal conditions. I think those two things are so fundamentally important because of what they guarantee for players … If [equal prize money] was the entire fight, it wouldn't guarantee that all players would receive part of it. But I think we should have a huge responsibility to hold FIFA's feet to the fire going into 2026 and 2027—we just can't let them off the hook.

One can't help but wonder if FIFA might try to weasel out of its promise to provide that equal pay. Gregorius:

> I'd love for them to try. I just think it wouldn't be tolerated. If we fail to get equal prize money in 2027, we also kind of win, because nothing will galvanise everybody against them [more than] if they renege on that particular promise. Because, like I said to them, at some point, surely, at the FIFA level, the fight for gender equality ends. Surely. And if not now, then when?

On balance, FIFA did implement vast improvements to the 2023 tournament conditions. Gregorius says that FIFPRO ensured that players understood what had been agreed to—for instance, business-class flights, which are pretty standard in the men's game but are crucial to any player travelling vast distances to Australia and New Zealand and needing to perform at the other end. She credits FIFA's swift and effective response when, for example, some players reached out because they had been given economy flights. The prompt response ensured the national federations' actions did not diminish players' experiences or the public's perception.

The tournament conditions themselves were outstanding. For some of the players, they were the antithesis of what they'd experienced before, and, Gregorius says, positively shifted their expectations of what an international tournament environment should be. The thinking behind the higher-standard environment was that it would ensure the players had their best-ever tournament. Based on what we saw, the improved conditions translated to improved outcomes on and off the pitch.

There is, as always with women's football, a 'but': some federations had to be dragged kicking and screaming to do the right thing in terms of pay and conditions. 'I mean, the obvious one is Nigeria,' Gregorius says, referencing the mid-tournament action FIFPRO had to take at the players' request because the Nigerian federation wasn't playing ball.[36] The Netherlands-based former Football Fern had vowed to try to have at least a couple of days off so she wasn't working a burnout-inducing five weeks straight through the tournament. Spotting a two-day window where she could travel to visit her Meanjin/Brisbane-based brother, she boarded a plane. After a single hour of offline flight time, she switched her phone back on to find messages from the Nigerian players, who wanted to put out a statement.

> So I'm waiting for my baggage, on the phone, trying to figure out how, communicating back to the Netherlands ... You can imagine the discomfort [of the players]. You are there in the group of twenty-three players fighting against the federation while still wearing the tracksuit, going out onto the field and playing on behalf of the country and the federation. There were those instances where I was a bit like, *I can't believe we're still here.*

12

THE OLYMPICS (AND THE KNEE THAT STOPPED THE NATION)

THE MATILDAS HAVE been on the verge of breakout success a bunch of times throughout their 45-year existence. The year 2007 and making it to the quarter-finals for the first time stands out; 2010 after they won the Asian Cup does, too. But the momentum and media coverage have invariably stalled after major events, which meant that many of us headed into the post–Women's World Cup Olympic qualifiers holding our breaths. Would the wave of support and interest continue beyond the World Cup, or would it dissipate as it had so consistently done before?

Our concerns were quickly allayed.

Through running the Olympic qualification gauntlet, the Matildas became the first women's football team to sell out Perth's Optus Stadium. (Research released shortly after the Women's World Cup demonstrated that support for the tournament had increased as the event progressed in all places except Adelaide and Perth.[1] It's almost as if Perth took umbrage at that: fans bought more than 100,000 tickets across the course of the Perth-based qualifiers—an unheard-of figure for the world's most isolated capital city.[2]) That ticketing appetite once again prompted the statement: 'We're going to need a bigger stadium.'

The juggernaut improbably continued as the Matildas made their way to the more central Melbourne home qualifier against Uzbekistan, resulting in calls for the home leg to be moved to the MCG, which has a capacity of 100,000. When asked about it in a press conference, Steph Catley joked that if Football Australia's CEO, James Johnson, was listening, he might want to get on that.

'If somebody had said to me twelve, fifteen years ago that you'd get 50,000 people to a game against Uzbekistan, I'd have said, "You're dreaming,"' former Matildas coach Tom Sermanni says. Kieran Yap recalls the Matildas' send-off match in Ballarat before the 2016 Rio Olympics, where the crowd comprised only a smattering of diehard fans. He muses on the likelihood that that match will be the last regional or small-stadium game they'll ever play: 'I don't think they're going back to that again. They might drop 20,000 supporters, like the Socceroos did, but I don't think they're ever going back to the suburban grounds or tiny stadiums again—it's a permanent shift.' Hannah Ferguson similarly terms it 'irreversible progress'.

Office for Women in Sport and Recreation director Sarah Styles identifies a key detail: fans were turning up to watch the team, rather than specifically to watch the team qualify for the Olympics. She points to the Bledisloe Cup, cricket one-day internationals and the Boxing Day Test, where crowd size varies depending on factors such as the quality of the opposition. By that measure, and with no disrespect intended, the Uzbekistan matches should not have sold out. Styles:

> When I watched Matildas versus Uzbekistan, I have never seen merch like that, I have never seen lines like that. They are there for them. It doesn't actually matter who [the Matildas] play. That's something I think is decidedly unique … As long as they continue to foster that, then that's where I think the Matildas have their trajectory.

Speaking of the 'star power' the Matildas command, journalist Samantha Lewis likewise says:

> I think the Matildas have reached a point where it almost doesn't matter any more how they go in major tournaments. Their celebrity is such that people will love them without medals. People will love them without World Cups. People will love them without [them] being world champions.

Post–Women's World Cup, Lewis has spent time reconsidering what this might mean for the team, and in terms of reimagining the definition of success:

> Success means silverware. Success means goals. Success means all these other metrics that the men's game has largely been defined by and built upon. But I think the women's game has necessarily had to build itself upon different ideas of success. What the Matildas have done and where they are now is a real testament to that alternative vision.

It's arguably reminiscent of what we're seeing with the women-led franchise Angel City, where the brand is about more than playing drawcard teams or even necessarily winning—although both are ideal. As Jean Williams says, with a team that has such a high profile and strong connection to the community, 'You don't need to win on the pitch to fill the stands every week.'

Continuing, Lewis references the 2024 Paris Olympics, the 2026 Women's Asian Cup and the 2027 Women's World Cup. Throw in the 2032 Brisbane Olympics and Paralympics on the Matildas' home soil and it's quite the lead-up:

> It would be great if they won some of those things, but it's not going to be devastating if they don't, because they have already achieved a level of success that winning those things is meant to do. Winning a tournament, winning a trophy, winning a gold medal is meant to bring you fans and coverage and investment and all that stuff. But they've already done that without having to win anything.
>
> So for me it's become much more about: What does the game do now, off the back of the Matildas' success, in order to

> continue this legacy? I know it's a catchphrase now, but [what do we need to do] to make sure this legacy is not just something that trickles away after a couple of years but is actually something that rolls on for generations? Then we can keep talking about the ways in which the Matildas, not just as this group of players but the Matildas as a concept, the Matildas as a team and as an idea, have continued to shape football and women's sport and women's participation in Australian society.

'I don't think it matters who the Matildas play,' Canberra United media manager and commentator Russ Gibbs, too, says of the esteemed position in which the Matildas now operate. 'The Matildas fans will watch the Matildas if they're playing a kick-around in a school car park—it doesn't matter. They'll turn up in their thousands.' Without casting any aspersions, he suggests the Socceroos don't currently have quite the same traction, perhaps in part because we see them regularly, and their opponents and matches are relatively routine. In contrast, he says, 'The Matildas, we don't see enough.'

Of course, the Olympic preparation wasn't all ascendant. Sam Kerr did her ACL ahead of the Olympic qualifiers, and the panic and despair this induced was equivalent to the calf muscle that stopped the nation. Amid feverish calculations of how many months it takes to rehabilitate a knee reconstruction and how many months until the Olympics (read: too many, so too few), Mel Buttle and Future Women (an organisation committed to achieving gender equality in Australian workplaces) both offered to donate an ACL to Kerr. Future Women, which had previously joked that it has morphed into being a Matildas fanpage, wrote, 'We volunteer as tribute.'[3]

Kerr's ruling-out was further marred by the announcement that criminal charges had been laid against her due to an allegedly racist tirade at a police officer over a cab fare the previous year.[4] The words she reportedly uttered were 'Stupid white bastard', perhaps not unlike the 'Suck on that one' comment she made post-match at the 2019 Women's World Cup—the 2019 comment being a response to the abuse she had experienced and experiences.[5] The words, if true, cannot be condoned, but were arguably multidimensional. Kerr is a person of colour—she has Indian heritage. She is also queer. She, more than most, keenly knows what it's like to be on the receiving end of racist, homophobic tirades. Is backchatting a white male police officer—a person whose authority must absolutely be respected, yes, but also a person who perhaps hasn't ever had to feel the sting of racism—in perspective here? Drawing on journalist and author Antoinette Lattouf's 2022 TED talk, the Missing Perspectives media company team questioned whether reverse racism actually exists.[6] Lattouf's thesis, visualised via a Venn diagram, was that white, able-bodied, cis-gendered, heterosexual males are 'not oppressed'.

Libbi Gorr comments on how the public-opinion pendulum swung: 'Day one, it was "Oh, how could she have been racist?" Day two was "Oh, did she really call him that? Good on her." It was really interesting to watch it flip-flop. And then day three it was "How come they've taken this long to bring it against her?" ... So she's just in the stratosphere now.'

The question for Football Australia was why Kerr had failed to inform it of the charge. Blindsiding her employer ahead of that employer fronting media to announce friendlies against China gifted the media clickbait headlines off the back of an otherwise innocuous press conference. But it must be recognised that Kerr is human and, for all her achievements, a relatively young human at that. She's also the first Matilda to have such a profile and therefore such a highly dissected existence. As some mused, maybe her self-image hasn't caught up with her impact.

The upside, if you can call it that, to the incident is that people are paying attention. 'This degree of scrutiny and analysis over the events surrounding Kerr's charge is that now everyone in the world *does* know who she is, which is a blessing and a burden for her,' Bridie O'Donnell says. Fan and photographer Kris Goman agrees and says it's a mark of how much the landscape has shifted and how heavily people are invested now: 'Five years ago, if that happened, it wouldn't have been in the news.'

★ ★ ★

Intrepid alumni Maria Berry, Heather Reid and Sue Monteath were among the 'Tenacious 10' (as coined by Reid) who travelled to Uzbekistan for the away leg of the final Olympic qualification round. In some ways, it was a return to the early-era national team trips: rugged conditions and a core group of savvy, plucky women heading to a game that would prove historic.

'I suppose similar to the early years was that people we spoke to hadn't heard about the game, didn't know about it, didn't really even know about the women's team,' football administrator and former national team manager Reid says. She equates the match to 'when we jumped in the car and went to Sydney in 1979. People were saying, "You're going where? For what?"' They had been headed to the match that would be etched in history as the Matildas' first A International.

Still, Reid was pleasantly surprised that there was actually a sizeable contingent of fans at the game in Tashkent—at least 2000, of which forty to fifty were Australians. The latter comprised expats who dropped in from Dubai and the neighbouring 'Stans, as well as the region's Moscow-based Australian ambassador. With the thermometer dipping well into the negative, there was a lot of discussion about the weather. It made for a memorable experience. Reid had to remove her shoes at half-time to try to wiggle and defrost her toes. Monteath says of the sub-zero temperatures in which the match was played:

> It was frigid. It was minus six. We couldn't sit down because [the] seats [were so cold]. We just had to keep standing and stamping our feet, so it was probably the most uncomfortable I've ever felt when watching a game. It would have been nice if [the Matildas had] scored earlier—we probably would have jumped up and down a bit more [to warm up].

Also aligning with the quintessential women's football experience, there was no food service at the ground bar a woman selling pastries outside the gates, and the women's toilets were locked.

None of this fazed Reid and co. For the toilets, they simply headed across the corridor to the men's bathrooms.

A 3–0 win in Tashkent, Uzbekistan—the team's first time encountering such chilly, snowy conditions—marked the fairytale return of 35-year-old Michelle Heyman less than ten minutes after she was subbed on. The flipside to Kerr's injury was that Heyman and Chloe Logarzo were called up to the squad in Kerr's absence—for Heyman, it was her first national team appearance in six years and marked a retirement reversal. She'd called time on her international career some years before to save face after not being selected.[7] Her return was as much a victory for elite athlete mental health as it was for the team—so often players' careers finish suddenly and absent a fairytale ending through ageing out, injury, or coach or team-combination subjectivity. Heyman had equalled Kerr's domestic record of 17 goals in a single season and become the first player to win the Golden Boot three times. And, as we've seen across their careers, Kerr's and Heyman's fates had always been inextricably entwined—this was the second successive time Heyman received a call-up after Kerr sustained an ACL injury.[8] In a gesture that befit the moment and a video that tugged at the heartstrings, Katrina Gorry's young daughter, Harper, who had previously been named the team's 24th player, announced the squad list for the Round 3 Olympic qualifiers.[9] Gorry was Heyman's Matildas roommate and had, as has been documented, struggled with her own mental health challenges in the team. Through the Olympic qualifiers (and, later, the Olympics), the two best friends were reunited.[10]

Heyman ran rampant in those qualifiers, scoring not just that goal on the first leg but following up with four on the return one. She was so dynamic in poaching goals in those statement performances that it was impossible not to ponder what might have been had she been in the squad during the Women's World Cup. (Fortunately for Heyman, she's getting a second chance many players don't get, and deservedly so. 'She's been such a good player for so long now,' former Matilda and Canberra United teammate Ash Sykes says. 'Goalscoring-wise, I've not seen many players who know how to put it in the back of the net so naturally. She makes it look easy.')

Fittingly, Reid, who had worked closely with Heyman for much of her career, was there to witness it. She'd even prepared homemade supporter signs adorned with Heyman's image:

> I couldn't get any of the commemorative masks that were distributed for the 100th [A-League Women's] goal, so I said, 'We'll make our own.' I had the image of her smiling face. We found some second-hand beach-paddle things, which were perfect because they were light but also reasonably strong.

A local printer helped Reid print copies of the image and she stuck them to the paddles and packed four in her suitcase for Tashkent. The image of her holding one of the paddles at the game alongside a beaming Heyman went global.

* * *

The 2024 Paris Olympics were the first to achieve full gender parity.[11] It was an important milestone, but at some 130-odd years since the first Olympics, representative of the glacial progress we're making. Women were not allowed to compete in the inaugural Olympics in 1896: their participation was deemed 'impractical, uninteresting, unaesthetic, incorrect'.[12] Even after admission, they comprised less than 10 per cent of Olympians until 1952 and were only allowed to compete in every sport as recently as 2012.

Curiously, gender inclusion/exclusion, visibility/invisibility has always been entwined with Olympics and Women's World Cup history. In its formative years, the Women's World Cup leveraged off the better-funded, higher-profile Olympics as it sought to create a sporting-landscape foothold. It brought otherwise disinterested audiences to the game courtesy of the Olympic Games Effect, a phenomenon that sees nationalism overtake 'No one watches women's sport' and 'Women's sport isn't as good quality or commercially viable' bias and has audiences engage with more women's sports through a gender-blind lens.[13]

The 2023 Women's World Cup flipped that neutral model, with gender front, centre and celebrated. Indeed, having been admitted equally to the Games, women athletes across the board seemed to pick up the mantle, with women carrying the medal tally as the tournament unfolded. The surge prompted media company Women's Agenda to create a women's medal tally.[14] Missing Perspectives posted a meme illustrating the back pain of Australian women carrying the medal tally load.[15] After Australian swimmer Cameron McEvoy won gold on Day 7, Missing Perspectives posted how he had swum 'like a girl' to win gold.[16] For its part, *The Betoota Advocate* highlighted the gender medal gap and questioned male athletes' commercial viability.[17] Meanwhile, women's financial advocate and expert Mel Browne inverted the dismissive tropes women have so often heard with a social media post espousing that 'Men should just work harder or choose less low medalling sports if they want more medals'.[18]

The gender-non-neutral model was also reinforced through the Matildas and not their male Olympic counterparts, the Olyroos, qualifying for the 2024 tournament. Evocative of journalist Shireen Ahmed's statement that football is for everyone, but sometimes it takes women to illustrate that,[19] Australia had but one football team to get around throughout the tournament, and it was, once again, the women.

It wasn't just the nation's hopes the team was carrying. The 2024 Olympics represented the last chance to win a major tournament for some of the players of the era that bridged the no-pay/some-pay/full-pay era, as they are likely to retire before the next Women's World Cup. Lydia Williams announced her post-Olympics retirement ahead of the event and received a heartfelt send-off at a friendly against China in June 2023 amid a standing ovation that included a guard of honour with alumni on one side and the members of Football Australia's National Indigenous Advisory Group on the other. In a moment that had most people asking if someone was cutting onions, tennis great and Wiradjuri woman Evonne Goolagong-Cawley presented Williams with a custom-designed and -decorated booka, an animal-skin cloak that signifies the continuity of First Nations cultures.[20] Williams later wrote, in an open letter thanking the Matildas, 'Obviously there is only one Cathy Freeman, but if I have inspired just one Aboriginal girl like me to put on her goalkeeper gloves, then that's an incredible thing.'[21] Williams wasn't the only player set to retire from the national team. In fact, the Olympics marked the start of a changing of the guard. Katrina Gorry had hinted at retirement; Clare Polkinghorne, Aivi Luik, Tameka Yallop and Kyah Simon, one had to wonder, might have been considering it, too.

★ ★ ★

And so the team ventured first to Spain to prepare for, and then to France to play in, the 2024 Olympics. Off the back of the Matildas' breakout Women's World Cup and succession of sold-out friendly matches conducted amid fan fever-pitch, fans' hopes and the team's confidence were high—as we would soon see, too high. Australia's group-stage opponents included Germany and the United States, then ranked fourth and fifth in the world, respectively, and teams that, as the Croissants identified, had between them won six of the nine Women's World Cups that have ever been played.[22] (Speaking of the Croissants, they sent one 'correspondent' to France, the hometown of their brand, which had been inaugurated for the French-hosted 2019 Women's World Cup. The name associated with the popular French pastry turned out to be unexpectedly apt. 'We were laughing because this is a five-year strategic long-term brand play that we've accidentally fallen into,' they say.) Just as noteworthy was that, as previously mentioned, the USWNT's fifth-place ranking, which came off the back of the team's poor 2023 Women's World Cup, was its lowest ever.[23] The team has more often been ranked in the top two. So while the term 'Group of Death' is invariably too liberally bandied about, the context such a term provided in this instance was that the Matildas' progression past the group was in no way guaranteed.

The initial hurdle the Matildas faced was that the team's luggage and equipment took an unexpected detour en route from Spain to France, leaving the team without, and scrambling to temporarily replace, necessities such as toiletries and underwear. Although it was an inconvenient disruption to the Matildas' tournament preparation, bigger issues soon engulfed the team and the women's football tournament as a whole.

Sweden had for the first-ever time failed to qualify for the Olympics—this after finishing third at the World Cup and second at the 2020 Olympics—and Women's World Cup runners-up England (or the Great Britain equivalent) were also out of Paris 2024. But their absences were scarcely noticed as controversy almost immediately erupted around reigning Olympic champions Canada. Canada were set to defend their title without the steady steerage of stalwart Christine Sinclair—a Canadian team without her was almost unimaginable—and against the backdrop of the unfolding lawsuit against their federation. But overshadowing both was the fact that Canadian staff were found to be using drones to spy on the team's opposition. Coaching staff were sent home, and FIFA deducted six points from the team and rebuffed an appeal.[24]

Spain were the most likely contender for gold after their Women's World Cup sweep, but Germany and the United States were seeking to make amends for their World Cup sputtering. The Matildas needed to overcome both of those motivated teams, as well as Zambia, to propel themselves towards the knockout rounds and the podium finish the team was intent on coming away with. Unfortunately, just as in the 2022 Women's Asian Cup, the Matildas' sights were set too far on the future.

A 3–0 loss to Germany during which Australia looked flat and fatigued while the German team looked clinical and cohesive started the team's tournament on the back foot. The Matildas conceded on setpieces they had traditionally been decent at defending—a bewildering new Achilles heel, the origins of which no one could quite understand or explain.

Katrina Gorry had played few (read: if any) minutes in the tournament lead-up due to recovering from an ankle injury sustained in club football with West Ham that had required surgery and a lengthy recovery. Yet she was the team's player of the match—her defensive coverage and double-up defending were crucial in the first half, and without her efforts Germany's score would likely have been higher.

Characteristic of how desperate the Matildas were and would be across all three group-stage games, defenders turned strikers. Tony Gustavsson substituted actual striker Michelle Heyman on in the dying stages of the game, and she immediately created a chance across the face of goal. But there were no Australian players there to capitalise—having been run ragged, the players were perhaps too fatigued or too stunned at how very wrong the match was going. Whatever the cause, what was clear the entire ninety minutes was that the Matildas were never in it. The German team played beautiful football, but the Matildas' performance was disjointed, muted.

The Germany game result was confidence-rattling, but not fatal (although we fans might say that having to wake up at 3 a.m. in winter to watch football in a polar-opposite time zone to witness your team humbled 3–0 felt absolutely dire). After that match, journalist Kieran Pender wrote that the Matildas have a habit of doing things the hard way, but presciently foretold that sometimes the hard way is too hard.[25] The Zambia game that followed the Germany one was, indeed, a textbook case of doing things the hard—almost too hard—way.

The flatness and difficulty in defending setpieces and containing on-running attackers the Matildas had demonstrated against Germany continued from the outset in the Zambia game. The Copper Queens' Barbra Banda scored within the first two minutes—a horror start to the second, and must-win, group-stage match against the seemingly beatable 65th-ranked team. From there, a frenetic number of goals were scored, mostly by Zambia courtesy of Banda and Racheal Kundananji, players who had also to date recorded the two most expensive transfers in women's football history at US$740,00 and US$860,000, respectively.[26]

Zambia led the Matildas 4–2 at half-time (including through a Banda hat-trick), a scoreline that felt almost insurmountable. As we turned our attention to whether it might be possible to make it out of the group if the Matildas were one of the two best third-placed teams, worries about the mounting goal difference nagged at fans' collective minds. Having haemorrhaged three goals in the first game and now four in the first half of the second, the possibility of even a third-place-based progression was looking bleak.

The Matildas needed an urgent injection of energy and new tactics. Gustavsson subbed on Heyman, Clare Wheeler and Kaitlyn

Torpey close to the 60th minute. The team immediately looked more spritely and Heyman soon generated a goal from Wheeler's cross in with a backheel, which forced an own goal through a Zambian defender deflection into the goalkeeper and in.

A heart-in-mouth flurry of chaotic awarded and denied goals ensued. By the match's end, the Matildas had gone from 2–5 to 6–5, which prompted *The Betoota Advocate* to publish an article entitled 'Matildas secure easy victory that was never in doubt after cruising past Zambia in group stage'.[27] Stunned fans and pundits alike wondered, *What did we just watch?* Gustavsson himself was blunt in his post-match assessment: 'Obviously, that was shit.'[28] In her subsequent analysis, like Pender, Lewis considered whether the Matildas were running out of miracles.[29]

That the first two matches weren't confidence-inspiring was doubly concerning as the Matildas then had to face their arguably toughest group-stage opponent, the United States. That team, which featured just eight of the players from the 2020 Olympics and ten from the 2023 Women's World Cup, was brimming with players keen to prove themselves. It was also operating under the assured guidance of the newly appointed former Chelsea coach Emma Hayes. The USWNT had already defeated both Zambia and Germany 3–0 and 4–1, which didn't bode well given that the Germans had themselves clinically defeated the Matildas 3–0. Australia entered the match needing the win, but knowing they could potentially sneak through to the knockout rounds with a draw, pending favourable outcomes in the other group matches.

The US game proved the Matildas' strongest of the tournament and the most like the form we know they can deliver, but as Pender had observed, it proved too little, too late on a progression pathway that had been made too hard. A setpiece was again the Matildas' undoing: having played defensively and kept the United States scoreless for the majority of the first half, an uncleared ball enabled Trinity Rodman to put the USWNT up 1–0 shortly before half-time. Australia had done well to contain the Americans to just one goal until then, but it was still oceans away from what the Matildas needed to progress. Also, the team played defensively at a time when it probably needed to throw caution to the wind and attack.

Brief distractions came through technical issues around the VAR after the Australians appealed that Rodman's goal had come only after Arnold's line of sight was interfered with. After much suspense, the VAR technical issues were resolved and the referee, after being able to review the footage, deemed that the goal stood. There was another bleary-eyed flurry as Australian host broadcaster Channel 9, perhaps recognising that the Matildas' tournament was all but over or at least relegated to being considered less important than the country's more successful swimmers, elected to cut to a women's 100-metre swimming final. Australian fans had to scramble to change to a secondary channel to continue watching the Australia v USA game. (Former Socceroo Robbie Slater appeared to be silent on the relegation. He wasn't silent later on the Matildas' disastrous campaign, conflating folding laundry and players having their own hotel rooms with the Matildas' poor on-pitch performance.[30] Er, as in the standard kit manager role within the team and the privacy and ability to rest that the men have always had and that is built into the collective bargaining agreements across the board? Make it make sense.)

There was also some witty side banter. Neither the injured Kerr nor her fiancee and former USWNT player Kristie Mewis were in attendance at the tournament, but a fan jokingly proffered a million-dollar payment for a stream of Kerr and Mewis watching the Australia v USA match together. Kerr's up-for-it response was: 'Where should we stream it?'[31] Thematically on par, Just Women's Sports reposted a famous image of Kerr and Mewis from the 2020 Tokyo Olympics, saying that they 'Missed this sportsmanship'.[32] The image shows Mewis consoling her 'friend' Kerr after the United States defeated the Matildas to secure the bronze medal. The image, albeit one initially misread by some not in the know, was one of the first hints that Kerr and Mewis were dating and garners mirth from savvy fans when it's referenced.

But those moments of levity offered only temporary reprieve.

Heyman was again subbed on in the 60th minute but, as with Gustavsson's panned hesitancy in the Women's World Cup and the two preceding Olympic group-stage games, the lateness of the substitution made it difficult for her to change the game. (Defenders Steph Catley and Alanna Kennedy would finish the tournament as the team's top goalscorers: across all three games, strike power was largely nullified or wasn't on the pitch.) Yallop took the field in the final ten minutes—her first appearance at the tournament after having been a late omission from the opening match through injury. The only player ever to have scored a winning goal against the United States, she wasn't on this occasion able to muster a game-changing goal. It was likely her final Olympics and possibly even national-team appearance.

The match finished 2–1, with goals to Rodman and Korbin Albert on the US side and Kennedy on the Australian one.[33] The devastated Australians' fate hung on the other group matches that had just kicked off. By those matches' end, it was confirmed that Canada had scraped into the knockout rounds in one of the third-placed positions, despite its points docking and drone scandal. (It had won all three games, but under the penalty, its nine points had been curtailed to three. Although the Matildas, too, were on three points, goal difference ruled them out.) Having recorded their worst result and earliest exit in twenty-four years (the last equivalent exit was at the 2000 Sydney Olympics), the Matildas were out of the tournament. Gustavsson, whose contract was up for renewal but was obviously not going to be renewed after such a poor tournament, was gone with almost immediate effect.[34]

For context, the match and the tournament outcome occurred almost a year to the day of the 'Miracle in Melbourne' Women's World Cup group-stage match where the Matildas had stunned Canada 4–0. Coupled with the fact that the United States and Germany had also recorded early exits from the Women's World Cup, the reversals of fortune could not have been more apparent. The United States, the team Gustavsson used to work for, was the team that delivered the final result and blow. The devastation wasn't contained to the Matildas: Brazilian great Marta was issued a straight red for a high-foot challenge on Spain's Olga Carmona in stoppage time. It looked set to be an uncharacteristically harsh end to Marta's glittering international career—but Brazil defeated France in the quarter-final to provide Marta with another chance to go out on a high.[35] Marta received a chance at redemption after the team progressed to the final. Brazil had gone from securing one of the third-place positions the Matildas had been chasing (the difference was a solitary goal) and overcame the favoured home team France and Women's World Cup champions Spain in the knockout rounds to meet the US in the gold-medal match. A single goal proved the difference there, too. Brazil dominated possession but were denied by, for example, an almost super-human, single-handed diving save by Alyssa Naeher, which saw Naeher parry an otherwise certain Brazil goal with the fingertips of her outstretched right hand. The save, and Naeher's form throughout the tournament, arguably provided some salve for the gutting penalty that had marred her 2023 Women's World Cup. Marta, meanwhile, took to the pitch one last time and received a silver medal and the tribute she deserved.

The Matildas perhaps took some small comfort from the final tournament results, too, with their early exit now providing some greater context: group-stage opponents Germany and the US won the bronze and gold medals overall.[36]

★ ★ ★

Gutting Olympic results and, as Lewis termed it, the 'reality check Australia has been bracing for'[37] aside, we need to reconcile the Matildas' stunning Women's World Cup success with the pragmatism that they are phenomenal athletes and humans, but they are not yet world champions; they are also young, tired women who have been operating under conditions and a physical and mental load we have not yet come to fully understand or appreciate.

In a masterstroke of lengthening the Matildas' and the sport's longevity and profile, Football Australia successfully bid to host the 2026 Asian Football Confederation (AFC) Women's Asian Cup.[38] The second time Australia will have hosted the tournament (the last time was two decades ago, in 2006), it will be the second major women's football event the country has hosted in three years, and will facilitate an important runway to the Brisbane 2032 Olympics and Paralympics.

The Asian Cup also marks something of a closing-the-loop moment for Sarah Walsh. She was fresh to the national team as a player in 2006. Now an experienced administrator, in 2026 she'll be at the event's organisational helm. That iterative career trajectory is one she can scarcely believe. It was when she was drafting what was, by her own admission, a fairly dry LinkedIn post announcing her Asian Cup role that her wife pointed out that that event will be twenty years since Walsh's initial pivotal tournament involvement. Walsh phoned a few of the alumni from that era. She says they gibed that they would never at the time have picked her to be the one running the show, but the calls did prompt important recollections that will inform her work.

It's not just Walsh who'll be closing the loop. Australia, then ranked fifteenth in the world, finished a surprise second at that 2006 iteration in Adelaide, a tournament run on a one-stadium, one-city shoestring. At the time new to the AFC, the team wasn't sure how it would fare against top-ranked Asian teams. A bit like its 2023 result, the Matildas outperformed expectations and both made it to the final and, through that top-two finish, qualified for the 2007 Women's World Cup. They went one better in 2010, becoming the first Australian team—women's or men's—to win the Asian Cup. The team admittedly underperformed in 2022, being routed in the quarter-final, which is preserved in the Disney+ documentary. So it will be looking to make amends for that and leverage its legion hometown support and 2023 gains to win the 2026 event.

Paired with a hopefully good showing at the 2027 Women's World Cup in Brazil (the first time the South American footballing great will have hosted a Women's World Cup), the major events and sustained investment and profile the Matildas will garner will cement the elevation of women's football in ways not yet seen.

13

OUR ROMAN EMPIRE

THE 2023 WOMEN'S World Cup might have finished, but the tournament and the Matildas have continued to capture and influence the cultural zeitgeist. Late in 2023, Google reported that the Matildas, Sam Kerr and Mary Fowler featured among Australians' top searches for the year.[1] 'Matilda' was chosen as Australian word of the year by the Australian National Dictionary Centre,[2] and the *Australian Financial Review* named Sam Kerr the most culturally influential person in Australia—beating even *Barbie*'s Margot Robbie.[3]

Soon after, Mattel, which had named women's sports its career of choice for 2023, released a Mary Fowler Barbie complete with high bubble braid and gloves.[4] (The doll's release gives renewed meaning to Samantha Lewis's quip to me about Fowler and her NRL-playing boyfriend: 'She's Barbie. He's just Ken.') Then, at their fourteenth consecutive sold-out match and having accrued $4 million in ticket revenue in four days, the Matildas, with 76,798 people in attendance, recorded their largest domestic crowd to date.[5] It was for a friendly. Against a team ranked nineteenth in the world. Played on a Monday night. During the school term. In winter.[6]

Amid this, we fans are starting to catch our breath and compare notes. Some stories people share are snippets, some are fully formed anecdotes. All are deepening our connection to, and understanding of, what just happened. For the tournament is, as Frimpong suggests, the kind of thing you might use to build immediate rapport and pass the time if you found yourself trapped with strangers in a lift. Indeed, the tournament and team permeated the cultural consciousness so much that they've arguably become women's 'Roman Empire'.[7]

★★★

'My favourite moment was when my partner would say to me every night, "So we're not watching the seven o'clock ABC News,"' laughs Marion Stell, academic, historian and co-author of *Women in Boots: Football and Feminism in the 1970s*.[8] No, they most definitely were not.

★★★

Football writer Kieran Yap was one of the few people in the country who wasn't trying to source Women's World Cup tickets as the tournament reached fever pitch. His first child was born on the first day of the tournament. He and his partner were actually at the hospital for the Matildas' opening match against Ireland but it was a false alarm, so they headed home—only to have to go back to the hospital a few hours later because this time it was the real thing.

Whether or not the adrenaline surge or stress surrounding that first game played a part in invoking Yap's partner's labour can probably never be quantifiably proven. Regardless, his son's well-timed arrival meant Yap attended a few games in person and watched many more via broadcast as he spent quality family time at home, albeit screaming into a pillow as he tried to contain his cheering enthusiasm and not wake his partner or child. There were upsides, too. 'I turned into Santa Claus for a few weeks,' Yap says of giving away some of his pre-purchased and now highly-sought-after tickets. 'It was actually pretty satisfying to be able to help people out.'

★★★

The buy-in to the Matildas has extended beyond city centres and is country- and culture-wide. Danielle Warby moved to a regional area a couple of years ago and has encountered not one, not two, but three questions about the team during her local trivia competition. One related to which athlete had a stadium named after them in Perth (A: Sam Kerr). Another asked participants to name two or three other teams that played in the group stage for the Olympic qualifiers (A: Philippines, Chinese Taipei). 'Not an easy question, like who scored the winning penalty would be. But everyone knew the answer. Nobody got it wrong,' Warby says. There's now so much information, distributed so frequently, that Warby can't stay across it all: 'People are telling me things I don't know. That's how far we've come.'

★ ★ ★

Long-time remote fan Louise Crawford[9] went two for two in choosing Matildas matches to attend in person. Her first live football match was the knife-edge Canada v Australia game, and her second was the heart-stopping Australia v France quarter-final. For the second match, she was coincidentally perfectly seated behind the goal at which the record number of penalties took place. They were immense, and the outcome just as much, but Crawford's appreciation of them held additional significance: having recently had to obtain hearing aids, she had been following Arnold's own hearing-loss experience with interest.[10]

Of Arnold going public about her experience, media manager Ann Odong tells me:

> I think she was just at the stage where she was ready to accept that this was something she needed. And she had a lot of support from the players, particularly Caitlin [Foord] and Alanna [Kennedy] who are her close friends and who really supported her in that decision and in that journey. Also, she just came out more publicly and decided to actually really own it. And the reception has been fantastic. The [response] has been incredible—the support from the Matildas community, from the public, but also seeing

> how it's really touched a lot of people [regarding] that visibility and representation for the hearing-impaired community.

Indeed, Arnold may have absolutely shone during the penalty shootout and the tournament as a whole (and that alone was impressive enough), but to Crawford, Arnold was a person whose similar experience and openness and normalising of wearing hearing aids importantly helped her come to grips with her own.

* * *

The Matildas' profile is now so elevated and, as with the helicopter intrusion that occurred during the Women's World Cup, so left field that media manager Ann Odong and digital lead Liana Buratti never quite know what their day is going to look like or what might pop up in their media and social media feeds.

Among the calls Odong has fielded in recent times is one involving Swedish royals' request to meet with Swedish-born Matildas coach Tony Gustavsson. Australian-Danish Queen Mary reportedly accepted a Matildas jersey gift, as did Taylor Swift. Those, like the helicopter, aren't covered by any handbook.

It all makes for long days and little sleep. 'Haha, what's sleep?' Buratti laughs, going on to say:

> But honestly, there wasn't much sleep happening [during the tournament]. Between the matches, training, press conferences and interviews each day, travelling, etc., the days were very long, usually 18–20 hours, but it's something you wouldn't do unless you're really passionate, and everyone in this team is. The players work hard and we want to work just as hard to ensure they're being promoted the way they deserve.

That promotion has seen an influx of media and fan interest. Buratti explains that the media and digital team's strategy was and remains consistent and human-focused, regardless of how many fans and followers the Matildas now have (although the team does try to provide additional or contextual information as needed to ensure newer fans are included well):

> Regardless of if we've got 100 or 100 million eyes on our Matildas content, that's why I'm so passionate about the phrase, 'Come for the performance, stay for the personality'. That is what underpins all of our content.
>
> Giving a behind-the-scenes view of the players meeting Cathy Freeman, showing the players so raw and vulnerable when reacting to the news they'd made the squad, even giving fans the ability to connect with the players via our #AskMatildas series, it [is] all about creating that connection and then letting the on-pitch performance speak for itself.

Something that is always fascinating to wake up to is the left-field content the team hasn't created or anticipated. An example of this is when US comedian Seth Meyers on his late-night talk show referenced getting emotional about retiring Matildas great Lydia Williams handing over the number 1 goalkeeper jersey to Arnold.[11] Meanwhile, Sam Kerr and Steph Catley are being mentioned in unrelated *Guardian* articles about sliced-cheese comparisons and taste-testing.[12] Really. Matildas Active Support member Majella Card describes it thusly: 'It's like, *What an odd place for this to show up*. They are now totally mainstream.'

★ ★ ★

Stadium grounds manager Matthew Oliver is among the people working behind the scenes whose integral work was simultaneously visible and invisible to us lay fans. The person tasked with maintaining the pitch to FIFA's exacting standards, he watched the Matildas' quarter-final penalty shootout from the north-east pitch tunnel. Like the rest of us, he rode every emotion after every kick. But he had some additional considerations, not least how the pitch held up: 'FIFA had very strict parameters for how the pitch needed to look (the mowing patterns were measured to the millimetre) and the field performance was tested daily during the tournament to ensure it met the required standards for a Tier One tournament.' That standard testing certainly came in the form of that longest-ever penalty shootout:

> The previous match we hosted a shootout at the northern end, so I was pleased this penalty shootout took place at the southern end of the pitch, which helped to balance and maintain the integrity of the turf for future matches across the tournament. I was always confident that the surface was going to withstand the rigours of a huge penalty shootout, and was particularly pleased with how it performed and contributed to such an amazing occasion.
>
> Also, fun fact:
>
> One of FIFA's strict regulations was that the pitch had to be mown daily using walk-behind cylinder mowers instead of our regular ride-on cylinder mower. The pitch was also mown post-match with walk-behind rotary mowers to collect any debris from the match. The team certainly got their steps up during the tournament, averaging 11 kilometres of walking per mow per day!

* * *

In terms of both frequency and omnipresence, Ash Sykes' experiences across the event are illustrative of many other people's. One match day, while waiting for a coffee at a cafe, she overheard a bunch of cyclists casually discussing the upcoming game. Another day, while she was walking through the Sydney CBD at lunchtime on a weekday, she heard three businessmen in suits talking about Kerr being out and potential replacements for her, including nominating the replacements by name. Sykes was stunned: 'They were talking about it like it was any other sport … and I was just like, *We've made it!*'

Former Matilda Jo Powell had a similar experience on a Melbourne street where she witnessed tradesmen lugging furniture who were discussing the upcoming game as they went about their work. 'It was amazing to hear that. So it's not like it's isolated to women or kids. It doesn't matter who you are—it's foremost in everybody's mind at this point in time.'

Karen Menzies observed the at-scale demographic shift, too. 'So obviously, you had lots of families with kids [at the games], but there'd be large groups of men around their thirties as well. This is the sort of demographic I would expect [to be] turning up to a [Men's] State of Origin, but it's a Matildas World Cup game.'

* * *

Illustrative of the early signs of what was about to happen as the tournament kicked off is the experience of Kris Goman, a self-described boomer who set up a private Facebook group for roughly thirty friends. Goman's plan was to coordinate Women's World Cup ticket purchases and seating logistics via the group, and provide the practical information people would need for a smooth tournament experience: when tickets went on sale, how to access tickets via the FIFA app, how to travel to and from the venues, how to sell tickets on the resale platform, whether fans could take a drink bottle and snacks into the stadium, whether they could sit a baby on their lap ... 'Just all these questions,' Goman says. 'So many questions.'

Characteristic of the pragmatic, community-service ethos that infuses women's football, as well as the underserved women's football market, the group became an unofficial but authoritative communication channel and conduit for crucial event information. Goman had expertise in this area, having photographed and plugged media gaps for A-League Women's games for some years. Goman facilitated the group but also empowered others to steer its direction. It was and is truly organic and collaborative: 'It's just a friendly environment, and people are nice, as opposed to being combative.'

Still, the group took on a larger life, and quickly. Those friends told their friends, their friends told their friends, and Goman was soon receiving requests to join the group. 'All of a sudden, there's a thousand people and it's like, *Who the hell are they all?*' Goman says. The group grew as each tranche of tickets was released, and by the time the tournament kicked off, membership was at around 20,000 and climbing. 'Then Facebook actually sent me a message and said, "We've noticed your group is one of the fastest-growing groups on Facebook,"' Goman says. 'And it's like, *What?* Dumbfounded me, the whole thing.'

★★★

Terming it one of the most meaningful roles he's ever had, Russ Gibbs helped provide invaluable audio commentary that for the first time made the tournament accessible to people with vision impairment.[13]

Gibbs is an experienced commentator, but this particular audio commentary required him to adjust his approach in a good-challenging way. With TV commentary, on-screen images traditionally do the heavy lifting and the commentary is supplementary. Descriptive audio commentary is doing all the jobs, which means there's no downtime. Gibbs explains:

> Where is the ball on the park? Who's got it? Who's making a run? What colour shirt are they wearing? What kind of boots have they got on? Do they have a ribbon in their hair like Hayley Raso? [I provide] those kinds of distinguishing things that you and me and everybody else takes for granted because we can see them.

Audio commentary is fatiguing but important work to enable people with impaired vision to join in the workplace or water-cooler conversation. Gibbs and his peers would work in five-minute bursts: 'On, off, on, off, on, off, on, off. That will give you a bit of a break, [allow you to] get a drink and re-evaluate.' In truth, it wasn't proper rest. Even while off-mic, they were watching for substitutions or additional important details, such as a key player warming up on the sidelines (for example, Sam Kerr about to make her highly anticipated entry to the tournament and the game), which they would silently draw their partner's attention to so they could incorporate it in their commentary.

The commentary also requires significant concentration because existing practices predominate, and it can be easy to slip back into habit of not describing the action because you're used to commentating for TV. As Gibbs says, 'When you're on TV, you don't describe where the ball is ... That was the thing I put at the top of all my notes—*Where's the ball?*—in big red letters.'

* * *

Academic Susan Harris Rimmer wrote the human-rights report submitted as part of the Women's World Cup bid.[14] In it, she stepped out the intersectional issues the tournament would entail, and the risks and rewards of hosting such a tournament. Major sporting events are often exceptions to any such human-rights rules, which means they can ride roughshod over human rights and decency.

The sense that something had profoundly shifted in this space came for Harris Rimmer when she visited the toilets at a match in Brisbane. There on the wall was a tournament-branded sign, complete with QR code, encouraging people to make contact should they have a human-rights issue. 'Well, I just cried,' she explains, adding that she took lots of photos of the sign. It was the human-rights report playing out in real life in the most needs-centric, accessible and heartening way.

Especially significant was that the organisers had achieved this in the relatively short timeframe they had for executing the tournament—three years from the mid-2020, mid-COVID announcement, compared with closer to an unencumbered decade for the men's equivalent. It would have been understandable, in the scramble to deliver, had the signs not been thought of, or been considered but omitted. Notably, human rights were also mentioned and therefore signalled as a priority in the tournament's opening ceremony. Picking up on that, Harris Rimmer says that, generally speaking, the tournament 'did what it said on the tin, which was provide a safe space to celebrate women's rights and women's excellence'.

* * *

Human connection was at the epicentre of the tournament. Many people who've been involved in women's football chronicle the number of friends and family—people who already had some connection to them—who sought them out for personalised and perhaps expert but accessible, non-judgemental insight into what they were witnessing, often through text messages and social-media direct messages. Isobel Cootes says, 'Rather than turning to Google, they apparently turned to me, which was fine. I was happy to fill in the blanks.'

Such curiosity and information-sharing introduced new dimensions to friendships. Friends who had previously not shown any interest in the game excitedly attended matches with Croissant Ciara O'Sullivan because she arranged tickets for them. They also collated a list of thirty questions for her as they sought to improve their football knowledge. 'We spent four hours discussing those questions,' O'Sullivan marvels. They'd gone from having no prior interest to giving themselves a comprehensive crash course in all things women's football. O'Sullivan offered to change the subject to something more in their wheelhouse, but the friends were adamant that no, they were genuinely interested. And thoughtful: they'd compiled the questions over a two-week period and put them to her over dinner at a later date because they didn't want to distract her while she was immersed in the tournament 'tour'.

The broader interest from such new fans provided more opportunities for journalists such as Cootes to pursue stories that, while fascinating, might not have previously been given prominence. 'People were just so hungry for content. It allowed us to do more human-interest stories or to write about "Strawberry Kisses" and things like that,' Cootes explains. (Such features included small but fascinating details. For example, that many of the players' preferred carbohydrate-loading dinner on the eve of a game is 'spag bol': spaghetti bolognaise.[15])

Cootes attributes that expanded, more nuanced demand to the newer audience—one that is perhaps more human-centric than football-centric. Said audience and the novelty of the game as a whole sent them and, subsequently, journalists down rabbit holes to sate their curiosity. 'If you'd told me, even at the France send-off game, that everyone would be obsessed with Mary Fowler's gloves and why she was wearing them … I was like, "It's cold. She's just wearing them,"' Cootes says. But the gloves turned out to be a topic of enormous interest and the topic took on a life of its own: 'That was one of our most well-read articles.'[16]

⋆ ⋆ ⋆

Journalist Samantha Lewis had had a plan heading into the tournament. It was composed of two pillars. Lewis explains:

> One was history—using the opportunity of the spotlight of the World Cup to teach people about the incredibly long, textured, interesting, vibrant history of women's football in Australia. Drawing upon all those old stories harking back to pioneers and generations gone by, and focusing on these moments that not a lot of people knew about. My second pillar was during the tournament itself: trying to capture how this moment really felt to people, and why it was important.

She leveraged her creative-writing background to produce stories that were heartfelt and compelling, to 'try and capture that lightning in a bottle'. There was an underlying motivation:

> I think for Australian journalists, in particular, it wasn't just that it was this World Cup on home soil. For so many of us who'd seen how apathetic Australians had been towards football over the years, suddenly seeing the whole country get behind this thing in itself was fuel. We felt in the media like we almost had a responsibility to keep people engaged and reading and clicking and watching, because this was our moment to show what our sport could be. We had to push ourselves to breaking point in order to do as much as we could for the sport, because we'd wanted a moment like this for so long, to be able to capture the imagination of the entire country. So I think a lot of us put our own welfare and our own physical wellbeing or emotional

> wellbeing or mental wellbeing aside because we had this bigger mission, this bigger fight that we were fighting.

Lewis's welfare allusion is to how privileged, but simultaneously how taxing, the work opportunity is. She says:

> Travelling interstate [with such a short amount of time between matches] was really tough. Checking in and out of hotels constantly, running on terrible 7-Eleven sandwiches at two o'clock in the morning because nothing else was open—that was always really tough. But you just have to push yourself, because even though it runs for a whole month, it is basically a month of sprinting. You just have to keep sprinting, because you know there is an endpoint and if you stop now, you won't have enough time to make it back to that speed.

Pokuah Frimpong, too, touched on how the tournament was fantastic but also tremendously hard work: 'It's incredibly draining, because it's not nine to five—you're constantly working.' Switching from researching to writing, teeing up interviews, filming, editing, attending press conferences, recording podcast episodes, watching games, publishing pre-game content, backing up after a game to create and publish content relating what happened in it, and producing preview content for the next day are just some of the things that occupy your time. Also, you spend so much time hurrying up and waiting. It leaves no time for laundry or rest. For Frimpong, the tournament was the best kind of whirlwind experience, but one that left her utterly spent.

★ ★ ★

Tracey Holmes, who pioneered women's sports coverage on such esteemed, long-running programs as *ABC Grandstand*, pays attention to the photographers' pen area size at matches and the number of photographers camped out along the baseline. 'I always look for that across all sports, because it is so telling,' she explains. It's telling of the value that is placed on particular sports and particular genders. That's something that would have been noticeable to original Matildas photographer Joseph Mayers, who *was* the pen for many years—he took photos of the team to redress the lack of media coverage and important historical documentation.[17]

Size and scale was something that was front of mind for the organising committee. In the seven weeks preceding the tournament, they hired and onboarded 700 people. That enormous undertaking was across security, catering and various venue roles, and swelled the team from 100–150 people to more like 800–900. 'Then you've got thousands of volunteers as well. So even that process of just inducting everyone, getting them up to speed knowing what they're going to do across nine different venues. It was a behemoth,' Kim Anderson says.

Even more of a behemoth was the Stadium Australia fit-out logistics. While we fans were happy that the Matildas' opening match was upgraded to a 75,000-seat stadium, the move ramped up the logistical complexity. Bump-in normally takes weeks, but the stadium was only available days ahead of the Ireland game due to a scheduled Men's State of Origin match. Co-COO Jane Fernandez describes the logistics with which the team had to contend:

> That was a huge, huge decision and had a huge impact on my operational team. To be able, in basically a five-day window, to fully brand Stadium Australia at its size and scale, ensure the pitch was ready to go and perfect and there was no sign of rugby league, get everything bumped in and ready, build media tribunes, ensure the tech was ready to go ...

She credits the team for its phenomenal work to achieve it, and acknowledges the weather gods, too: 'It was wild what [the team] had to do. If the weather had turned, it wouldn't have gone in our favour. It would have been really, really touch and go.'

★ ★ ★

Anderson and her peers had a mission: to showcase the world's best women footballers, engage audiences with exceptional storytelling, and blaze a trail for female empowerment. She says, 'In short, I think it was very intentional, the choice to celebrate greatness on and off the pitch.' Central to that was the Women's World Cup brand, which the local organisers were seeking to leverage and build on:

> When we looked at the brand, we were like, 'This is the foundation of everything.' It was literally the first thing I did, on day one. [The bosses] were like, 'Right, can you launch the brand in two months?' I was like, 'OK, great, yep, I'd love to do that in a pandemic where I'm in lockdown with no team.' It was a crazy time, but it was the biggest, meatiest task I'd ever been given.

The brand Anderson launched—the one Fernandez and her team worked so hard to ensure was implemented in a tight turnaround before tournament kick-off—contained vibrant, vivid, contemporary First Nations artwork etched on backgrounds of orange and hot pink. Launched long in advance of the tournament, it provided a hint of the celebratory, energising and inclusive environment the event would entail. Kalkadoon artist Chern'ee Sutton's work was also selected for the match ball, an LED lightshow projected around the stadiums, message sticks and boomerangs given to players and dignitaries, and limited-edition coins.[18]

The upside to that frontloaded brand deliverable was that the bulk of Anderson's work had been done by the time the tournament rolled around. Her peers' workloads had been a slow build that peaked during the tournament itself:

> The nature of marketing [means that] 90 per cent of the work is before the tournament starts. So I think [I] and my team actually had an amazing experience during the tournament because we could relax and go to lots of games and enjoy ourselves a bit more. I think I got to sixteen matches across the two countries, so I was pretty privileged. I'd often be sitting next to Jane [Fernandez] and her phone would be blowing up with transport delays or this and that and whatnot. So, yeah, I certainly didn't have it as tough as others during the tournament.

It wasn't without its challenges, though: 'My boss would call me "the believer". I always knew we were going to be amazing and it was going to be a huge cultural moment. I definitely had that sense of belief from the beginning, and I think the signs were all good,' Anderson explains. Case in point: the strong Australian ticket sales. 'Typically, you would see 50 per cent of sales for a major event happen from day one of the tournament when people were like, "Oh, it's on."' But fans had already tipped in to buy upwards of 1.4 million tickets by that point[19]—meeting the stretch target, and then the stretch target's stretch target. The final ticket-sales figure would end up close to 1.8 million.[20] (Historian Marion Stell astutely observes, too, that the children who were at the tournament were there of their own volition—they weren't being given complimentary tickets and bussed in to fill the stands, as has seemed to happen in previous tournaments.)

There was incongruity between Australian and New Zealand ticket sales, which is where Anderson's belief was perhaps most evident. 'All the data, all the consumer insights, everyone I was talking to was saying, "Kiwis buy late—they will not jump on the bandwagon until the eleventh hour." We did see that in the last couple of weeks before the tournament started. They bought in droves,' Anderson explains. She acknowledges that the nervousness around the New Zealand ticket sales wasn't unfounded: 'The Football Ferns hadn't played there in years, they didn't have the profile of the Matildas. So it was all perfectly logical, you could tell a story around it. But that didn't mean that people weren't nervous about it.'

Also, the undertaking in condensed, COVID-exacerbated conditions was enormous. Anderson explains:

> The whole two years of planning felt like sprinting a marathon every day. So even when you were confident, like I was, there were still four million things to do every single day. We were tired, we were stressed, and it was tough at times. But we really believed in what this amazing event was going to do. We knew it would be incredible, and that as soon as the first ball was

kicked, the magic would take over. It was going to be an incredible sporting event.

Still, some aspects took even her by surprise:

> I mean, New Zealand scoring an end-to-end goal in their first match and beating Norway like that—I did not script that. Sam [Kerr] being out and Steph [Catley] having to step up, and all the things that happened with the penalty shootout … I think that's where I probably had great confidence in what we were doing from a marketing perspective to fill the stands to create the great atmosphere, even in those neutral matches.

Scintillating neutral matches were a recurring theme. David Davutovic and others nominate the Nigeria v Canada game held at lunchtime on a weekday in Melbourne that was packed and riotously well supported; Mel Buttle similarly experienced a surprising swell of emotion when her train was full to the brim with families on the way to a match for a non–State of Origin game and for a sport 'that no one had heard of when I was ten'.

'We all knew the Matildas were going to sell out. That was never a problem. That was always guaranteed. It was more around how all the other games would go,' Fernandez says, picking up on a similar theme. She points to a weekday lunchtime game between Korea and Colombia in Sydney. 'We were watching that one really closely. And my goodness, it was almost a full house. It was pretty chockers as the Colombian fans came out in force—it was almost like it was a public holiday.'

Even so, the tournament exceeded Anderson's most ambitious beliefs. 'Did I think we would get to two million ticket sales? No. In my heart of hearts, I thought, personally, that we might get to 1.75, 1.8. But two million was … I think there is an element there of the Matildas Effect that is undoubtedly huge and can't be underestimated.'

Yes and no. The Matildas swept the country into a frenzy, but Anderson and her team also employed the strategy and created the conditions that facilitated it. As she says, 'Our marketing plan was all about attracting what I called 'the convinceables'—people who were not your regular Matildas fans.' So going beyond the diehard fans and reaching non-traditional and new fans, or fans who otherwise had not yet had an opportunity to engage with women's football. That targeted crossover with other cultures and popular culture would bring new audiences to the game, grow the game itself, and also help fill the stadiums.

'It was wonderful. I loved being in the stadiums,' Fernandez says. She cites a couple of examples: the positive energy surging through the venues from start to finish, and the patriotism with which people belted out their national anthems. Witnessing that firsthand, she knew they were onto a good thing: 'What we wanted to do was bring people together to unite through football, and we totally achieved that. We always said we wanted to entertain and inspire, and I feel like we did that. It's great to be able to sit back and reflect and know that you achieved what you set out to achieve.'

⋆ ⋆ ⋆

Security concerns that fans' fever-pitch excitement might engulf the team reportedly almost prevented the Matildas' quarter-final matchday walk, but the players apparently insisted the traditional team walk was a must—superstition and needing to work off some nervous energy overrode the abundance of caution. It was a new scenario among many new scenarios for a team that had previously moved through the world relatively anonymously due to wider disinterest. No doubt the reversal was slightly baffling and also raised unanticipated security conundrums. How, for example, does one contend with saying no to small girls wearing Raso ribbons and tugging on the heartstrings with puppy-dog eyes—girls who are likely too tiny to fit on theme-park rides but perhaps small enough and deft enough to duck and weave through security guards' grasps?

One of the people whose job it was to consider such scenarios was Australian Federal Police (AFP) officer and football fan Sarah McKenzie. She was one of the all-female security detail assigned to the sixteen Australia-based teams (plus the four that travelled over from New Zealand for the tournament) under FIFA requirements.

Describing it as both a once-in-a-lifetime and a once-in-a-career opportunity, McKenzie was selected after submitting an expression of interest to the AFP. She was assigned to the Canada team.

During her introduction to that forty-strong Canadian contingent, she told them that she had travelled in a personal capacity to the Canada-hosted 2015 tournament (and the 2019 France one), and that she had a Canadian jersey she had bought in Montreal that she planned to wear in support of the team. McKenzie qualified the jersey statement with the detail that, with the greatest respect, that jersey *didn't* (unlike most) have the great Christine Sinclair's number on it. Instead, it had that of former Canadian player and Canadian domestic league founder Diana Matheson, primarily because at 153 centimetres tall, she is a 'more compact' player akin to McKenzie's own size than Sinclair, who is 175 centimetres.

True to her word, McKenzie wore said jersey (concealed under her uniform). After the team made it through its opening match without a loss, she was informed she needed to not wash the jersey as it qualified as a good-luck charm. The charm ran out at the Australia group-stage game that ended Canada's tournament run, but McKenzie showed enormous emotional intelligence by arranging for a friend to bring their golden retriever to the hotel afterwards. She couldn't change the outcome—which was particularly gutting as it ended Sinclair's peerless career—but she could give the team an invaluable hour of canine therapy before the players dispersed.

★ ★ ★

Hayley Raso is comedian Mel Buttle's favourite player. Buttle joked on her social media that as Raso hadn't responded to her messages, Buttle had elected to marry her partner instead. In a brilliant response, Raso engaged and commented on the post with a hi and a congratulations.[21]

Such witty repartee is counterbalanced by another of Buttle's posts, which spoke to the bittersweet experience of so many women that the quantum leap forward simultaneously highlighted: that of thwarted opportunity. In the post, which included a black-and-white photo of Buttle trying on a Matildas jersey in a retail change room, she spoke of being simultaneously stoked for the Matildas and angry-sad for her younger self, for whom a playing career or even serious participation hadn't been an option.[22]

'There were a lot of women around my age who were like, "Yeah, me too. It just didn't exist."' Buttle explains: they were in a small town, or the sport wasn't offered where they lived, or there was a dearth of information about how to get involved. Quite simply, girls and women playing wasn't promoted or even visible, and it certainly wasn't a viable career. Buttle:

> I don't think people understand that back in the 90s or late 80s you had to, unless there was a notice on the [billboard] of the shopping centre or you looked up a club in the Yellow Pages and rang them up, it was actually quite difficult to get information. So a lot of the responses [to my post] were the same feeling of what could have been.

Bridie O'Donnell experienced similar feelings. In 2022, SBS was one of only two networks to stay in France to cover the Tour de France Femmes, the inaugural women's version of the famed multi-stage cycling event. With fewer stages and no live broadcast, the Tour de France Femmes was still the diminutive of the men's competition. O'Donnell recalls:

> But it was getting a launch and a platform and a broadcast globally that women's cycling had never before experienced. I'm going to cry thinking about it again. Standing on the Champs-Élysées in the very early morning of Sunday, the final day of the men's race, which is more of a procession or a ceremonial stage, I knew the team presentation for the women was going to be underneath the Eiffel Tower, and then they were going to race on the Champs-Élysées. That just felt so monumental.
>
> I felt a terrible pang of jealousy. And I felt immense pride. And I felt rage that it had taken more than a hundred years. So I can only imagine women football fans, and parents of kids that play round ball in this country, must have felt that times

> a hundred last year at the opening game, not only with the Matildas but to be in full stadiums, to be walking to events with scarves on and seeing the whole population wearing Matildas jerseys. [It] would have been for some, on a surface level, an amazing moment of joy and patriotism and pride in our national women's team. But I think at a deeper level, it would have been a very emotional and perhaps even confronting time for many women who have been involved in the sport.

★ ★ ★

Experienced administrator Nicki Bowman says:

> I cried a lot. I cried when I saw it take over Sydney. I cried when I looked out my window and there was a mural emerging of Caitlin Foord taking up the whole side of a building. I cried when I got to the stadium … I think it's because I'm the kind of person who has a really clear picture in their head of what things can be. What I didn't know was how long that road would be.

It was unquestionably long, and its turns remarkable, as Bowman says:

> To go from barely being able to fill half a stand in Wollongong [for some pre-2012 Olympic friendlies with the Football Ferns]—I remember they had no money, no budget, scrambling around to put together even a camp in Wollongong [and one of the matches was played behind closed doors because they couldn't afford security and ground personnel] … To go from that to this in ten years, it's like bamboo—you know, the legend of bamboo that you've planted in the water and you look after it and nothing happens for forever, and then all of a sudden you walk outside one day and it's ten feet tall? That's how it felt for me.

(At the time we spoke, Bowman was driving hours to cheer on the Wellington Phoenix A-League Women's team at an away game. Her Wollongong mention was particularly poignant given the

Phoenix had been based near her home in Wollongong in its inaugural year due to COVID travel restrictions, and she was appointed its local liaison and player welfare officer. In a way, it was the team that realised her ambition, years before, in attempting to get up a Wollongong-based expansion team.)

Bowman acknowledges that the meteoric trajectory must be especially bittersweet for the players who *just* missed out on it—the Walshes, the Garriocks, the Barbieris who were right there in 2011 and 2012, but whose international careers ended just before the women's game really kicked off. They were the pioneers who started to force people to consider such elements as pay equality, appropriate levels of support staff, and maternity leave. 'But when you're in that position, you never get the best of it, right?' Bowman says. 'You fight the hard fights and you lose most of them, but you've broken the ground that somebody else can finally build the building on.'

Tom Sermanni addresses this from a complementary angle. 'They've been quite successful for twenty years,' he says, listing the Matildas' consistent quarter-final appearances since 2007, and in 2010 winning the Asian Cup. 'So I think there's a difference between recognition and achievement.' With this tournament, they experienced the double. Sermanni says he feels pride not for himself but for the players, who've achieved so much on and beyond the pitch. 'I feel delighted for them, and for what a lot of players have achieved—players who didn't necessarily get much out of the game.' He's referencing the ones whose careers were shortened through injury or lack of opportunities but who have pivoted and improved things for everyone coming behind them.

Bowman notes that a lot of naysayers have argued that of course Australians showed up—it was a World Cup, and we have a history of watching major tournaments. During the Olympics, for example, we'll show up to watch relatively obscure sports such as European handball, curling and Greco-Roman wrestling. But for the stadiums to continue selling out post-tournament is another thing. 'Not even in my wildest dreams did I think we would be saying they'll be selling out [Stadium Australia] for a friendly, and in the same breath saying the Socceroos won't fill a Western Sydney stadium for an actual World Cup qualifier against Lebanon,' she says, noting both that it's not a zero-sum game and, interestingly, that the latter was despite Western Sydney having a significant Lebanese population. She says what a lot of us are starting to dare think: 'It feels unstoppable.'

The only (but very unlikely) thing Bowman thinks might see this fall away is if the team underperforms for a protracted period of time and Football Australia hasn't put the other necessary connections in place. Sarah Styles makes a similarly pragmatic observation. 'At one point, maybe they won't sell out. And you know what, that's still OK and still phenomenal,' she says, hopeful that tall poppy syndrome won't kick in. Bowman, too, points to the normalising of the new standards: the hedonic adaptation 'where you think everything will be great when you get to the next level, and you get to the next level and you normalise it really quickly. You also tend to forget how hard it was to get there.' Now, Bowman notes, we're normalising selling out 80,000-seat stadiums.

Bowman, like many, points out that the upside to Kerr's injuries is that it's allowed other team members to shine, that the brand and ultimately the ticket sales are enhanced by not relying on one or two superstars. Eleni Psaltis calls it similarly: 'Everyone stepped up and played differently without her [during the tournament]. She's definitely the star. But I think the team became the star.' Another interviewee phrases it as feeling like a bomb went off before the first game that then freed us up to imagine other possibilities.

Bowman, too, has been analysing the elements that combined to build to the breakout 2023. She says:

> First of all, for many years the Matildas have worked incredibly hard to build a very direct connection with their fanbase. If you attended a game, you were almost guaranteed to get an autograph or a photo with a player. The explosion of the game internationally has created new career paths, markets and fanbases, and the players and their teams are more media and brand savvy and are leveraging those elements. The Matildas are appearing outside of the team, and they're also appearing inside

> the team more than once or twice a year as there are more games. That is bringing in money as well as exposure, because women's football is being seen as a marketable product.

She recalls that as recently as even a few years ago, there wouldn't be a screen at Matildas games, which meant no pre-match packages or replays. (That transports me back to looking after the team's social media. I half-seriously said to the players that it would really help me if they could make it obvious who had scored and provided the assist, because if I happened to be looking down at my keyboard or away at the precise moment, there was no replay against which to check information before I tweeted it.) They'd be in a really inferior stadium, Bowman continues. If the match was on television, which it often wasn't, the coverage would be poor. There would also be next to no Matildas-specific merchandise to purchase—if there was any, it would be Socceroos merchandise. She says:

> The best components of all of those things weren't in the women's game. I say that with great respect to those who were in the women's game back in the day. You went there because you had a real passion. Often, you went there because you were a woman. But you weren't necessarily getting the mentoring and the training and the expertise and the exposure to the best of the best that the men were afforded.

(A related issue was that the women's game was seen as an apprenticeship for coaches, in particular, before they 'upgraded' to the men's game.) Bowman continues:

> So it becomes this virtuous cycle. Because every point that makes the game better, the players better, the experience better, every touchpoint of that is now starting to inhabit that rarefied air at the top, where they're learning from the best and becoming the best.

Also, people are no longer looking to move on from the women's game, and may even be looking to move *to* it. 'Because increasingly the money's in the women, the prestige is in the women,' Bowman agrees.

It's night and day compared to the 2011 tournament, when Bowman and Heather Reid, who were at the time in the Football Federation Australia women's advisory group, were provided an all-expenses-paid trip to represent the federation at the Women's World Cup symposium due to lack of interest from other administrators. Now, Bowman says, she wouldn't be invited into the VIP area and she struggles, as do many early-adopter fans, to even secure match tickets.

FIFA invites two delegates from each member federation to a symposium that runs adjacent to the tournament. 'It's kind of like the FIFA [Noah's] ark,' Bowman explains. The seating arrangement in 2011 was alphabetical by country, so she and Reid were up the front in prime position with their translation headsets on. Next to them were Aruba and Austria. Bowman was much amused, 'because I thought, you know, good old powerhouse the USA will be shoved up the back next to Uzbekistan.'

★ ★ ★

Sue Read recounts a conversation she had with one of her clients who happened to be at the Matildas' first game. When the team scored its first goal, the players ran over to celebrate in front of and pay tribute to a particular bay in the crowd. 'I hope that was to the alumni,' the client told Read. 'And I'm like, "Sure, let's go with that."' The idea of intergenerational acknowledgement was a lovely sentiment, but it's a connection that's yet to be fully cemented. 'They possibly don't even really know who we are at this stage,' Read says of the current Matildas. 'But I didn't say that, because I didn't want to ruin my client's dream.' Her point is valid: the alumni collective is a relatively recent creation and there's still a small disconnect. 'Once they start to retire, when they start to join the alumni, I think there'll be an amazing cross-pollination. But at the moment, it's probably the current team and the alumni separate. I'm looking forward to that kind of coming together a bit more.'

Janine McPhee mentions that there have been some concerted efforts to bridge that gap. Alicia Ferguson, for example, set up

Zoom calls a few years ago between past and present Matildas for some intergenerational knowledge-sharing. Ellie Carpenter joined one of the calls; so, too, did Lydia Williams, the former with a long Matildas representative future ahead of her, the latter who recently announced her post-Olympics retirement after almost two decades in the team, 103 caps, and five Women's World Cups. Williams was the Matildas' longest-serving player who, along with the team's most-capped player, Clare Polkinghorne, lived and shaped the pay-and-conditions parity advocacy that yielded the Matildas' current elevated threshold.[23] (For comparison, just months before they had to strike in 2015, the players received $750 each for making the 2015 Women's World Cup quarter-finals. The 2023 team entered the tournament knowing they would receive a minimum of $45,000 each for making the tournament; $135,000 was the figure attached to making it to the semi-final; $247,000 the final figure for fourth place.[24])

Read wore a long-sleeved green shirt to our interview. It was a distinctly Matildas colour and goalkeeper jersey style. 'I often wear this colour and when I do corporate presentations I usually joke that as a past Matilda, we, by law, have to wear green for the rest of our lives,' she says. It's a moment of levity, but she soon makes a quite serious and valid point about the invaluable aspects the alumni offer, should Football Australia adequately recognise and leverage it: 'Support the group well and you've got more than 240 priceless advocates uniquely placed to promote the women's game, especially in our local communities and media.'

Certainly, the alumni are a relatively untapped resource. Although they are now being given game tickets, they're still being treated as adoring fans allowed to cheer on the team from the outside, not bastions of the game brought into the fold. Imagine the wisdom they could impart and the rousing inspiration and welcome they could provide to current and future generations within and beyond the team if they were given the chance.

Apart from noting that the alumni definition only includes players, and that it should be extended to key coaches and administrators without whose contributions the national team would not have existed or thrived, now would also be an appropriate time to consider paying at least some alumni a stipend for the significant media and other unpaid ambassadorial work they're doing from which the current generation and Football Australia are benefiting greatly. One option that would also generate Football Australia some positive PR could be to direct a percentage of ticket sales from certain matches towards a fund alumni could draw on. There is precedent for this: such an approach has already been taken for the ParaMatildas, the Australian national team for women and girls with cerebral palsy, acquired brain injury and/or symptoms of stroke. Or the fund could, for example, be similar to the 'post-career goal' fund the USWNT negotiated as part of its 2022 collective bargaining agreement.[25]

★ ★ ★

Fatima Flores marvels at the sudden and varied media interest in the women's game and in Matildas Active Support as the team's officially recognised supporter group. 'Initially, that was really awesome, because we're trying to spread the word and get more people to join in and create more noise for the game,' she explains. (So committed to supporting the cause is Flores that she at one stage wore a QR code that linked to the Active Support group's lyrics. These are team-themed lyrics set to famous songs such as 'Waltzing Matilda'.[26]) Fellow member and co-organiser Majella Card agrees: 'The media interest was next level. It was something we'd never experienced before and it was coming fast and furious. Matildas fever hit for sure.'

The edge was taken off slightly over the course of the tournament, but Flores was strategic:

> They wanted to make us fit whatever their story was going to be by getting us to chant on demand for the TV. We were kind of sick of doing that—we wanted to save it for the games and for the players, not just do it for the TV. But we took that opportunity as well to try and spread the word about supporting the players at the end of the tournament, supporting women's

> football in general [from the grassroots to the elites], and to get out and watch our local players. I was a bit cheeky, and at times I did bring up with media about how you've got to be there to support the game domestically as well, as in: 'Where have you been all this time? … But now that you're here, keep it going. Don't let this just be a one-off, because it's one of the biggest sporting events in the world.'

(Adding to Flores's point, we also need to broaden support and coverage to other teams such as the ParaMatildas and create the ParaMatilda Effect. Australia also has deaf, blind and homeless World Cup football teams we should be getting around.[27])

* * *

The team behind the pre-eminent *Vogue Australia* masthead was all in on the Women's World Cup. In some ways that wasn't surprising—executive editor Jess Montague has a background in sport, having covered multiple Olympics. She even experienced her first taste of a top-tier tournament courtesy of being a basket carrier[28] for, would you believe, Cathy Freeman's 400-metre final. (Nor is Montague the only *Vogue* team member who repped the 2000 Olympics: her predecessor as deputy editor was in the torch relay, and one of her team members was a dancer in the opening ceremony.) 'I think that is still the most amazing moment of my life, walking out for that race,' Montague says. 'I just remember I was shaking, my teeth almost chattering from the sound—it was a physical response to the noise.'

The intersectional nature of the Matildas' appeal means they span football, culture and fashion, which made *Vogue* an appropriate fit and champion. (That's an 'infiltration' and theme that's infusing *Vogue* more widely, with global editor-in-chief Anna Wintour hosting a sport-themed 'Vogue World' entertainment extravaganza in Paris to coincide with the 2024 Olympics.[29]) Working with the publication also represented a symbiotic opportunity to achieve the Matildas' wider tournament goals. 'The strategy that I had was to take the players out of the sport pages,' Ann Odong explains. The team already had good traction with sports media. 'I felt like if we were going to take this team to another level, to be able to unite the nation, then the nation needed to know who they were.' Odong surmised that that required going to where the audience was. *Where are they?* she asked herself. *Where are we not penetrating? Where are we not connecting? Are we not connecting in pop culture and Aussie culture?* 'It's going: *Where is Australia? Let's go to them without expecting them to come to us.*'

There was precedent in *Vogue Australia* for covering women in sport: the publication shot the Australian Women's Rugby Sevens team after they won in Rio in 2016, and has featured women sports administrators and other athletes, including swimmer Cate Campbell OAM, wheelchair racer Madison de Rozario OAM, and boxer and AFLW star Tayla Harris. Like Odong, Montague could envisage a way to strengthen the reach and impact by bringing together seemingly disparate worlds, and she initiated months-long planning for *Vogue Australia*'s tournament content.

The fact that many of the top Matildas were sponsored by Nike represented a targeted cross-promotional opportunity. The *Vogue* team asked themselves: *Who's on our dream list? What would we want to do?* That led to a London-based shoot with Sam Kerr, Steph Catley, Kyah Simon and Hayley Raso a few months before the Women's World Cup. Timing for the shoot was tight, with the players, then in the middle of their WSL season, converging on the space for a matter of hours from their disparate UK locations in between training and other commitments.

The *Vogue* team had to implement the shoot with precision. Usually with shoots of this scale they have fittings the day before and the talent is available for up to eight hours. It was an exclusive with Kerr, in particular, who was in unrivalled demand. But even the best-laid plans come with plot twists. 'Where she'd be coming from training was not actually close to where we booked the location. We had her for ninety minutes. There was traffic,' Montague explains. 'I found out later, the night before Nike even contemplated: "Do we get a chopper? Do we helicopter her in?"'

It wouldn't be the only time helicopters would feature in Kerr's immediate future, but no one was to know that then. In the end, no chopper was required, but that it was even considered speaks to Kerr's profile.

Vogue published its Kerr/Raso/Catley/Simon stories and photoshoots across its print, web and social media channels.[30] (Montague says the content proved so popular that Channel 7 News picked it up.) Then, during the tournament itself, the *Vogue* team created supplementary and extending content, such as videos and articles about how to style your jersey and street style from the games.[31] Montague says, 'People couldn't get enough.' The teal away jersey, in particular, was a sensation.[32] (In the original shoot with Catley, *Vogue* had paired the teal jersey with a red sequined skirt to great effect.)

Montague credits her sports-mad team, which is spearheaded by young women and young men creating the content, for driving much of this engagement. Former *Vogue* head of digital Mahalia Chang, for example (full disclosure), commissioned me mid-tournament to write a listicle about seven of the most game-changing Women's World Cup moments in the Matildas' history for their website.[33]

One *Vogue* digital team member representative of the broad and emerging Matildas fanbase is Will Lennox, who is in his mid-twenties and a massive Arsenal fan, and therefore completely across the football stats of 'Ausenal' players such as Catley. Like so many of us, Montague can't wait to see how that gender-specific cultural shift continues to play out—and *Vogue*'s ongoing connection to, and in-depth innovative coverage of, the team and the sport.

★ ★ ★

Western Australia–based Kris Marano specialises in how sport and storytelling have the power to create social change. Prior to the tournament, she worked with the State Library of Western Australia and a social enterprise to create a ten-episode podcast featuring WA women's football trailblazers.[34] Themes that emerged from the episodes were a microcosm of those we saw emerge throughout the tournament: sacrifice, self-belief (including through surrounding yourself with people who support you and having positive self-talk on and off the pitch), and storytelling that humanises the players and highlights them as role models.

Such storytelling transcends what Marano terms the 'physical playing element' that centres on match results. The feedback she's received is that the very human stories she captured for the podcast are resonating. (Marano credits Odong with influencing the high-quality work around the Matildas, including the ABC-TV *Australian Story* episode featuring Katrina Gorry that followed the tournament,[35] which led to all the feels. It's almost incomprehensible now, but Odong says Gorry wasn't the player on whom the episode was originally planned to be based. However, Odong says Gorry's was a story that would really resonate: it was both unique and universal in that Gorry walked the motherhood path alone but also, like so many, had to balance career and family life. As Hannah Ferguson says, 'Oh my god, I had a hundred people send me that reel ... Because watching that episode of *Australian Story*—my whole house watched it together. We don't care about free-to-air TV [but] we planned our day around that. We all sat down and cried about four times.' One of the most outstanding elements of the episode for Ferguson was that 'it was one of the first times we've seen a woman have a baby and her workplace help her to come back stronger. She was *better* at her job after having a baby. And that has *never* been the messaging.')

Marano nominates Instagram as the most powerful platform for conveying such connective stories throughout the tournament, but then nominates another less obvious one: LinkedIn. There, many of what she calls C-suite women, meaning administrators and academic researchers of the game, shared their post-tournament highlights. It was compelling: professional women who are carving out careers in space previously restricted to them sharing striking, unparalleled career insights. There will hopefully be even more women able to make such career-highlight posts in the future.

Ever aware of using her opportunity to help address the under-representation of women and non-binary people in media, Odong advocated for Football Australia to create a program for women and non-binary writers and photographers that ran throughout the tournament.[36] (She also partnered with the [Female] Athlete Project to feature women who work behind the scenes in the women's football space in a podcast series. The podcast guests included team manager Gina Rees and assistant sports scientist Georgia Brown.[37])

Great minds think alike: Nike and social-media-based news service the *Daily Aus* collaborated to create a similar program to redress underrepresentation in the space.[38] Just 10 per cent of sports journalists identify as women, and they comprise just 27 per cent of by-lines despite being 62 per cent more likely to provide women's sports media coverage.[39] That too-little is reminiscent of a report Shona Bass, Janine Mikosza and Heather Reid produced in the 1990s for Womensport Australia called *Inching Forward*.[40] The title had a dual meaning: newspaper column inches, or lack thereof, in relation to media coverage; and incremental progress. The Football Australia program was so successful that two of the photographers who participated in it now have contracts with worldwide photography agency Getty, says Ann Odong.

The progress, however incremental, is visible to sports journalist and gender-equality advocate Kieran Pender, something he both spoke about in our interview and has written about separately.[41] He requested data on the gender split for accredited media while at the 2018 Men's World Cup in Russia and the 2019 Women's World Cup in France. While FIFA didn't have the data to hand for those, Pender personally noticed a difference at the first press conference he attended in 2023: there were more female than male journalists in the huddle. While he recognises that the sample size was small and we have a long way to go to reach true parity, that was a brief moment signalling that we are at least making some advancement. For him, that moment, absent fanfare and which otherwise likely passed unnoticed, was more significant than the spectacle of sold-out stadiums (although those were impressive, too).

Interwoven with that is Pender's wider consideration of what form good allyship takes—that is, how you raise the representation of women and non-binary folk in the usually cisgendered middle-class-white-male-dominated media space. Whether only women should be writing about women is one of the questions implicit in that. Neither he nor anyone has the answer to this conundrum (although, being completely transparent, I probably land on the side of men being in the women's sports space provided their inclusion is appropriately considered and complementary), but Pender makes a thoughtful point about it. A fellow journalist reminded him of a quote that periodically pops up on the internet: male allies don't need to be awarded space in feminism—they need to make feminist the societal space they occupy.[42] That broader thinking shift perhaps aligns with Sarah Walsh's belief that the Matildas and the tournament are reshaping the sporting ecosystem. It also aligns with former USWNT player Tobin Heath's observation that women's sport isn't about women—its progressive, inclusive multitudes represent a more abundant, welcoming rethink of the future of sport as a whole.[43]

★★★

Rebecca Yolland works at major events around the world. She backed up working on the 2019 Women's World Cup in France with working at the 2023 one on home soil before heading back to France for the 2024 Olympics. Being the competition manager for the 2023 Women's World Cup in her hometown of Melbourne was something distinct. 'Operationally, it was one of the smoothest tournaments I think I've ever worked,' Yolland says, crediting for this her team and the volunteers who worked with them as well as FIFA and the local organising committee. She notes that it wasn't just those attending the tournament who had a good experience; the people working behind the scenes did as well.

On a personal note, working in a stadium in her hometown when she has spent the majority of her career working overseas meant it was the first time Yolland had family and friends in the crowd:

> Basically, I've never had that. Not that I think it made any real difference. I don't know that they noticed where I was. But it was nice to be able to share that, and [it was] great to hear afterwards how much they enjoyed it, as quite a few had never been to a football match before.

Yolland is one of many behind-the-scenes people whose contributions ensure a tournament experience is seamless. Julie Dolan witnessed firsthand that small army of people and the preparation and hard work that go into every aspect of a tournament, when she agreed to be among those who performed the 2023 tournament-group draw. Thinking the draw a unique opportunity and perhaps even a bit of a junket—pulling a country's name out of a bowl would presumably be relatively straightforward—little did she know how comprehensively she would be put to work.

The draw preparation involved three full days of training. 'It was just astonishing, because we all met each other and thought, *Right, we'll get this nailed today in the first hour or so*,' Dolan says. Instead, she, alongside Australian swimmer Cate Campbell and football greats such as former England player Ian Wright, had to attend not just a full first day of training but then a second and a third. '*Nothing* was left out of that training,' Dolan explains.

Across those three days in October 2022, Dolan and her peers were taught everything from which camera to look at and which light would come on to provide their cue to how they couldn't leave their hands in the ball container for too long or be seen to be rummaging about in there too much. Draws are highly scrutinised and potentially contentious, and it takes little for actions to be misinterpreted and invoke accusations of cheating. The draw balls themselves, Dolan learned, are guarded 24/7 to ensure there is no interference. Nothing, she says, is left to chance. 'Every single thing was pointed out, and we had to practise and practise and practise. This went on for three days—and they were eight-hour days,' she says.

Consequently, Dolan and co. were incredibly well-rehearsed by the time the draw came around. People tuned in to the live stream from around the world. ('It was like, *We've got this.* Because we'd practised so much that we knew everything. I guess that was the benefit of all those hours of training. It was just second nature to go out there and do everything the right way.') Each country draw took but a moment, but it was a consistent, well-executed event where we witnessed Dolan and the others reach into the container, select and retrieve a ball in an appropriate manner and timeframe, unscrew the ball, unfurl the paper inside containing the country name, hold said piece of paper in front of them with the name displayed the correct way up, and look down the barrel of the requisite camera. They did that over and over again until all thirty-two teams were assigned their group.

While the experience might not have been a junket, it did ultimately prove unique and also contained some unexpected highlights. Dolan was in her dressing room—a first for her, given change rooms had been pretty much absent for the entirety of her football career. 'I saw the mascot at the watercooler,' she explains. Tazuni, the penguin with the blue coiffure, had not yet been publicly announced, so Dolan's water-cooler encounter was something of a preview. She had thought that was the highlight and was messaging friends to tell them to keep an eye out for the mascot to be revealed, then in walked Aotearoa New Zealand prime minister Jacinda Ardern. Dolan, who isn't often starstruck, was so astonished to be in the impressive Ardern's presence that she couldn't get out of her chair.

* * *

Symposiums ran concurrent to the tournament—a value-add designed to maximise people's keenness to engage and to help enact wider social change. One symposium featured a range of panels and panellists discussing gender equality, including appearances by former Afghanistan national football team captain Khalida Popal and basketballer and First Nations person Patty Mills.[44] Jane Fernandez oversaw the 'Beyond Greatness' speaker series.[45] 'I really wanted to do it because we wanted to connect sport, art, music and culture, and also showcase female leaders from different industries,' she says. Those leaders included actor/comedian Celeste Barber; former Australia Post CEO Christine Holgate; Hello Sunshine's Sarah Harden, whose work concentrates on using storytelling to change the narrative for women; and politician and diplomat Natasha Stott Despoja AO. 'I was really determined to make this happen, for my sins,' Fernandez laughs. 'I don't know why I needed to run another thing on top of [the tournament].'

Another of the symposiums, entitled 'The Winning Playbook', included presentations about programs such as Dads and Daughters, which is designed to provide a safe sporting space for fathers and daughters to connect and break down gender-delineated sporting stereotypes.[46] It also featured the Sports Bra Project, which supplies vital sports undergarments to teams that might not otherwise be able to afford them or have them supplied as part of their uniform, in order to overcome a ridiculous barrier to participation.[47] (Case in point: the project donated to the Zambian team that participated in the Women's World Cup and that was the Matildas' 2024 Olympics group-stage opponent.) 'The things you take for granted,' Sue Monteath says. The session yielded this pearl of wisdom: it turns out a sports bra's lifespan is only about twenty-five laundry cycles.

* * *

Vicky Hewitt, Jodie Hammond, Joanne Kopp, Narelle Sibson and Nicola Zammit have been friends and football teammates for, they estimate, in the vicinity of thirty years. Having met through football (and, more specifically, futsal) when they were teenagers, they've played alongside each other in various club, representative and masters teams. Repartee and familiarity infuse their friendship, where discussion of old injuries sit easily alongside discussion of what stage their kitchen renovations are at. Some of them now have kids of their own whom they have introduced to the football community and fandom.

For Hewitt, one of the tournament's key selling points was its affordability. She bought seven stadium passes for her family and if there were any games they couldn't attend figured she'd give the tickets away or, worst case, forfeit the $30. Not that either happened. As we all know, attending became everyone's priority and tickets were highly sought after. (Hewitt may or may not even have known a teacher who may or may not have spent some in-class time on their phone in a cupboard refreshing the resale platform in an effort to secure last-minute tickets. The main change Hewitt has witnessed since is her friends' increased willingness to watch women's sport. That and the fact that they now say, 'Next time, I'll listen to you and buy tickets.')

In spite of being a football player, supporter and coach, Zammit didn't rush to buy tickets, mostly because she wasn't certain her daughter Peyton, who's spent a lot of years being dragged along to Zammit's football matches, would be all that interested. 'Well,' Zammit says, 'that was wrong.' Peyton not only wanted to attend games, she made a sign requesting the jersey of her favourite player, Kyra Cooney-Cross. Zammit had spent the day leading up to the match trying to manage Peyton's expectations: 'There will be 50,000 people in the stadium, and it's unlikely Cooney-Cross will see your sign or hand over her jersey', and so on. It turns out she was wrong about that, too: Peyton is now the proud owner of signed Cooney-Cross kit.

Heading into the quarter-final, Hewitt's mother bought face paint to put on Hewitt's kids. They duly painted the kids' faces, then bumped into her kids' friends outside the stadium. Hewitt says, 'Somebody was like, "Oh shit, can I have some of that?" So literally, the face paint got passed around and we were like, "We don't need it any more—here, take it."' The friends who inherited the face paint in turn passed it on to others in the stands near them.

Hewitt also dug out her old football representative jerseys for her young sons to wear to the matches. Some were slightly perished when she retrieved them, but the ones in decent shape provided a throwback. In some ways, the kit, which was men's cut, fit their growing bodies better than it had ever fit Hewitt's.

Although Hewitt's, Sibson's and Zammit's children's awareness of the Matildas was already high given their mums' involvement in the game, awareness among the kids' friends escalated throughout the tournament. 'Definitely before the tournament started, most of the kids only knew who Sam Kerr was, if anyone,' Hewitt explains. 'When we had that friendly against France just before the World Cup, I sat a bunch of [my son] Lucian's mates down.' She went round the group and they all identified a player they knew: Sam Kerr, Sam Kerr, Sam Kerr ... 'I said, "OK, every game we're going to focus on another player, and by the end of the tournament you will know them all." But I didn't have to do that. By the second game they already knew who everybody was.'

Among wider tournament highlights the women mention was the refreshing collegiality: 'The men's is obviously usually a lot more segregated because there is trouble, but people were all just sitting in amongst each other and it was like, "Oh, unlucky—that was a good shot." It was all very supportive.'

Another night, Hewitt, who has English heritage, was trying to do the double: watch England play live, then race home to watch Australia on television. She and one of her sons were watching a live stream of the start of the Australia match on the bus on a phone. Australia scored just as they hopped off the bus and they screamed and started running down the street towards home with renewed urgency:

> People near us on the street were like, 'Shit, has the game already started? I'm just going to get supplies!' So they started running and we were running. You wouldn't usually do that with kids—talk to randoms while running down the street in the dark at night near a pub—but we definitely did that night.

⋆ ⋆ ⋆

Three generations of women journalists provided informed coverage for followers and fans of the Women's World Cup before, during and after the tournament. One of them provided invaluable industry mentorship, the other two invaluable next-generation foundations and nuanced insights.

Tracey Holmes and Eleni Psaltis spent months preceding the Women's World Cup researching and creating a television series to provide sociopolitical background, history and commentary on the Australian national women's football team and the Women's World Cup.[48] (Speaking of Holmes and her generosity in mentoring other women journalists and in inviting her to co-create this show, Psaltis says, 'If she says jump, you say how high?' and adds, 'People sometimes describe her as a sports reporter, but she's more than that: sports, politics, diplomacy, geopolitics …')

Preparing the show was meaningful to Psaltis, who grew up in a Greek-Australian family immersed in football and knew the power of the world game well. But, as with all of us, she still found that the history of the women's world game was something that required detective work. Psaltis spent vast portions of her pre-tournament Mondays wheeling her son in his pram to the State Library of New South Wales so she could scour the microfiche for information on, for example, an early tour to Taiwan by the Australian national women's football team. What she found was sobering: 'All I could find were articles on the [male] Ming Dynasty,' she begins, before outlining an experience that is bona fide reflective of wider women's sports statistics: 'There were more reports on horses than female athletes ... I learned a lot about horses, that's for sure.'

Pioneering women's sports journalist Abbie from *Her Way*, who has designed a T-shirt and hoodie that aptly say 'Invest and She Will Do the Rest', is at the vanguard of the next generation of women's sports media workers and advocates. She launched her media platform in 2021 at the age of eleven in response to the dearth of women's sports coverage. She explains:

> When I first started going along to women's sport, I was so excited when I saw women with long brown ponytails, with names like mine and voices that sounded kind of like me yelling out to their teammates. It was one thing to see it at a local sports ground, but I didn't understand why that wasn't translating to TV, media and magazines.

Disappointingly and nearsightedly, FIFA did not accredit Abbie for the Women's World Cup due to her age (she was in her early teens), but Holmes offset that slightly by inviting her to do a live cross with her to ABC-TV's *News Breakfast* as well as appear on Holmes' tournament podcast series. An absence of FIFA accreditation notwithstanding, these were some of a number of opportunities Abbie was granted in recognition of her dedicated work providing coverage not just to women's football but to women's sports as a whole. She says:

> I had known journalism legend Tracey for about a year after chatting at various events, but to actually sit down with her at 7 a.m. on a school day in front of Sydney Harbour to discuss

> the Brazilian team's performance and how we would talk about it on live television together was one of many surreal moments during that month.

Other major media channels and programs, such as BBC World News, Optus Sport and ABC Radio National invited Abbie on their shows, and naming-rights sponsor CommBank asked her to be part of content it filmed with fans and Sam Kerr. (Of the latter, she says, 'Filming that content gave me invaluable experience as a host and presenter, as there was a lot of dialogue to recite!') Abbie:

> The chance to chat and learn from producers, journalists and presenters across all of those media outlets was a fun and invaluable experience. While my schoolfriends and I were really enjoying hanging out and watching games together, yelling and screaming, those media opportunities essentially forced me to do lots of research on players and teams while I watched, so I could feel well prepared for those appearances. Getting to be in such a professional environment where women in sport were the focus was inspiring, and I was really aware, as it was happening, what a special period of time it was. To finally experience what I'd wanted to happen since starting my media platform was pretty cool and surreal at the same time.

14

THE MATILDA (AFTER) EFFECT

SHORTLY AFTER THE 2023 Women's World Cup, an image emerged of winning penalty taker Cortnee Vine during a visit to an all-girls school in Sydney. Taken from above, it shows Vine high-fiving the outstretched palms of a multitude of schoolgirls in tartan uniforms and Panama hats. The crowd is simultaneously parting to allow Vine passage and pressing towards her to be in proximity to greatness.[1]

The adulation captured in that image wasn't a one-off. Throughout the subsequent A-League Women's season, children swooned after Vine signed their memorabilia. Even while she was playing, they called out to ask for her autograph. 'It was hysterical. It was like a rock concert,' Kris Goman says of witnessing it week in, week out. Majella Card, who co-leads both the Matildas Active Support and Brisbane Roar Supporters chants, notes Vine's post-tournament pull, too: 'It's not just Sam Kerr. I think maybe leading up to the World Cup, it was largely just Sam. But now Cortnee Vine … Being at the Brisbane Roar games it felt like, *Oh, no one's going for the Roar here—everyone's going for Cortnee Vine.*'

★ ★ ★

Catherine Ordway is an academic whose expertise is sports law and ethics. Prior to her academic career, she worked as a lawyer for the Organising Committee of the 2000 Sydney Olympics. In 2018 she asked one of her university classes to complete a risk analysis for the 2023 Women's World Cup. Almost all of the students' analyses recommended not to bid for the tournament as the financial risk was too great, primarily because there would be inadequate time for sponsors, broadcasters and fans to best leverage their support.[2] (This aligns with UK-based women's football academic Jean Williams' interview observation that 'Women's football has always been perceived as an economic drain'.)

That risk analysis was also conducted in real life and likely for a lot more expense. In the initial bid-planning stages, one of the Big Four accounting firms was commissioned to write a report quantifying the potential Australian economic and cultural impact of the 2023 Women's World Cup. 'At that time, the company said we would get 600,000 people to the tournament. I was like, "That's just not right,"' co-COO Jane Fernandez recalls. 'I told them, "I just don't think you're visionary enough."'

To be fair to the students and the accounting firm, few of us were.

In my book *The Matilda Effect*, I predicted that these Matildas and the 2023 tournament would not be a curtain-raiser to men's sport or a scant-on-detail footnote in history. I predicted that they would instead be the main event and story, and would give new meaning to the term 'the Matilda Effect'.[3] That's both in relation to raising awareness of women's extraordinary contributions and positively influencing women's sport and gender equality.

Not only have they given new meaning to the term—'the Matilda Effect' is now shorthand for breakout, universal, sporting, media, funding, game-changing, audience-attracting success[4]—but they've also catapulted the term into the cultural lexicon. The team and the 2023 Women's World Cup exceeded all expectations and crossed into uncharted territory. The tournament was as much a cultural movement as a sporting event. It changed sport *and* society.

So what just happened? And how?

Marion Stell says the event was a 'textbook case' of elevated media attention attracting serious audience interest and engagement, and showed how a tournament could be embraced by a receptive audience:

> It was confirmation during the World Cup of something that some of us have known for a long time: that if you have this confluence of things—like the extra media coverage, the ability to get the personal aspect and the personal stories—there is a product here that can take off.
>
> Of course, the other really key aspect was that there was success. The Matildas were doing well, they were playing a brand of really attractive football.

'I don't know about you, but as a historian, it's very hard during something as exciting as the World Cup to say, "I'm a historian. I'm not a fan",' Stell laughs. She's not wrong. All objectivity went out the window.

'Investment' is the word Fernandez lands on to articulate the what and the how. Also 'quality':

> I think it's a step-up approach that happened over time. FIFA invested significantly in the development of the women's game. Then Football Australia invested once we started bidding. So the brand started getting built. One of the key things was the change in the actual football itself and how bloody good it was. I think that surprised people, because back in the day, people would watch it and go "Oh, it's *OK*." But now, it's an unbelievable product, and a product people want to be attached to.

True. We now have the previously elusive proof that the secret sauce isn't so secret: if you invest in women, if you consistently provide the requisite funding, media coverage and wraparound conditions that are standard in the men's game, women's sport can and will thrive. (For so long, surfer and gender equality advocate Lucy Small explains, it's as though men's sports have been provided a thoroughbred and women's sports a Shetland pony and then made to race. 'It's not rocket science,' Alicia Ferguson says of what you get when you compensate players properly and enable them to focus solely on their football job. You put them in a high-performance environment and provide them with high-intensity, competitive training with and against international players, 'and hey presto, you get some really bloody good footballers'.)

Indeed, we have the data now. Before this tournament, we couldn't indisputably demonstrate the strength of the audience numbers. We couldn't point to robust jersey and ticket sales. We couldn't tantalise government or private investors with guaranteed GDP-boosting revenue. But off the back of this tournament, which boasts a truckload of impressive figures in all areas, we can quantify that women's sport is big, good business. (Were we being passive aggressive, it would be tempting to tell all the male administrators and media gatekeepers who are scrambling to adjust: 'Per my last email ...' Or, to cite the great Elle Woods, 'What, like it's hard?')

But the Women's World Cup's influence is not confined to or even best explained by data. 'Still processing' became the catch-cry as the moments were so momentous and so successive that no one has yet been able to fully absorb their enormity. 'Still buzzing' was what people were saying almost a year on. But articulating it? That was another thing. Summing up so many of our experiences, John Didulica says, 'I haven't really properly built an intellectual framework for what this all means. I can speak to how I felt.'

* * *

Malcolm Gladwell popularised the concept of the tipping point—the moment when an idea or a movement that has been steadily building crosses a threshold and spreads like wildfire. The Women's World Cup absolutely set the world alight. 'It was water-cooler talk for an entire month' is how David Davutovic defines it, while Janine McPhee says, 'The Matildas got into the hearts of all Australians, into their DNA.' As a member of the team that attended the 1988 pilot Women's World Cup, the tournament that proved the Women's World Cup was feasible as a concept, she would know.

Back in the day, Danielle Warby provided some of the Matildas' earliest media coverage: she started their Twitter account and reached out to players via MySpace to collate and report news about various women's sports. So she has long known the potential and been advocating for the uplift we witnessed. But even she was caught by surprise at the tournament's success. 'For this to happen, for it to be the most watched television event in our entire history of television—I'm sorry, what?! I mean, it's like, *I'm glad you're all here. But now you're really all here.* I mean, *Oh my god*,' she laughs. Warby touches on the elements so many others have touched on: 'I knew the Matildas games would sell out. What I didn't know [would occur] was the cultural moment [and movement] around the whole thing.'

That cultural moment and movement had been aspired to. Pre-tournament, when its success was hypothetical and when most of the planning and preparation were executed from people's lounge rooms amid pandemic-induced lockdowns, co-COO Jane Patterson set out to foster a tournament as penetrating as the 2012 Paralympics had been. That London-based event rewrote the book on how traditionally undervalued, undermarketed athletes could be seen and celebrated; it was a breakout athletic and perception-changing success. By any measure, the 2023 tournament was as tectonic as the 2012 Paralympics. It became the new beacon for shifting attitudes and actions, and for bringing new audiences to sports and sportspeople who don't generally receive as much funding or media coverage as others. For there was an undeniably magnetic pull to the tournament. Engaging with it became about much more than football; news cycles briefly became joyous and compelling instead of contentious and divisive.

Still, it's one thing to see it on paper—it's another to experience it. Journalist Samantha Lewis says:

> To see it go from the seedling stage to becoming this absolute forest was extraordinary. Thinking back even just a couple of

> years, watching the Matildas playing games in largely empty stadiums, in timeslots that no one cared about, receiving hardly any clicks on stories about the national team, to now it being literally the most famous sports team Australia has, with some of the most recognisable names and athletes—I almost have whiplash from how quickly it's happened.

Experienced sports administrator Eugénie Buckley, too, is somewhat stunned by the accomplishment. 'I knew it was going to be big, but 11.15 million watching the Matildas? The total Australian population is only 25 million. The AFL on Grand Final Day gets close to *four* [million],' she says. (Williams similarly observes of the commercial success and the groundswell of emotion and celebrity it entailed: 'It was like your Women's Euros were for us.' She is referencing the breakout success of the 2022 Euros. The UK hosted the tournament, which the Lionesses ended up winning. Matches sold out, the football quality was exceptional, and the entire nation fell in love with the tournament and the team.)

Fascinatingly, and importantly, the outstanding broadcast figures weren't the end goal. 'It wasn't an objective of ours. We didn't talk about it, because if you only talk about numbers, you don't build moments,' Sarah Walsh explains. 'We talked about how we wanted to bring Australia together like the Cathy Freeman race did. That's how we talked. People thought we were crazy.'

The first of Dator's Laws of the Future dictates that the future cannot be predicted because it does not exist. The second of Dator's Laws deems that any useful idea about the future should at first appear ridiculous.[5] Prior to 2023, hosting such a wildly successful women's football tournament that replicated the united euphoria around Freeman's race would have met both definitions. The 2023 tournament results are impressive, too, when you contrast them with the Women's World Cup product of just four years earlier. 'The 2019 tournament was wonderful. I think people really loved it. The fans had an amazing time,' says FIFA marketing professional Evie Chamberlain. 'But in 2023 the spread was bigger, right? It wasn't just, *OK, I've arrived at the stadium and I'm now surrounded by 70,000 excited fans.* It was, *The plane is landing in Sydney and I'm already surrounded by thousands of excited people talking about it—and talking about it openly, casually, like it's regular news, like it's any other sporting activity.*'

The cut-through was indeed phenomenal. 'I'm not educating people that this exists any more … I don't have to do that huge heavy lift of "I need to introduce you to the concept of this event,"' Chamberlain says. 'In 2019, it felt like people were interested in discovering it. In 2023, you were hearing casual experts on the street.' Uber drivers, for example, would regale her with their and other passengers' tournament stories; she'd overhear people discussing it avidly while waiting for coffee. 'It was much more immersive,' she continues. 'It felt like we got past the stadium perimeter in a way that I didn't really experience in 2019.' She credits Australia with getting on board and behind the tournament. 'France was excited, but Australia saw it as a real growth opportunity. [The local organisers] recognised the potential and they went for it … So I felt like we got much deeper into the market, but [also] deeper into people's psyche.'

'Society will never be able to say that women's sport is not commercial any more. That's what we and the team did,' Walsh says of that penetration. She makes the point that the results come when you design the game how it should probably have been designed in the first place:

> We're now speaking to a broader market—you know, mums who were told they were not sporting fans can now go to sport, football, watch Matildas and enjoy that with the whole family. It turns out that they do control the purse strings. They buy for the family, not just for themselves.

Whichever way you try to elucidate it, the tournament yielded something objectively fantastic. 'Maybe [the reason] why it's been really difficult to intellectualise the Matildas is because we haven't seen this before in Australian women's sport,' Lewis offers on the effect they've had on the sporting and cultural landscape:

> They kind of shot through this ceiling of their own sport and this ceiling of disinterest from those outside to make themselves unavoidable, to make themselves unignorable. They are in front of you now. You don't have to go and google them. You don't have to go and do research or ask people. They're just there. That is such a novelty for any women's sport, let alone football. I remember saying to a friend halfway through the tournament, 'Is this how it feels to be a fan of men's sport?'

Part of the surprise everyone is mentioning is perhaps the fact that the success, which had been decades in the making but excruciatingly incremental in gains, seemed to go from not much to everything all at once. There were some milestone events around the 500-, 100- and 25-day marks, Lewis explains,

> but then it was like a whole movement of people becoming aware of this thing at the same time. That's kind of what's happened with the Matildas more generally, I feel. There have been moments scattered throughout the last couple of decades for the Matildas, but all of a sudden, in this rush of time, they've gone into this other stratosphere of being known and being watched and being loved that I think a lot of us, we're still like, *Fuck, is this real?*

So meteoric and genre-defying has the Matildas' rise been, and so comprehensively have they drawn us into their orbit, that Lewis wrote an article detailing the 'Swiftification' of the team.[6] She says, 'Taylor Swift really is the only comparison point I've got, because she, just like the Matildas, has transcended the industry she's in. She's not just a musician—she's this pop culture figure, this icon, this leader. And the Matildas have done the same.'

That includes bringing non-traditional fans to the sport—fans who would never previously have considered buying a jersey, much less viewing a footballer as a role model. Indeed, the team now engenders boundless goodwill; the players are giving main-character energy. Lewis continues:

> That, I think, is where the real power of the Matildas is. They've been able to, in a unique way, open up the biggest participation sport to half the population of the planet and of the country and of the workforce. That kind of cultural shift is immeasurable. So when I talk about the Swiftification of the Matildas, the fandom element is also a really significant part of that parallel. Because Taylor Swift's fans are not just fans of her music—they're fans of the [Swiftie] community, they're fans of her principles, they're fans of so much of what she represents. That's what I think of the Matildas as well. [Fans] might not know the first thing about the offside rule or 4–4–2 or any of that. But they are so emotionally invested in this team and these players and the community that's been built around them that I don't think anything [the Matildas] do on the field is going to rattle that any more.

★ ★ ★

In the same vein as Dator's First and Second laws, there's the Overton window. Its six stages outline how something goes from unthinkable, radical, to acceptable, sensible, popular and policy.[7] Align those stages with the pendulum swing of women's football over the past 100 years, and a picture of the 2023 tournament sensation starts to materialise. First, the notion of it being unthinkable, 'inappropriate' or even 'unsafe' for women to play football. Back then, the game was played by a radical few. Now, girls and women playing the game is not just acceptable and sensible, but wildly popular.

Such concepts and explanations, along with Venn diagrams of overlapping conditions, are what we seem to be reaching for as we try to explain the elements that combined so perfectly.

Certainly, the wider cultural conditions were favourable. 'I think we'll come to look at 2023 as an example of many interconnected, interdisciplinary and intersectional mainstream cultural moments that galvanised women and non-binary folk in really different ways across a variety of fandoms,' sports academic Kasey Symons says. The convergence of wider social, cultural and political machinations contributed to that. Symons explains:

We're so often existing in alternative spaces and trying to find community, because mainstream pop culture doesn't give us enough content or representation, But I reflect on the NFL Super Bowl in February 2023 and seeing Rihanna performing while pregnant, then of course the *Barbie* movie and Beyoncé's record-breaking Renaissance tour. Then we have the juggernaut of Taylor Swift bringing her Eras tour around the world while also occupying a space we didn't expect of her.

Swift's relationship with Kansas City Chiefs [American football] player Travis Kelce opened a point of entry to one of the most hypermasculine sporting spaces in the world by Swift being visible and active in the fan culture and not caring if her presence annoyed a few 'Dads, Brads and Chads'. She undeniably brought new fans to the NFL and gave them a model of how to do fandom differently and not conform to the expectations often put on women in men's professional sport to fit in. But this kind of diverse fandom has long existed in women's sport, and the 2023 FIFA Women's World Cup having a moment to shine in the middle of all those moments put these fans in a spotlight we haven't seen before.

Hannah Ferguson paints a similar picture:

I do think there's much to say for that succession of the *Barbie* movie, Matildas, Taylor Swift tour, Beyoncé … So much culturally happened in a six-month period. I think the feeling in the air was so safe and so joyful and so positive … from my perspective, it was the thing that defined the year, because directly afterwards was [the horror of] Gaza, and the [failure of the Voice to Parliament] referendum.

It was also, she says, a revelation for women that this could be our new normal, that it was possible to have this experience all year round: 'It was the first time in my life that I'd felt truly safe in a sporting environment. And I felt like men gave a shit about women.'

Journalist Patricia Karvalas termed the tournament a 'feminist cultural reckoning'.[8] Small, too, references the fever-dream-like experience so many of us had throughout the tournament: 'I felt like I was in this parallel-universe heaven where everyone was obsessed with women's sport.'

'It was like a utopia' is how Warby describes it. 'This is what it could be like if we had more equality in sport and other areas, because the more women you have in a public space, the less likely things are to go to shit. It's science.'

Journalist Eleni Psaltis, who primarily covers politics, also touched on the soft diplomacy and confluence of events. 'Covering Gaza a lot, it has struck me how the social fabric of Australia and social cohesion are at risk right now. There are a lot of people who seem unwilling to come to the table and talk to the other side.' She says the Women's World Cup countered this:

> There was community, there was commonality, and there was connection. It's really struck me how we consume news and entertainment these days: it's all fragmented, and we're all in silos, we're all on different streaming platforms. There's just no sense of community. You can't talk to a stranger down the street and go, 'How good was X/Y/Z last night?' You can't assume they watched the same bloody thing. But these moments in sport *are* those conversation starters, and the things that produce community, commonality and connection. We can watch them in real time and celebrate in real time. I just think we need to lean into sport more than ever, because I think people are yearning for those things, especially after being isolated during COVID.

Former Matilda Sue Read similarly sums up the timing this way: 'So many positive things came together at the right time. We'd all just come out of COVID, but hadn't yet been allowed to really connect. We all wanted to experience some joy and do it together. And that is what the Women's World Cup and the Matildas gave all of us in the best possible way.'

Indeed, COVID may well have aided the 2023 organisers, although it wouldn't have felt like it while they were grappling with the logistical challenges of lockdowns and border closures while preparing for the event. That COVID benefit dates back to the bid itself. (Coincidentally, Fernandez was speaking to me for this book when the FIFA Congress was announcing Brazil as the 2027 host. For the 2027 bidders it was the equivalent 'on tenterhooks' scenario she'd lived through for the 2023 bid she steered. But this time, she was able to enjoy it as an interested observer.) 'I think [COVID] definitely helped us. It meant we were a lot more targeted with our campaign around the FIFA Council members and making sure we produced great content that was targeted to the region, to their countries,' she explains. Everyone was assessing the bid remotely from their own location, so it made sense to make it context-specific:

> It made us think a little bit differently. And I think, as you rightly say, people wanted something to celebrate, they wanted good news, and we were able to provide that. Then, of course, the Matildas—I mean, unbelievable role models, unbelievable footballers. When you have someone like Sam Kerr backflipping around the place,[9] it also helps.

★ ★ ★

Rebecca Shaw (aka @brocklesnitch on social media) wrote that what we experienced during the Women's World Cup wasn't so much that men finally got on board and 'validated' the game—it never needed their approval—but that something had shifted in the sociocultural sporting landscape.[10] It certainly felt like some of those zombie value arguments had been vanquished. As more than a few social media threads have asked, have guys who hate on women's sports finally started to realise that's not—and never has been—the flex they think it is? The language also shifted. 'Men's sport is "passionate". Women's fandom is "hysterical",' Ferguson points out; women and the things they are interested in are consequently diminished. But in 2023, being emotional about women's sport was commended and stigma-free.

That returns us to the fact that many people operating in the space knew the event would be big but still couldn't have imagined such a best-case scenario. 'I don't have the answer, but there's obviously many factors. What I think is that a true phenomenon is never quite predictable,' Ferguson says. Perhaps we were also in some ways primed in a post-COVID, post-Scott-Morrison-government world. That is, the social, cultural and economic factors aligned, Overton window style, to yield the unifying opportunity the Matildas were seeking, and they and we took it.

Analysing the event as it was unfolding, academics synthesised a number of factors pointing to why everyone got around the Matildas and the tournament—not least of which were a social contagion of positive emotion around success and an inclusive, accessible common goal. There was also the attraction to good-news stories, the positive social cohesion sport imbues, and shared experiences that broke down barriers and facilitated connection and camaraderie.[11] Visibility, escapism and dopamine-inducing experiences were also contributing elements, as were the inspired, positive sportspersonship on display and the teams' and tournament's ability to invoke an all-encompassing sense of joy and hope.[12]

All of those are true. But to distil that coming together in wonder might well come down to the winsome confluence of three elements: bandwagons, beer and non-violence.

Ferguson makes the point that the 'things that women enjoy aren't gatekept'. That lack of ringfencing means fans of women's sports aren't expected to have expertise or to avidly follow a single team—two exclusionary elements, alongside violence and homophobia, that otherwise alienate people from the men's game.[13] (As comedian Mel Buttle puts it, women's sports fans are like, 'Great, come in. Welcome, we need you.') Ferguson continues:

> It's about just having the knowledge to converse. If we want this to stick, the view and the approach have to be that no matter what understanding or level you're at, you could start watching a game tonight. All my approach ever has been, all I'm trying to do, is to make someone feel comfortable to try the next game.

In a similar vein, journalist Isobel Cootes repurposes the 'gateway drug' reference to the 'gateway game' that matches such as the France quarter-final were in terms of hooking in new fans.

That 'try the next game' philosophy aligns with the Matildas Active Support approach. In contrast to the alienating, aggressive culture that tends to dominate men's-sport supporter groups, Matildas Active Support fosters a convivial atmosphere and offers a low barrier to entry. It deliberately offers an alternative way of doing fandom. 'A bandwagon?' Matildas Active Support co-organiser Card says. 'No, it's just new people being introduced to something amazing. One day a bandwagoner, the next day a diehard Matildas fan.'

Which brings us to beer and aggression. Alcohol consumption and violence were not prevalent around the Women's World Cup, yet the tournament was a resounding commercial success. One of the abiding takeaways of this is that it's possible to enjoy a beer without being aggressive. What stood out for Williams in this respect was that it was so safe at stadiums that she could see a woman breastfeeding in the row in front of her during a match. Fan Nicola Zammit had an equivalent experience after the Australia v France quarter-final:

> Walking around the streets then was just a really different vibe to [Men's] State of Origin or anything like that. It was friendly. There weren't any drunk people and you knew there wasn't going to be any violence, so you could let the kids walk a few steps in front of you in a crowd and not be overly worried.

Ferguson compares the experience of attending the Women's World Cup with that of attending a recent Men's NRL Grand Final, where she was in the eighth row and at one point caught the ball, which she jokes made her fear for her life. She references the hypervigilance that's second nature to women: studiously ensuring we don't respond to wolf-whistling and catcalling, tensing because we sense a fight could break out any moment ... 'We all know that feeling. It's something that men would be upset to hear us describe. Truly, we are not the emotional gender.'

Read also points out that the women's game and the Women's World Cup model better modes. 'It was a more positive spectator experience: safe and fun for families, women and men. Everyone was just so happy, and related very differently on and off the field,' she says. For example, she observed players not just celebrating their own team's win but also recognising the other team's loss:

> The thing for me is that sport teaches you how to win and still be humble. It teaches you how to learn from your losses and be better. But also when you win, how to be compassionate to the other side. Just the fact that women did that, that was a total mental shift, and something I don't think people were used to seeing on the international stage. It felt quite different compared to what we often see, which is more of a power and domination thing of 'We're awesome and you're terrible'.

She illustrates that point by describing the emotional intelligence shown by England supporters in the immediate aftermath of the Matildas' semi-final loss. 'We did a little bit of gibing with the English supporters, but they were like, "Actually, seriously, guys, we're really sorry."' In the post-match press conference, England coach Sarina Wiegman likewise politely apologised for ruining the Matildas' fairytale run, and earned a few chuckles. Gracious coaches and fans in women's football—it's a thing.

Read continues the story about the fans:

> We were like, 'Oh, look, we'll go for you *even though* you were really brutal to us.' It was a way to bond instead of a way to actually denigrate each other. We were all there for the same positive outcome, and we were all in awe of the massive outpouring of emotion from the country and the overwhelming support for women's sport. There was no violence, no negativity. It felt like a different kind of crowd. All the men I saw supporting teams were really enjoying themselves, but there was no sense of aggression or agitation, whether we won or lost. The English

> gibing was more like a fun acknowledgement of our sadness than any kind of negative experience.

That aligns with Pokuah Frimpong's sentiment that it 'feels like war, but it's beautiful. Like, "Oh, we're playing you. I love players from your team."'

Photographer Madeleine Penfold compares two identical assignments she had that illustrate what we saw play out at the tournament: documenting the experience of a men's club game and a women's club game on consecutive days. Shooting the identical briefs, differentiated only by gender, was, Penfold says, 'like being in a time warp'. The men's game was characterised by day drinking, littering, and men and boys in the crowd screaming unrepeatable things at players. Penfold:

> Afterwards, I didn't even want to be there. It was carnage on the streets. Then I go to the women's game the day after, and it's calm and peaceful and beautiful. Everyone wants to chat. Then you watch the game, and it's nice and it's peaceful. I appreciate that some people say we need to close the gap and bring that passion and anger and aggression through, but maybe it's, like, 'Leave the aggression but bring the passion.' Look how much passion we saw at the [Women's] World Cup.

That aggression-free passion is what former Matilda Alicia Ferguson picks up on. Speaking about the France v Brazil group-stage game but as an example of the layering of the aforementioned conditions, she references the brilliantly refreshing atmosphere.

> I've been to a lot of [Men's] State of Origins with a lot of alcohol in me, but the vibe of Caxton Street leading up to a women's sporting event, and football specifically—it still gives me goosebumps now—is the [reality of] no gender bias in sport [in action]. This is where you go into an amazing sporting event and the dirty Cacco [Caxton Hotel] with the sticky floor is *heaving*.

As Ferguson summarises, 'No aggression. No fighting. The mixture of fans. The good party vibes. And the amazing football on show, played by women.'

This is in sharp contrast to the documented statistic that domestic violence rates increase by 40 per cent on Men's State of Origin night.[14] (I'd infer that the domestic violence rates did not spike in the same way on Women's World Cup game nights.) Admittedly, this issue is not confined to one sporting code or country. UK-based domestic violence prevention groups highlighted such violence in the groundbreaking campaign 'He's coming home' released for the 2022 Men's World Cup.[15] It featured the English flag strung up outside a house, with the words on it that were a play on the English saying about the trophy returning to the country were the team to win: 'It's coming home.'

Here, the first half of 2024 involved Australians witnessing an ever-increasing number of women killed by men.[16] At the time of writing, a seemingly light-hearted social media trend was posing the question: Would women rather take their chances in the woods with a man or a bear? It was indicative that—for a range of reasons, which included that bears see women as human and that if the women were attacked, no one would ask them what they were wearing—most women elected to take their hypothetical chances with the bear.[17]

Such challenges are why advocacy around the women's game is important. As Small posted on social media, sport is 'a kind of signal, a microcosm of the broader community of where we're at in terms of gender power relations'.[18] (The Matildas and the Women's World Cup are nothing if not the sporting MacGuffin of gender equality.[19]) That has in turn informed Small's advocacy: equal access to pools or pitches isn't about access to sporting spaces or evenly splitting prize money—it's about 'trying to transform our communities to be better, safer places'.[20]

Indeed, many have noted that the Women's World Cup showed how sport could be, or that this is what we always knew it could be but couldn't prove until now. This idea was supported by post-tournament research that found more than one in three boys and men agreed the tournament may have shifted their attitudes towards, or stereotypes about, women's societal roles,[21] and earlier research in which it was found that survey respondents saw women's sports as more progressive, inspiring and inclusive, and cleaner than men's sports.[22] (As Cheek Media observed, male sporting codes have previously been able to ignore or skate over inappropriate behaviour because 'revenue is their only moral code. Suddenly an alternative is on the table.'[23])

This warm counterculture was attributed in part to being a direct response to the hostility and exclusion to which women have traditionally been subjected—both explicit, through active prevention of access to pitches and playing, and implicit, through an alienating culture of machismo, sexism and assumed knowledge and attire requirements that are exclusionary to newcomers not acquainted with the culture's intricacies.[24] That tracks: it turns out 20 per cent of the population hates (mostly men's) sport for such reasons as its hostile, toxic culture.[25] (Sport is, after all, largely an environment built by and for men, so 'its inequality and inequity are baked in'.[26]) Akin to the headline at satirical news site *The Betoota Advocate* 'Local woman actually enjoys watching sports now that messy buns and people being nice to each other on the field exists',[27] a female friend of Kieran Yap texted him a revelation they had mid-tournament: 'I thought I hated sport. It turns out I just hate men's sport.'

That's not to say this happened by accident: there was clear strategy underpinning it. Sarah Styles believes its formation was seeded back in 2016 or 2017, when the Matildas played some friendly matches in Western Sydney and deliberately fostered strong community ties. That 2017 period coincided with when Football Australia began seriously marketing the Matildas; the team subsequently sold out Penrith Stadium with what was then a record 17,000-strong crowd.[28] (Gosh, that crowd figure now seems quaint.)

A key milestone in that approach came in 2024, when the team marked its fourteenth consecutive fully subscribed match, which was played in front of some 75,000 fans.[29] Fascinatingly, adoration had so advanced by that time that journalist Abbie from *Her Way* observed Men's NSW State of Origin players leave their hotel un-swamped by fans, while at the same time fans clad in Matildas colours gathered around the hotel entrance for glimpses of their heroes.[30] Days later, commentator Robbie Slater complained that Network Ten had relegated the Socceroos' match to a streaming channel as it privileged coverage of the Matildas.[31] Cue polite narrowing of eyes and subtle head tilts as those of us who've spent decades not being able to easily watch Matildas matches considered whether we had entered an alternative universe. (If you have time and some popcorn, it's worth delving into the comments sections on articles and social media posts about it—some of the responses are *chef's kiss*.)

Styles attributes the build to the team developing and sustaining deep community connections: 'For me, that's almost a bit that I feel doesn't get enough credit—that it's not just this past three years. It's off the back of this thing that then hit an incredible tipping point.'

Like Fernandez, Styles references another fascinating interwoven aspect: Sam Kerr's signature backflip. 'I'm kind of oversimplifying this, but on the other hand, I actually don't think I am,' she says, pointing to the much-photographed backflip Kerr performed after scoring a hat-trick of goals for Chelsea in the 2021 FA Women's League Cup final.[32] The same or equivalent picture was projected on the Sydney Opera House sails as part of the 2023 Women's World Cup bid.

> That photo is on the front or back page of every newspaper in the country. All of a sudden, Sam, in particular, is starting to cross through what is a really big psychological barrier for some sports fans in this country of respecting women as athletes. Because deep down, plenty of people, plenty of men, ultimately are like, *Actually, I could be better than that. I'm better than that.* As silly as it sounds, that idea of saying Sam could do a running backflip actually breaks through [and makes people realise] *Oh shit, I can't do that. I actually can't do that.*

Styles references the intersection of the admiration for that elite skill level and the fact that football is now socially acceptable for

Australian girls and women to play, which created the conditions for the team to build its following ahead of the Women's World Cup. Her point is that the Matildas' breakout success has come from more than a plan to play Top 10 teams in the lead-up to the Women's World Cup: it's built off a clear, multifaceted, long-term strategy to set the team up for success. She pinpoints that it's also 'built off some superstar players helping to really build that momentum, which then extended to how strong the awareness is across the full squad'. We saw that awareness accelerate when Kerr was unexpectedly unavailable for a large portion of the Women's World Cup.

Styles identifies another crucial aspect—one that was on her radar because her previous role was in elite-level cricket, with the Australian women's cricket team long being equally groundbreaking in its pay, conditions and on-field accomplishments.[33] The tide was rising before and alongside the Matildas, not least because of the Australia-hosted ICC Women's T20 Cricket World Cup in February and early March 2020. 'There's an element of people forgetting what 2020 looked like for them,' she says of the Australian women's cricket team, which not only won the final but, perhaps supplemented by the crossover drawcard appearance of pop star Katy Perry, almost also filled the MCG.[34] It was a then-unheard-of feat and popular-culture collaboration for an Australian women's sporting team.

> What was happening there, what was happening with football, with netball, in the Olympic sports, with the Matildas—each of these was lifting the others. And then we have that absolutely incredible, honestly life-affirming, soul-enriching experience of [2023].

Styles worked at Cricket Australia for the five years prior to that T20 tournament. The MCG idea came about just after International Women's Day (IWD) in 2016, which prompted Styles and her peers to consider what day of the week IWD would fall on in 2020. 'I literally pulled out my phone and scrolled through a couple of years quickly,' Styles explains. The 2020 IWD would be a Sunday—so a good day for hosting a sporting event that might attract fans and families. Enticing 95,000-odd people to attend was ambitious, but Cricket Australia very nearly managed it.

Of that T20 final, Styles says, 'I sometimes say it was one hamstring away from the perfect match—Ellyse Perry, who was arguably cricket's Sam Kerr in that journey, missed out because of [a hamstring injury].' Also, while my own mind went to the inclement weather that very nearly cancelled the semi-final, Styles's went to wider events and the benefits the Matildas have been able to reap that the Australian women's cricket team haven't. 'That's the week COVID hit, so the ability to truly capitalise on that moment got smashed ... I've seen quotes from the tournament's CEO, Nick Hockley, that if that match had been scheduled forty-eight hours later, they probably would have had to cancel the whole day.'

Tracey Holmes, too, positions the Women's World Cup's success as standing on the shoulders of other women's sports, and events such as the T20 World Cup: 'It's part of that journey. You can't separate football all by itself. There are stepping stones from some of the other sports as well.' And there are the stepping stones *to* other sports. The Matilda Effect is starting to be felt. The Wallaroos national women's rugby union team and Australian Diamonds national women's netball team, for example, leveraged the Women's World Cup media interest and the compare-and-contrast options available to them for their own battles over conditions and pay. The cricketers tipped in to create a 'fighting fund' for the netballers.[35] (Leading national women's cricketer Alyssa Healy told ABC-TV's *Offsiders* that she's witnessed the quality of, and interest in, netball and refuses to believe the sport can't be profitable.[36])

The Diamonds won the netball World Cup—for the twelfth time—the night before the Matildas' Round of 16 match against Denmark. But unlike the Matildas, the Diamonds received no money for their achievement and relative silence when it came to media coverage, except to contrast their results and recompense to the juggernaut that was the Women's World Cup.[37] (Academics Kasey Symons and Bess Schnioffsky attribute this to a number of factors, including the fact that there isn't a similarly strong or stronger male equivalent against which to compare or foster netball's development.[38] This is concerning for a number of reasons, not least because netball is often the entry point for Australian girls and women to sports participation and fandom.)

In the same suit, and in words that could be transposed to almost any women's sporting team, the Wallaroos penned an open letter to Rugby Australia that players posted on their social media accounts calling out the empty-pockets argument that sees money spent hand over fist for the men's team while the women are told they can only be afforded part-time wages and subpar treatment: 'You told us flying anything beyond economy was too costly. Then you flew the Wallabies business class on a trip shorter than ours.'[39] They also pointed to the Matildas as an example of what's possible when investment is adequately made.

The effects continue and are expanding. In 2024, the Women's State of Origin rugby league series was increased to three games (instead of the nonsensical two that precluded there being any true victor) and run as a standalone rather than a curtain-raiser event. Approximately 25,000 people turned up to watch each of the three games, despite inclement weather for all of them (25,492 for Game 1, 25,872 for Game 2 and 22,819 for Game 3, if you want to be precise), the impressiveness of which was surpassed only by the broadcast figures of, at their peak, more than 2 million[40] (and 6.38 million TV viewers across the three games).[41] Basketball has similarly exploded. In priceless cross-code admiration, Kerr posted images on social media of herself wearing a jersey supporting US collegiate basketball star Caitlin Clark.[42] (Significant, too, is that Seven Consulting, which was one of the switched-on early investors in the Matildas, recently started sponsoring the Opals.[43] 'When we started that sponsorship, we spoke about hopefully being joined and then replaced by major Australian companies, which could give the team the support they deserve, but in the meantime, we would start the ball rolling,' says Seven Consulting founder and executive chair Declan Boylan. 'Indeed, in time, Commonwealth Bank, Coles and others recognised the value of the team and the wonderful women who represent our country. We are starting to see the same momentum of true believers in our work with the national women's basketball team now, the Seven Consulting Opals, who also had no sponsors when we started with them in 2022 just before the FIBA world Cup in Sydney.')

(Speaking of crossovers and team and tournament champions, Matildas Women's World Cup support traversed sporting and cultural arenas. AFLW players Chloe Dalton, Tayla Harris and Darcy Vescio were in attendance. Basketballer Patty Mills repped a jersey,[44] so too did US singer Macklemore.[45] Lydia Williams presented a jersey to singer Pink—an equally trailblazing, empowering woman—and her daughter while Pink was touring Australia in early 2024,[46] which spoke volumes of the elevated status at which the Matildas now operate. Taylor Swift also reportedly accepted a jersey—although it wasn't publicly worn, it was one of the few gifts Swift accepted while in Australia. Also, we've had a Matildas/Wiggles crossover with the Wiggles playing the national anthem at a Matildas friendly against the US in 2021.[47] Might we see one for *Bluey*? After all, that show's two main characters are young active girls (OK, girl dogs) and the show is set in Brisbane, the city where the palpitation-inducing penalty shootout took place, and the location of the newly commissioned Matildas statue.)

Importantly, the Matilda Effect is starting to cross into policy. Thanks to the advocacy of and savvy leveraging by Lucy Small and journalist and fellow gender equality advocate Kate Allman, the NSW state government (like the Victorian and now federal governments) requires peak state sporting bodies to provide a plan for equal prize money and for board gender equity as part of grant funding applications.[48] Small and Allman's timing was uncanny, as Small explains:

> We had a meeting with the NSW sports minister that we'd had lined up for months and just happened to fall a day after the World Cup final. Walking into that meeting I felt like there was literally nothing the minister could say to push back on us, because we had the strongest example to show that investment and a commitment to equality will deliver outcomes, and the World Cup had just captured the imagination of almost every

> person in Australia. All of the old arguments, like 'Women's sport just doesn't get the eyeballs' or 'But the women just aren't as good', were out the window, and we had the strongest case study to prove it.

Yes, yes, they did. Small expresses the sentiment so many of us are experiencing right now: 'I feel the World Cup has emboldened me. None of the armchair economists in comments sections or in conservative media have a leg to stand on any more, and I feel I can be more forthright because I can always say, "Did you watch the World Cup?"' Indeed, it feels a little like the *Simpsons* meme 'Don't make me tap the sign'.[49]

Bridie O'Donnell concurs. 'I think that I felt—and, of course, the hundreds, thousands of other people who've been advocating for gender equality in sport felt—vindicated and inspired and smug,' she laughs when I put to her that the Women's World Cup fostered a pretty good feeling for those of us who have traditionally been told there's no market for women's sport. She runs through a list of results and data to which we can now point to permanently put that argument to bed:

> The millions of people who were tuned in, the photographs of people at the G [MCG], watching the games on TV instead of watching the footy, or people on aeroplanes watching it, except for that one guy who was watching *The Lord of the Rings*. That data around the number of people who were watching, the attendance, the sold-out stadiums, even at the [Olympic qualification] game that we had here in Melbourne against Uzbekistan, which was sold out. People I know were texting me during the day like, 'Do you know anyone who's got tickets?' And this was going to be a 36-degree day.

Without wishing to overgeneralise, the sentiment appears to be growing. The theme for IWD 2024 (which was, incidentally, the day I spoke to a number of people featured in this book) was on point: 'Count Her In: Invest in Women. Accelerate Progress'.[50] On that day, Office for Women in Sport and Recreation director Sarah Styles called for conditions that would enable women to 'finally be able to put down the mental load of having to justify our place in participating in certain sports, of justifying our right to be leaders, our right to be fans in the way we choose … and instead just be able to get on with it'.[51]

That IWD followed the first-ever mandated release of Australian companies' gender pay gaps, which made for sobering reading.[52] While Styles went for the classy speech, some savvy women went for the classy troll and delivered the companies with the largest gender pay gaps the age-old and slightly offensive IWD treat: cupcakes. Except these cupcakes came with a twist: they were iced with the companies' pay gap percentages.[53] Weeks later, on April Fools' Day, the [Female] Athlete Project similarly spoofed entrenched attitudes by asking whether we were aware that men have been playing sport professionally for decades.[54]

★ ★ ★

Another noteworthy aspect of the 2023 Women's World Cup was the tournament's and the Matildas' normalisation of queerness. That's a sign of the times, yes, and the tournament took place just months after the historically symbolic 45th Sydney Gay & Lesbian Mardi Gras, which celebrated the original marchers and was held during Sydney's hosting of the annual international WorldPride event, one of whose displays featured a meme-inspiring rainbow-flag-outfitted 'Progress Shark'.[55] But still, it was a marked difference.

'Obviously, marriage equality [being made legal in Australia in 2017] really shifted the dial. But even after that, people were still not that open. But this group of players, they're all getting engaged and posting on Instagram … It's just there, as it should have been all along,' Warby says. Nor is being openly queer identifiably hampering players' careers. Warby: 'I think what's really interesting to me is that the cultural moment the Matildas have created means that if you're going to give some blowback, you're going to look like an arsehole.'

(That Warby uses a swearword is also relevant: including swearwords in the Disney+ documentary was true to who the Matildas are but also meant the program was given a mature rating, which potentially made it less family friendly. To their credit, Football Australia committed to it.)

'I think the Matildas are a bit of a shorthand for queer, in some ways,' Mel Buttle says. 'But also not. It's not just about that.' She mentions a Matildas bit she has in her stand-up comedy show. She had included one previously and it didn't land, but off the back of the tournament's success, she tweaked the segment and tried again. It's been a hit. The premise is that Buttle knows everything about the Matildas. She rattles off names with details that hint at her next-level knowledge—'Hayley Emma Raso'—and alludes to being so immersed in the world that she's still following Mackenzie Arnold's ex-girlfriend from three girlfriends ago: 'I just get this sense that everyone in the room knows exactly what I'm talking about. I don't have to explain who they are any more. People know all these characters.' In fact, they know and relate to them so well that they light up when they realise Buttle is wearing socks embroidered with images of Matildas players. (When we spoke, she'd just come from a meeting where the Caitlin Foord socks she was wearing proved the ultimate icebreaker.)

One reason, perhaps, that players' sexuality was a non-issue was that the quality of the football and the event itself were so good that there was plenty else to talk about. Overall, the event was variously described as 'queerly thrilling', and the most openly queer ('really, really gay') sporting tournament yet.[56] As Buttle says, it platformed 'lesbian excellence'. (Compare that, if you will, with the absence of out players in the 2022 male equivalent event held in Qatar, where homosexuality is illegal.) So normalised was queerness throughout that fan Alicia Webb, who identifies as gay, posted a conformity-flipping quip about Steph Catley's apparent heterosexuality in her friendship group chat: 'Catley [is] the only one who's out as far as I can tell. I'm very proud of her. I don't understand her lifestyle but I am an ally.'

Diversity is improving, too, including in relation to cultural background, disability and marital status. For example, Katrina Gorry had a child on her own, Arnold wears hearing aids, and Mary

Fowler and Kerr have Papua New Guinean and Indian heritage, respectively, and have inspired girls who haven't seen themselves represented in sport before. (As journalist Marnie Vinall pointed out in relation to Kerr, it warranted taking a moment to appreciate that the nation's hero is a queer woman of colour.[57])

The nonchalant acceptance of queerness was a marvel to former Matildas Karen Menzies and Sue Read, who played in an era when you couldn't bring your whole self to the game. Menzies, who left the game in the 1990s in part because of the homophobia she encountered, also references the volume of, and normalisation within, the media coverage: 'I think that for the entire month, the person who hit the national headlines the most was an Australian lesbian. I can't imagine that happening ten years ago. Certainly it wouldn't have twenty years ago. And when it did for the entire month, nobody blinked.'

Read nominates the players' self-assuredness: 'They've been a beacon of positivity, at exactly the right time, but not preachy about it either. Just like: "This is who I am." I think that's immensely empowering. I have found their openness so inspiring, and validating. It's amazing to live to see a time where we can all be celebrated, and selected on our performance, without fear of exposing our sexual orientation.'

Speaking more generally, Libbi Gorr observes that whether it was the Taylor Swift or Matildas audience, neither was burdened with or had a sense that they had something to prove: 'It was just "We're here".' Referencing the football club at which her daughter Dali plays, Gorr is now witnessing at a grassroots level the flow-on effect of such normativity: girls who are attuned to and confident in using their bodies; girls for whom 'athletic' and 'feminine' are not mutually exclusive. Illustrating this, she speaks with admiration of the girls' confidence in using their bodies to compete on the field and their 'very strong eyelash and ponytail culture'. While she is not entirely sure how the girls can see through their fulsome lash extensions, she's aware that it's striking and thought-provoking that these girls will never know a time when it wasn't possible to play, or to not play on their own terms.

Engaging girls in sport on such terms, and keeping girls and women engaged lifelong, is something that is on Read's radar not just as a former elite athlete but as a practising psychologist. She well knows that participation in sport leads to better physical and mental health outcomes:

> From a psychology perspective, we know if we can keep girls in sport from the ages of thirteen—where most drop off—to twenty, we see better outcomes in nearly every area of life—including career trajectory, leadership, completing studies, health-related outcomes, and of course improved body confidence, mental health and resilience. For that reason alone, we should be investing more seriously in all levels of women's sport.

(Indeed, given the underrepresentation of women at senior levels, it's also worth noting that 94 per cent of C-suite professional women have played sport.[58])

Initial signs are promising. Post-tournament, football participation rates have increased by about a third in Australia.[59] That volume may go some way to addressing the almost-vertical attrition rate for teenage girls that Read speaks of.[60] It won't be easy or straightforward, though, and it's important not to conflate advances in high-performance sport with community participation. Research has consistently demonstrated that translating enthusiasm for elite on-pitch feats to amateur off-pitch participation isn't linear.

Still, the Matildas' Women's World Cup heroics may prove the crucial participation and puzzle-piece-shifting catalyst.[61] Early anecdotal indications support this. David Davutovic, for example, recently witnessed firsthand a 700-player all-women outdoor football competition held at his local club where numbers were capped only due to the physical field numbers and therefore the number of matches that could be scheduled.

15

NOT DONE—NEVER DONE

WRAPPING AROUND THE tournament, and providing a fresh take on the Matildas' long-held 'Never say die' motto, was a goosebump-inducing marketing campaign. The ongoing campaign, which later won a Bronze Cannes Lion for its inventiveness and effectiveness, comprises three deceptively simple words: 'Til It's Done.[1] The truncated ''Til' doubles as a reference to both 'until' and the central syllable of 'Matildas'. 'It's' is deliberately undefined. Combined, the three single-syllable words focus on the work done, and still to be done, in and around the women's game.

Cortnee Vine famously pinned a list of career goals on the back of her childhood bedroom door. They included being a consistent starting W-League player, being invited to a Matildas camp, making the Matildas squad, and being selected for a Women's World Cup and Olympics.[2] Not dissimilarly, the 'Til It's Done campaign contains a goals list, this one in poster form and demarcated as if written with chalk on a chalkboard:[3] ''Til we … play our first international match; score our first World Cup goal; get a write-up in the papers; get our own jersey; [are crowned] women's Asian Cup champions …' The goals the Matildas have already achieved are struck through, evoking a deeply satisfying summary of the team's to-date achievements. The ones still to be completed sit unaltered to spur them on until they, too, can be crossed off. The most recent entries to the living campaign, penned as the Matildas' historic 2023 tilt unfolded, reference the country sitting up and taking notice, and men's sports pausing to make way. Through such forward and backward examination, the campaign celebrates the Matildas' wins while setting their sights firmly on the future and the legacy they seek to leave.

'When we were developing a brand strategy [in consultation with the players] four years ago, they spoke a lot about how, when they were playing as kids, they didn't really have any role models in football other than men, and their female role model was Cathy Freeman,' Football Australia's head of marketing, Peter Filopoulos, says. Four key themes emerged from the discussions with the players: that the Matildas wanted to be understood as professional footballers; that they were a team, not a brand; that they wanted to generate inspirational moments for future generations; and that they wanted to leave a legacy.

Football Australia took the four pillars that emerged from those discussions and briefed external agencies to come up with a campaign. (Implicit in that and the wider marketing and communications plan was an aim to foster not a miniature or mirror Socceroos brand, but an authentic, standalone marque comprising and leveraging the twenty-three individual personalities and their interests that would connect strongly with a range of audiences and fans.) The budget was modest, characteristic of everything in women's football, but the aspirations were big. 'We wanted a rallying call, but something that wouldn't put pressure on the team,' Matildas media and PR manager Ann Odong explains. The campaign also had to do a number of jobs: it needed to be flexible enough to work from the high performance to the grassroots; it had to be open-ended and align with the purpose of uniting the nation; and it had to work not just for the 2023 tournament but, potentially, beyond it.

Ogilvy was the agency that came back with the goods. 'I got that sense that they [had] nailed it within two or three sentences, a couple of slides in,' Filopoulos explains of the meeting when Ogilvy pitched the 'Til It's Done concept. Odong concurs that she very quickly knew it was the one. Those three words powerfully met the flexible, rallying-cry, nation-uniting, pressure-less brief. She knew, too, that the campaign comprised language people could use. 'Everyone can provide their own "it" and "done",' she explains. And it enables the team to define its own end point and success. Put simply, 'it's only done when we say it's done'.

Filopoulos had to take the concept up the chain for final approval. He recalls being nervous presenting it to the leadership team—without its buy-in, the campaign wouldn't fly. Fortunately, the group had the same reaction he'd had and immediately, unanimously approved it. 'They just loved it from the first moment,' Sarah Walsh says of the team's reception to the campaign, 'because they've reached equal pay and conditions, but it doesn't stop them caring about other parts of the game.'

'I got a voicemail message, which I still have today,' Filopoulos continues, referencing a message Matildas head coach Tony Gustavsson left him after that meeting. Having thought more on the campaign, Gustavsson complimented Filopoulos and his team on landing the brief. He was already envisaging how he could incorporate elements of it into his work. 'That was a moment where I thought, *Right, yes*,' Filopoulos explains.

And so, as the Women's World Cup unfolded to equal parts anticipation and unforeseen elevation, from banners to social media posts to bus-stop signs, Football Australia unveiled the 'Til It's Done campaign to enormous uplift.

* * *

The Matildas' 2023 Women's World Cup campaign was a huge success by any metric. With the team going from sold-out match to sold-out match in record-breaking strengths never before witnessed, it would be easy for us to view women's football as not just on its way, but too big, too momentum-fuelled, to slide backwards.

On the fiftieth anniversary of the perception-changing Battle of the Sexes tennis match, tennis great and gender equality advocate

Billie Jean King said that when it comes to the work in and around women's sport and gender equality, it's not done—it's never done.[4] In fact, every decade or so headlines proclaim that women's sport has made it, but then support recedes and the conditions and coverage return to stasis.[5] So although the Women's World Cup and the Matildas' involvement in and around it felt exceptional, because in many ways they were, we know that the job of ensuring the further success and longevity of women's football is far from done and that the advances made will backslide should we not manage this next stage carefully.

We're only a few years on from when men's sports were prioritised in COVID bubbles and women's sports were all but cancelled,[6] but issues continue to accrue. In early 2024, for example, the Young Matildas had to play a rather bizarre match in Uzbekistan in uncleared snow.[7] Men's-centric thoughtlessness saw the Ballon d'Or ceremony scheduled at a time when women footballers couldn't attend due to international duty.[8] The Manchester United women's team was displaced to a demountable so the men could have the women's facilities while their own were refurbished.[9] Meanwhile, France sought to ban the hijab for its 2024 Olympics athletes. Individually and collectively, these are the kinds of infuriatingly regressive moves that make you want to, in a bit of subversiveness, put fake Picassos in women's bathrooms.[10]

Academic Fiona McLachlan, who has researched the 'boom time' progress narrative,[11] is, like all of us, grappling with what we just witnessed, what it might mean and whether it will last. Is it boom time again, or even finally? 'I think what we've got is an anomaly,' she tells me. 'So the Matildas Effect is very real.' That is, the team brought the nation together in ways never before seen; it demonstrated that people can engage with and get as excited about women's sport as they do about men's.

So far so good.

'Where the boom-time bit comes in for me is: Does that translate broader than this particular group of women at this particular time?' McLachlan says. Will it translate to other women's sports and to levels other than the elite? Prefacing it with the statement, 'This is the controversial bit', McLachlan says, 'My heart sank a little bit at the excitement.' That's because progress narratives, boom-time narratives, counterintuitively act as a form of resistance: they allow people to say, 'We don't need to take action on endemic issues such as gender inequality, because we've already made it.'

McLachlan has seen that resistance rear up post-tournament in grassroots settings in which she's working. She explains that the opportunities for girls and women to play are now there, so a form of inclusion has definitely been enacted, but that inclusion is undermined by the heckling and misogynistic, homophobic language girls and women encounter in many of those still relatively hostile environments. There are also the less obvious but entrenched aspects, such as clubs not enacting equal access to the best pitches or the best training times, so girls and women are relegated to the poorer and poorly lit pitches, and only at times when the men don't need them.

McLachlan gives another concrete example of that subtle but identifiable inequality: some clubs she's visited have different-sized trophies for their girls and boys teams. Unsurprisingly, the boys' trophies are larger. 'That one blew my son's mind,' she says. McLachlan's five-year-old son is aware of the work she does in age-appropriate brushstrokes. She explained to him: 'I go to these football clubs, and I try and get them to share. The boys and the girls need to share, right? And he's like, "Yeah, that makes sense."' He intuitively understands that girls and boys should be granted the same amount of time and the same number of turns. 'Do they listen to you?' he asked McLachlan. Her response: 'Not really.'

Such experiences and conversations have prompted McLachlan to consider at what age we start to accept the socialisation that girls are 'less than'. She notes, too, that even when inequities like this are pointed out to clubs, they're reluctant to make change, citing issues such as lack of funding to have trophies remade. So the status quo and the subtle messaging this value-laden sizing difference sends remain ingrained.

McLachlan is conscious that by raising these issues she might seem as if she's being a 'Debbie Downer', but it's a necessarily pragmatic lens to look through to help us stay the gender equality line. Ultimately, through her research, she will be seeking to better understand the question none of us have quite yet been able to answer: whether the Matilda Effect will prove to be more than a one-year or one-team flash in the pan.

Such ephemerality is what Kieran Pender identifies as the element that makes it so challenging to articulate the tournament's enduring legacy. Citing the way the Matildas captured the nation's attention, he says it certainly suggests the team has made a positive impact. Adapting a famous line from a speech given by former prime minister Julia Gillard (after she lost the Labor leadership in 2013) about gender not explaining everything, not explaining nothing, but explaining some things,[12] Pender says, 'It won't change things overnight. It won't have no effect. It will have some effect.'

'It's definitely crashed through in terms of popular culture,' Danielle Warby says of what she's witnessed outcome-wise so far, but she notes that there are other ceilings—some obvious, some less so. Infrastructure and managing demand are among the more obvious ceilings. And ticketing. Ticketing is a big one. You have to run, not walk, to buy international women's football tickets now, as demand far outstrips supply. As a number of crossover fans have observed, logging in to purchase Matildas tickets gives anxiety-inducing Taylor-Swift-ticket-waiting-room vibes.

While such strong ticketing interest is the stuff of dreams, it's also the stuff of nightmares. How do you balance welcoming new fans to the mix while retaining access for the people who've been there all along? Who should be getting tickets? The Croissants suggest a kind of loyalty advantage: 'So if you've been to X amount of games, you get an extra ten minutes to try and get tickets.'

Adam Costin is one such fan whose loyalty should be considered. An early adopter and longstanding male ally of the women's game, he missed out on tickets to the Matildas' Women's World Cup games. He continued to support the team through the mediated experience of TV, but his missing out gives me pause: Costin is someone who should absolutely have been in the stadiums to witness the matches firsthand. Less concerned about his own circumstances and more keen to see the game cement sustainability and longevity, he is thoughtful about what it all means:

> I haven't seen much in the way of negative outcomes from the explosion in popularity, except for an administration perhaps struggling to properly take advantage of it. If this level of popularity is to be maintained, improving resources for player development in the A-League [Women's] is crucial to that. Fifteen years ago the vast majority of the Matildas played locally. Now we hear it's a big leap for the local players to step up into the team. If we are to keep producing world-class players, we need to have a local league that is of a higher quality than most world leagues. That requires resources.

Costin has touched on the most pressing of legacy challenges still to be resolved: infrastructure, development pathways and participation rates, with the first of these straining under the latter two. Didulica similarly muses: 'Functionally, how do we get more pitches? How do we build a better pipeline? How do we make sure girls build proper careers out of football in Australia and then into the world? That's where my head's gone.'

Accommodating the surging grassroots interest sustainably and appropriately will be tough. Pitch availability is a pernicious issue, and local and state governments are unable to manufacture new, centrally located, suitable vacant land.[13] (After all, if they could solve the pitch dearth issue, they could solve the housing crisis.) Still, the Malthusian trap has been set—if we can't stump up for some patches of grass and conditions to enable girls and women to play, the obstacles that scarcity presents will hobble the game.

None of these challenges can be solved in isolation. Throughout the tournament, Didulica could see a straight line from grassroots football to the Matildas: 'There was such goodwill.' But he notes that hasn't been accompanied by the structural alignment he was hoping for. 'So while there's unified goodwill, I still don't see everybody working cohesively.' The silos continue.

Warby credits Football Australia for its efforts in and around the tournament, but echoes Costin's sentiment: the national body probably hasn't capitalised on the tournament enough. She rightly cites the goalkeeper jersey as an example:

> How hard is it? It says to me that it's broken through to a certain level but there's still a bunch of people making decisions about some of this stuff who are not quite connected with it. Anyone who truly gets it would have been like, 'So we're going to be printing a huge run of goalkeeper jerseys, right?'

Indeed, while the surge of interest is no doubt unprecedented, it does seem like bodies such as Football Australia are playing catch-up on the professionalism required, and on understanding and catering to the transformed demand. Bridie O'Donnell agrees:

> My takeaway from the World Cup is that the paradigm has shifted. Now people want more. They want to see more of the best women athletes in the world. They want it to be marketed professionally. They want to be able to buy those tickets, see those athletes, buy the merchandise. There's a standard now that is lifting. Supporting organisations are going to have to decide: 'Are we on board with that or not?'

Being on board must include consistent, high-quality, accessible media coverage that strikes a balance between ensuring commercial viability and audience need. Optus reportedly paid $13 million for access to all sixty-four World Cup matches, on-selling the rights to the Matildas matches to Channel 7 for an estimated $4–5 million.[14] Given the broadcast figures the Matildas matches yielded, the duo's arrangement was later dubbed the broadcast deal of the century.[15] (The two 'paid peanuts and received gold'.[16] In fact, the $1 billion benefit Optus reaped through its investment all but offset the losses and reputational damage it sustained from earlier hack damage.[17]) CommBank reportedly achieved a similar boon, paying an estimated $1–2 million for a four-year sponsorship deal that includes naming rights.[18] (One wonders if it may also garner an entire generation favourably viewing the CommBank brand akin to that of the bank's defunct Dollarmites school banking program.[19])

Tracey Holmes notes that it was fan interest in the Matildas and the Women's World Cup that drove the tournament media coverage. 'I think the media was late to that party,' she says. It goes a lot of the way to explaining why the broadcast rights were sold so cheaply and why the anti-siphoning laws weren't activated. (The Women's World Cup wasn't considered to be nationally significant enough to enliven the anti-siphoning laws. That meant that aside from the Matildas matches Channel 7 subleased from Optus Sport, much of the Women's World Cup was accessible only to those who could afford an Optus Sport subscription or who were able to attend live sites. Tangentially related, Australia's first women's-sports-dedicated bar recently opened in Oxford Street in Sydney, providing an ongoing venue at which to access women's sports, including those behind paywalls.[20])

The Optus broadcast deal translated to subscribers watching twenty-one hours of matches each, which led to the company recording its largest-ever month in terms of overall minutes streamed.[21] Interestingly, Optus found that the broadcasts attracted many more women viewers while simultaneously retaining its existing, largely male subscriber base. Its audience didn't shift—it grew. Finally, some 75 per cent of viewers watched the matches on old-school televisions, which suggests in some ways that the viewing experience was large and communal.[22]

Those stats align with Australian Sports Commission research that found that although just 48 per cent of the population had intended to engage with the tournament, 78 per cent ended up doing so. Almost the same number (75 per cent) said that what they witnessed made them feel proud (and yes, that prompts questions of that apostate 3 per cent).[23] In short, the event was so compelling that three-quarters of the Australian population was drawn in. 'I don't think there was a household that wasn't watching it on those nights. It was like, "If you're not [watching], well, what are you doing?"'

Davutovic says. Indeed, the Matildas' late-stage matches such as the quarter-final lent themselves to something cinematic: peering into the windows of houses around the otherwise still country would have revealed families and friends crowded around televisions for a collective viewing experience akin to those in the 1950s.

Journalist Waleed Aly posed a rhetorical question about what would have happened had the Matildas' feats been broadcast solely on pay TV. He surmised they would have retained their merit but not their cultural currency.[24] One upside of the enormous response to the Matildas' matches is that it reinvigorated 'dinosaur' free-to-air television, which had been barrelling towards extinction.[25] It also demonstrated that terrestrial television provides an invaluable, equitable national service that subscription services don't. (As Cheek Media wrote, 'Free to air will never be this relevant again'.[26])

★ ★ ★

In the pre-tournament human-rights assessment, academic Susan Harris Rimmer noted that no single tournament could solve the myriad and intersectional human-rights issues that permeate the space. But the tournament was such a resounding success that at times I wonder if it did more than nudge things. Harris Rimmer's immediate, appropriately pragmatic response to my getting carried away was: 'It wasn't enough to stop sexual harassment at the final.'

'I think we've still got a way to go in the way we describe women's skills,' she adds, citing the insinuation that it is astonishing that Gorry can be both a mother and an elite athlete. She also notes that there are improvements to be made around normalising talking about women's skill and competitiveness, especially the constant—if unspoken—comparison to the men's game it invariably entails.

That lurking comparison extends to the quality of the media coverage. Journalist and gender-equality advocate Kate Allman was one of the members of the all-women commentary team that covered A-League Women's matches for the first time ever in the months following the 2023 tournament. She's since pointed out what had been hiding in plain sight, which explains in part what has provided fodder for arguments that women's football is 'less good' than men's: 'You might not be able to articulate the problem, but when watching a football match with fewer camera angles, no matter the gender of the players, the play will appear slower and less exciting.'[27] Later she reminds me of research that has demonstrated that when gender is removed by changing live footage of athletes to stick figures, fans don't just enjoy women's sports, they prefer them.[28]

Holmes suggests that we should be fostering an illustrious, standalone future rather than a replica of the men's game. 'Is that the best we can imagine?' she asks rhetorically. 'Why don't we do it better or differently?'

Harris Rimmer also cautions against trying to mould women's football into a simulacrum of men's. She instead encourages galvanising football for the better for both, and even engaging in some out-of-the-box thinking. Imagine, for a moment, a place where mixed sports are normalised and gender delineation is no longer the yardstick, she says:

> Can you imagine a world in which we have a football tournament where there are men *and* women on the teams? And that's perfectly normal? And we don't have huge expectations about what men and women can do? It does always get to me that sport is one of the last gender-segregated areas of human society.

Representative of this fresh perspective, Team Heroine—an agency led by former Football Fern Rebecca Sowden that, among other things, is responsible for the 'Correct the Internet' campaign, which seeks to address online gender bias—published a 2023 Top 10 women's sports campaigns listicle.[29] (For the record, I would like to correct the internet around the mispunctuation of 'Matildas'. And yes, I am nervous that somewhere buried within this book will be an inadvertently placed apostrophe, thereby undermining this argument. If you find an errant 'Matilda's', please don't tell me.) Among those the listicle highlighted for their perception-shifting originality was the campaign that saw an AI-generated football expert called Hope Sogni nominate for a hypothetical FIFA presidency.[30] The campaign's aim was to redress gender inequality at senior sports levels and inspire new ways of operating. Better yet, it was trained on data input from women who have already had an impact on governance and gender-equitable representation, including former Matildas vice-captain and former FIFA Executive Committee member Moya Dodd, and former Lewes Football Club CEO Maggie Murphy. (Lewes is a community-owned, semi-professional club that was the first to implement equal distribution of resources and pay for its women's and men's teams.[31])

Other featured campaigns included the ad by French telecommunications company Orange that engendered awe at the skill of the male players' technical capabilities. Reminiscent of the aforementioned stick-figure research, the amazing player-beating, goalscoring feats are revealed to have been performed not by men but by women, once the ad's superimposed settings are corrected.[32] 'That still brings tears to my eyes,' Psaltis recalls. 'It's just a masterpiece of deception, forcing us as viewers to unsee and see again.'

(While not wishing to detract from the largely positive reaction to the ad, it is worth noting that, as Dodd explains, the ad catered to men's sports fans and 'newbies' to women's football. That is, it overcame the common misperception that women aren't skilled at the sport. But the 'truebies' (true believers) well versed in women's football found the ad slightly patronising, or at least still far behind where the modern game and sophisticated women's football fans are.[33])

Not on Team Heroine's list but worth a mention are the efforts of the Women in Red project to redress the bias in Wikipedia entries.[34] Just 16 per cent of Wikipedia contributors are women; just 15 per cent of Wikipedia entries are about women.[35] (That too-little representation is indicative of the factors that act as barriers to participation, and correlates with women's history being undervalued and under-documented.) In early 2024, Angel City Football Club and the Los Angeles Public Library co-ran an inspired Wikipedia edit-a-thon to improve the number and quality of women's football entries.[36] (Former Matilda Sally Shipard can attest to the import of having representation in the form of Wikipedia entries for women.

When she first starting dating her partner, April, April's sister Bree was awestruck: she'd never known anyone who had a Wikipedia page.)

Of course, the flipside of fans, sponsors and media alike finally seeing (or no longer ignoring) women's sport is sustainably managing expectations and demands. Catley spoke of the emotion she felt during the Women's World Cup seeing the number of people supporting the team out on the streets and in the stadiums.[37] Sam Kerr spoke of how people were approaching her and Mackenzie Arnold to say 'Thank you' rather than 'Well done'.[38] It certainly felt as though the tournament and the Matildas were at the centre of an all-consuming vortex and everything else was standing still. But as many people have wondered aloud, in terms of players being both able to engage with fans and asked to give away jerseys by little girls in the stands who have spent hours crafting heartfelt, imploring signs, how does a team and a brand built on being extremely accessible to fans balance that now that the volume and parasocial demands of fans are impossible to meet in a genuine, workable way?

There's a converse layer to this heroism: the higher standard to which women athletes are generally held. They are expected to be good people, not just good athletes. This role-model behaviour is often largely derived from uncompensated labour borne of players' love for the game and their desire—and wider embedded cultural expectation—to both grow it and leave it better for those coming behind them. But this is a heavily gendered issue. For men, the inspiration often lies in rousing others to individual excellence. For women, it's selflessly benefiting the community and the sport despite the demands this puts on their more precarious, less-well-paid careers—the emotional and mental labour and the time involved, such as staying back to sign jerseys or even give up jerseys of which they have few or that hold sentimental value.[39]

For commentator Russ Gibbs, the difference is the expectation versus the reality: the egoless, approachable Matildas are and would be happy to spend time with fans, signing and giving away memorabilia and posing for photos. The issue is that we shouldn't *expect* them to do it. Also, we need to find ways to make it scalable.

'It's harder to get an interview with a Matilda than a Socceroo now,' football writer Kieran Yap observes. Some players are now in the upper echelons and accordingly more difficult to gain access to. He situates the helicopter flying overhead at training alongside an in-game moment when Kerr came off the bench and the crowd 'went ballistic' (as Yap put it) when she removed her substitute bib in readiness to take the pitch, and then actually ran on. With the exception of perhaps Cathy Freeman, never has a woman athlete warming up so overshadowed on-field action. As Yap defines that heightened level of scrutiny, anticipation and expectation, 'This is proper rock-star level now.'

Former Matilda Jo Powell, too, cautions that there's potential for glamorising the job without focusing on the hard work that underpins it and the rarefied air in which the players are now operating: 'Kids assume that what they see is just how it is. You know, you just rock up, you get paid, you go overseas, and you play for other teams ... But it hasn't always been that way.' It still isn't. Players such as Kerr sit within the 1 per cent. The other 99 per cent, if they make it and if injury and/or non-selection don't scupper their career before it's really begun, are scraping by. For instance, a 2024 FIFA/FIFPRO report identified that more than a quarter of elite-level women players work secondary jobs to supplement their football career, and 73.9 per cent earn less than US$19,000 annually from football, which puts them in the ballpark of the poverty-line pay the Matildas had to strike over back in 2015.[40] So setting realistic expectations about what's possible and feasible both in terms of career opportunities and player–fan interactions is yet to happen.

At the same time, you want everyone—especially the current and past generations of women through whose unpaid or underpaid labour and out-of-pocket expenses all of this has been built—to be able to capitalise on the surging commercial revenue and growth. As Didulica notes, 'The energy for women's football is incredible.' Putting aside the ongoing elevated incomings such as the $4 million in revenue the Matildas generated in their four-day, two-city 2024 China friendlies for a moment,[41] Football Australia has estimated that the Women's World Cup provided more than $1.3 billion in economic benefit and unlocked $398 million of government funding for women's sports.[42]

Domestically, A-League Women's memberships for the first post–Women's World Cup season increased by 669 per cent.[43] More than 300,000 people physically attended matches across the entire A-League Women's season and finals—the most spectators for any Australian women's sport.[44] (PFA co-CEO Kate Gill makes a valid point: this growth was wholly organic—the A-League Women's was absent from Football Australia's legacy plan.)

There are also women-specific considerations around revenue growth and the attendant fair distribution. Former FIFPRO women's player union advocate Sarah Gregorius says current forecasts project that 60 per cent of revenue from the women's game will be generated from commercial income and sponsorship, with 30 per cent to come from broadcast deals—the inverse of the men's game, for which broadcast rights drive revenue. There's more: women's game commercial revenue is driven by deep engagement with the players, which translates to fans following and buying merchandise related to specific players rather than clubs. 'Nobody buys a T-shirt of the [American] NWSL', says Gregorius. 'They buy the shirts of the players, and they follow the players from club to club, environment to environment.' This gives new meaning and complexity to the issues around fan interactions and jersey signings and giveaways.

Gregorius talks, too, about the lens women footballers bring to such commercial discussions—that the players advocate for prize money from, for example, FIFA Club World Cups to be apportioned not just to already decently funded teams that are likely to win, but to national teams and leagues that don't yet have appropriate resourcing. There's that admirable but challenging 'Leave it better' mentality/requirement again. 'They're bloody socialists,' Gregorius jokes. 'Really, they look at it through this [incredible lens of] where we have solidarity, where we can have this mentality of a rising tide lifts all boats.'

One can't help but think it's unlikely the men's teams are thinking that way or having such conversations. Gregorius agrees, but, as she also points out, they don't have the 'historical baggage' they need to shed in order to succeed.

The Matildas are arguably the country's highest-profile and most valuable brand right now. Football Australia is certainly approaching interactions with the team as a revenue-driven partnership. 'We're in business with our female players now,' Walsh explains. She unpacks the considered approach they've taken to building that brand, exposure and related revenue streams, including signing with Network Ten and free-to-air TV. 'Then we decided to do the documentary with Disney+, who have markets in the UK where all of our [top] players are. So [we're] being strategic.'

Football Australia is also thinking and operating equitably. The Matildas achieved equal pay and conditions in 2019, but equal is different from equitable. 'So they have equality now but, actually, the needs differ for the Matildas and the Socceroos, and Katrina Gorry is a perfect example of that,' Walsh notes of Gorry's caring responsibilities—she is the primary carer for daughter Harper. In practice, the teams are treated differently, but with a wider approach of entwined improvements and benefits. Walsh explains that a current example is the collective bargaining agreement negotiated in 2019 that initially saw the Socceroos take a brief pause in payment so Football Australia could overinvest in the women's team. As a result, the industry's and Football Australia's total revenues grew, which everybody now shares in. With revenue now shared more equally, the Socceroos are benefiting from the Matildas' commercial incomings. Tournament ambassador Kate Jenkins has separately espoused that no Socceroos were harmed in the making of the Matildas—gender equality is good for everyone.[45] Or, as Walsh puts it, 'If one succeeds, they both succeed.'

Still, and as Gill has already flagged, that success is yet to translate sustainably to the domestic league. Exhibit A: Canberra United, a club that pioneered operating as a standalone model.[46] (Canberra United was the Australian equivalent of Angel City decades before there was an Angel City, minus the celebrity investors.) In early 2024, it found itself the afterthought characteristic of the women's game when its fate became tied up in the politics and machinations of whether an A-League licence would be granted to a men's equivalent.[47] Things were so badly handled and so bleak that former Matilda Sue Read and her peers had to launch a crowdfunding campaign to ensure the club's survival. Her Save Canberra United group raised over $90,000 for the team and lobbied government to contribute a further $200,000 to help keep it afloat.[48]

It's hard to fathom how we got there, and so quickly, after the Women's World Cup we'd just had. It exposes the tenuous circumstances undermining so much of women's football and the blood, sweat, tears and goodwill by which it is driven. Canberra United's absorption into the mires of the men's association was also reminiscent of how the original association that ran women's football in Australia, the Australian Women's Soccer Association (AWSA), was bankrupted in the early 2000s after being subsumed by Soccer Australia's politics, financial woes and mismanagement.[49]

The ACT government eventually provided the $200,000 to see Canberra United through the 2024/25 season, but made it clear it was a one-off payment and a long-term solution needed to be found.[50] The scenario raises again the question of bundling versus unbundling of women's A-League clubs from men's, especially in light of the growth of women's football and the increasing appetite for investing in women's clubs as standalone ventures, as we've seen with Angel City and San Diego Wave.[51] (See, you know, the other sections that discuss how refreshing it was to attend matches without toxicity, gambling and violence.)

It's not just funding. A related measure to ensure the safety and sustainability of the game is the urgent and ongoing need to address the ACL epidemic that plagues women's football.[52] Fundamental to that is the need for women-specific research, given that most scientific research concentrates on men and simply 'adds in' women after that.[53] For instance, only recently have researchers begun to consider if there's any correlation between the type of bra worn and ACL injury. (Early indications are yes.)[54] Incredibly, testing menstrual products with real blood has only occurred since 2023.[55] (Not dissimilarly, white shorts are not yet entirely obsolete, and the Matildas' kit has also only in recent years had period-proofing technology built in.[56])

Thankfully, FIFPRO has launched the three-year, women-specific Project ACL. Player travel time and intensity and other conditions and environmental factors will be under the microscope as the project seeks to understand the entwined elements and mitigate ACL injuries. Load, particularly, is an emerging issue as the calendar is becoming more congested by the day. Watch this space as the congestion is increasingly contested as player safety needs to be balanced with profits.[57] (The slightly perverse upside Psaltis points out is that because we've fallen in love with the players, we're more attuned and affected when they are injured. This greater scrutiny may apply increased pressure to federations, funders and researchers to address the widespread issue.)

Concussion, too, is an escalating issue as the game speeds up, more people are playing, and our understanding improves of the injury's vast and long-term effects. Matildas goalkeeper Teagan Micah suffered a pre–Women's World Cup concussion via a boot-to-face connection that left her with symptoms so acute she was out of the game for six months.[58] Grassroots teams are even less well equipped to spot and address such injuries. National Premier League Women's (NPLW) goalkeeper Noran Buttle, for example, had to medically retire from the game and reduce and then cease work after three poorly diagnosed and managed concussions sustained in short succession left her with post-concussion syndrome.[59] The syndrome is a long-term health challenge that includes vision issues and debilitating headaches and migraines.

Less obviously, but increasingly pressingly, climate change is looming as an issue as the nature of footballers' work means they are at greater risk of exposure to, and injury from, for example, more volatile weather and heatwaves.[60] The 2032 Olympics host, Queensland, is not only hot and humid but also the most disaster-prone state in the country;[61] people, animal and property damage and trauma aside, floods or fires wouldn't make for a good showing.

Also unresolved but urgent is the need to establish a sensible, sensitive way to facilitate playing opportunities for transgender athletes, which has traditionally been positioned as the tired 'inclusion versus fairness' trope in and around women's sports.[62] (Is there anything more starkly at odds with the radical possibilities the Women's World Cup demonstrated than the ongoing transphobia permeating our culture and media?) Former Western Australian Cricket Association CEO Christina Matthews has judiciously recommended saving women's sport by investing in it, not scoring political points at trans athletes' expense.[63]

But deep breaths. Concentrating on the never-done nature of the advancement of women's football is to do a disservice to the incredible gains and glimpse of a possible future the Matildas and the Women's World Cup brought us.

Moya Dodd once said that trying to stop women from playing football is like trying to defy gravity.[64] In 2023, we witnessed what working *with* rather than *against* gravity could entail. The Matildas and the Women's World Cup previewed a world where there are no grass ceilings holding women's sports back—the quality of play, the ticket and merchandise sales, and the broadcast figures are now undoubtedly, point-at-ably there once you give women proper access to resources. They've also moved the conversation and planning from being focused on trying to demonstrate value and justify funding and focus and mere existence in the space, to expansive possibilities.

Pointing to the phenomena that were Taylor Swift, the Women's World Cup and *Barbie* as well as women's estimated $128 billion of untapped potential because women are, for such reasons as lack of affordable childcare, prevented from working to their full potential, Angela Priestley of *Women's Agenda* surmised that if a relatively small segment of women can so significantly boost the (apparently all-important) economy, imagine what fiscal and other benefits removing the barriers hampering millions of women could do.[65] Anyone who's been in and around women's sports and has experienced the full force of being worked *against* rather than *with* probably felt that in their bones. As recently as May 2024, 89 per cent of women working in football reported experiencing gender-based discrimination, and of those who reported discrimination, more than 60 per cent said no meaningful action had been taken as a result.[66] Indeed, Future Women posted a meme riffing on the famous Victoria and David Beckham 'Rolls Royce' scene from the *Beckham* documentary series.[67] The meme opens with Victoria stating, 'Gender equality already exists.' David interjects with 'Be honest' and she responds with 'I *am* being honest.' His reply: 'What do we call a professionally ambitious woman?' 'Bossy.' 'Thank you.'[68]

And so, with grass ceilings not made entirely obsolete but at least impressively thinned out as the Matildas and their peers continue to shore up their conditions and commercial outcomes, we can turn our attention with renewed energy to tackling the other big-ticket elephant in the room: glass ceilings and their accompanying problematic cousins, glass cliffs. Progress is, as ever and please excuse the unintended pun, glacial. There's mandated parity at the Football Australia board level thanks to the 2018 constitutional reform that enshrined 40:40:20 (that is, members comprising 40 per cent men, 40 per cent women, and 20 per cent of any gender),[69] and former sex discrimination commissioner and Women's World Cup ambassador Kate Jenkins has been named Australian Sports Commission chair.[70] But they're outlier highlights. For the most part, women are under-represented above middle management. We're yet to consistently see women appointed to head coach and other authoritative, decision-making senior administration roles. So there have been few women at the apex of the pinnacle parts steering the women's game.

Encouragingly, the absence of women in principal decision-making and governance positions seems to be on the radar and a focus of Football Australia's not-yet-done list. As Filopoulos says to me towards the end of our interview, '"No glass ceilings" is where [we're going] next.'

16

THE PAST, FUTURE AND PATRIARCHY

DAYS BEFORE THE Australia v France quarter-final in Brisbane, Melbourne-based Tal Karp phoned fellow Melbourne-based alumna Shona Bass and asked if she was going to the game. Bass's response was no, she couldn't afford it. Karp issued a cryptic question: 'If I could get you to the game, would you come?'

Karp, then CEO of Y Australia (formerly known as the YMCA), had been double-booked. Her day job required her to run a forum for the Y's national movement; her alumni allegiances pulled her towards supporting the Matildas. She instinctively knew she needed to be there in person—watching on TV wouldn't be the same—but she was not going to be able to finish one gig in time to fly up to attend the other. 'There was no way I was going to get to Brisbane in time,' Karp tells me. 'I had to see that game. It was such a critical moment for the Matildas. But I didn't know how I was going to be able to keep my day job and get to the match.'

Karp happened to mention the conundrum to Malcolm Sharp, whom she bumped into one morning while buying a coffee. Sharp asked her if she was going to the game, and Karp mentioned her disappointment. To her shock, Sharp—who turned out to own an aviation company—later texted Karp with an impossibly generous offer: to fly her to Brisbane on a private plane once her day-job forum was finished. The quid pro quo was a Matildas scarf and a ticket to the sold-out game.

'I obviously said, "That's beyond crazy. There's no way in hell that I can accept something like that,"' Karp says. She was profusely grateful for the offer, but it was too lavish, and it felt very uncomfortable. She had necessarily lived so lean when she was a Matilda, moving out of her rental accommodation each time she travelled overseas for tournaments, boxing up her possessions and leaving them in friends' garages to save on rent when she was away with the team. This kind of offer was in a realm completely at odds with her prior experience or comfort level. 'But after a few attempts to reject the offer, the discussion turned into how we could create an opportunity to support Matildas Alumni who couldn't otherwise afford to get to the game,' she says.

Karp contacted all of the other Melbourne-based alumni, one of whom was Bass. The incredulous Bass said, 'Seriously?' and Karp said, 'So are you in?' Scarcely believing it would materialise, Bass said yes and duly followed the instructions to turn up at Essendon Fields airport. Sure enough, there was a private plane there for alumni Karp, Bass and Selin Kuralay, and Young Matildas physiotherapist Belinda Pacella. Moments after her forum finished Karp traversed the short walking distance from the Y Australia office to the airstrip, and the four women joined Sharp on the plane. As Karp describes, 'It was an epic trip', a moment when 'your wildest imagination becomes reality', and one that the four, and Sharp, won't soon forget.

★ ★ ★

Private jets might be an outlier, but it's such experiences and stories that illustrate just how fundamentally public perception and recognition shifted throughout those few weeks in July and August 2023. They illustrate, too, how alumni—the women who pioneered this, who made those crucial first forays into splintering grass and glass ceilings—began to see themselves and their contributions. And so, it's worth finishing where we started: juxtaposing the tournament with the experiences of the alumni.

As the Women's World Cup unfolded, interview requests for alumni and pioneering administrators came in thick and fast. (Heather Reid, for example, completed some twenty-two interviews over the course of the month and recommended other alumni and administrators for many more.) The alumni had a common shared goal through those interviews, of course: promoting women's football and the Matildas.

As the inaugural Matildas captain and one of the better-known alumni, Julie Dolan was perhaps one of the greatest in demand. She didn't find it burdensome (although she did chuckle that she can no longer rock up to airports without having at least done her hair, because people now tend to recognise and come talk to her), but did find the newfound interest a little surprising after forty-something years of relative radio silence. She acknowledges that it was at times difficult to keep up with the demand. 'I tried to do it all, because no one had ever asked questions before,' she explains. 'Finally, women's football was on the map.'

Karen Menzies was another alumna who was regularly contacted. She begins our interview by humbly saying that although she was in the team, she by no means considers herself one of the greats of the era. But she is aware that her story as the first Aboriginal Matilda, and one for whom football was an escape from removal and institutionalisation as a member of the Stolen Generations, is intriguing to domestic and international media. She hopes, too, that it is helpful for people from marginalised communities who may hear it and are able to take away useful elements.

'People actually wanted to know our story,' Janine McPhee says. It was a novel experience and one that positively influenced the alumni's own perceptions and involvement. McPhee notes that when her generation played, the team wasn't even called the Matildas. It was—among other patronising names, such as the Soccerettes and the Lady Socceroos, that were bandied about back in the day—known as the less colourful but somewhat-of-a-mouthful Australian Women's Soccer Team. '[Prior to the tournament] a lot of players actually didn't feel like they were part of the history of the game,' McPhee says. 'They didn't feel like they'd left a legacy, and they didn't feel respected.' That altered somewhat over the course of the tournament, including for some players who may have previously felt on the periphery.

'Our policy at the PFA has always been to be as inclusive as possible,' Rita Mankowska says of the organisation's efforts to show players how much they and their contributions matter. 'We don't mind if you have one cap or a hundred, if you are a 78er or on the honour roll. If you are a past player, then you matter, you are important, and you should be celebrated and supported. We hope that this philosophy helped to remind the alumni of their value.' With the significant exception of Elaine Watson, the inaugural matriarch of women's football in Australia, who passed away mere weeks before the tournament kicked off, most of the women who started on this road are, fortunately, still around to experience this important cultural shift.

'It was just unbelievable. [We went] from being invisible to visible. It was the most bizarre thing,' Bass says. She exemplifies that with a story about wearing a shirt inscribed with 'Matildas Alumni': 'I was wearing it on public transport and people were coming up and chatting to me about the game and asking me if I was a Matilda. This time last year, I could have worn that T-shirt and no one would have said anything to me.'

The alumni hoodies particularly contributed to that visibility and warm public reception. Alumni such as Carol Vinson and Renaye Iserief road-tripped their way up and down the east coast for the group-stage games, and the hoodies were a staple part of their travel outfits. 'We were constantly stopped in the street by people asking what it was like to be a former player and wanting photos with us,' Vinson says. Jo Powell reports similarly: 'Obviously, we would wear those to the games and on public transport regardless of where we were. We would jump on a train and not so much the really young generation but the parents of those kids were like, "Hey, do you realise that this person here is a previous Matilda?"'

Sue Read's experiences mirror this. It recently took her a while to figure out why people at the gym kept saying hello. She later realised she'd thrown on her Matildas Alumni hoodie before walking out the door to her early-morning training. The warm reception might have been enhanced by the fact that the Canberra-based former Matilda, who has short blonde hair, is often mistaken for current Matilda Michelle Heyman. 'I don't know why, because I think we look completely different,' she says. Fascinatingly, Read recently became the frontwoman for the effort to save Heyman's imperilled Canberra United.

The recognition continues. Bass recalls another experience where she was heading out with friends and was giving one of them a lift. Said friend asked Bass if she could spare five minutes to pop into the friend's place when she arrived to pick her up. Bass agreed and was greeted by a group of eight-year-old girls outside the house:

> There's a huge piece of cardboard about two metres by two metres stuck on the fence [illustrated with] soccer balls and my name … These little girls had done all these things and were just so excited to meet me. And it's like: *Go figure. Who would have thought?* So I got out and had my photo with them and went into the backyard and had a kick with them in my going-out shoes.

Whomever you talk to, their marvel at the recognition and reconnection is apparent. McPhee says:

> To have that pre-game tournament reunion, when everyone was in the same room—it was probably 150 alumni in that room—was something special. There were tears shed, a lot of laughter, a lot of banter. Just being able to reconnect with old teammates you hadn't seen for that long was such a special feeling.

Having not kept in touch with anyone in the interceding years, Menzies was worried the alumni events might be a little like awkward school reunions. Fortunately, her wife encouraged her to attend, cautioning that she would regret it if she didn't. 'Of course, I went, and I had the most sensational time,' Menzies says. Jane Oakley agrees:

> Catching up with the alumni was such a positive experience, reflecting a little on the past, but more so we were all taken by the level of public support and diversity. (One comment that worked its way around the alumni very quickly was that a young boy had been overheard asking his mum whether there was a boy's/men's Matildas.) The alumni were just overjoyed to see how far women's football has come. The current and future Matildas have a gift awaiting them, which is the ability to reconnect through the alumni program—it's so special. Even though we don't see each other a lot, there's an undeniable bond. For some of us, it's been a long time since pulling on the green and gold, but during the World Cup [and the recent Olympic qualifiers] many stories were shared, which takes you back to what was a magical time in your life.

Ellen Beaumont's experience is an example of that reconnection and that cross-generational recognition. As someone who played in the early 2000s, she's seen the middle parts of the Matildas' history, and she says that 'meeting Matildas who had played in the 70s, 80s and even 90s was a great history lesson' for her. She only knew players from her era, so learned firsthand from pioneering players whose experiences had involved different but relatable challenges and yielded new perspectives, such as having to decide between football work and paid work, couch-surfing to save money, completing individual training programs alone, and never or rarely meeting as a team before games. Beaumont continues:

> Other stories we heard were of how difficult communication was back then. There were no emails or mobile phones—past players had to wait for a letter in the mail to see if they'd got the call-up to the team. I realised how many things I took for granted as a Matilda. Even during my playing days, we didn't have to pay for our expenses and logistically we met frequently to train at the AIS ... Past players didn't have our luxury.
>
> What I reflect on, and what I saw were recurring themes for every decade of Matildas, is that every player made personal

> sacrifices, every player did it because they loved to play for Australia, no one complained, and each decade it got that bit easier for the Matildas as development of the structure and environment they played in also improved—equipment, jerseys, training, travel, communication, level of opposition—essentially from amateur to professional.
>
> It really made me feel part of the Matildas family again. After retiring over ten years ago, time has gone on and life has changed, but this provided a reminder of my playing days and how fantastic it was to be a Matilda—how much fun we had with each other, how much hard work, training and dedication we all put in towards a collective goal. I was so proud to be a Matilda. I even delayed getting a [new] job so I could take a month off and go to all the 2023 World Cup games.

Beaumont has subsequently inked a permanent reminder of the experience with a tattoo of a magpie wearing a Matildas beanie. More widely, the tournament enabled her to 'sneak in' a whole new wardrobe of football jerseys. She now has Steph Catley, Christine Sinclair and Marta jerseys, as well as ones for Germany, Jamaica and Japan: 'I felt like a kid in a candy shop, and my twelve-year-old self who only ever wore football jerseys came out!'

The convergence and catch-ups were arguably especially important to players hailing from regional areas who might not often cross paths with other past players. That includes Amanda George, who was the only player from the Northern Territory in the 1987 Taiwan tournament team:

> I last saw the others in 1989, when I played my last nationals tournament. It was quite hard to recognise most of them. It was also great to meet players from other eras. We all got on as if we were family. Sitting with everyone watching the game was awesome—lots of chatter and cheering. It was the first time we had been together as a whole of the past Matildas. I loved every minute of it. I have many new friends that I would never have

made if not for the tournament. We all look forward to catching up at Matildas games, and regularly correspond in between.

Alumni are also increasingly being officially recognised, including those who may not have played A Internationals or ever received caps. Since 2018, steward of the game Heather Reid, along with alumni such as Iserief and McPhee, have worked to identify, locate and contact more than forty players who never received their caps. This process has facilitated recognition for players in the first named Australian team from 1978, as well as others who played in non–A International games. George received her cap at the 2024 Olympic qualifier in Melbourne, thirty-seven years after her 1978 appearance. Monika Werner was similarly capped recently. She played in 1978, the year before the first official A International, and says, 'It was truly amazing to be acknowledged in front of a crowd of 54,000 people. The atmosphere was incredible. Given that we played in front of crowds of around a hundred back in my day, it was truly wondrous.' She says she's currently the most famous person in her hometown, with radio stations and newspapers interviewing her and the local pub installing her as its patron.

'It's pretty funny, because it's not something we expected,' Powell says of the recognition of the alumni's trailblazing ways. 'In our day, we just did it because we wanted to play. We didn't expect to be the pioneers of anything. So it's pretty amazing. I mean, you don't generally expect to see anything in your lifetime.'

Powell's story might be new to the general public (and she, along with Read, was only officially presented her cap in 2024), but she acknowledges that it has taken on new resonance in her hometown of Grafton: 'Everybody who has seen my journey probably realises what it was about now.' (Ash Sykes, now a commentator, had an equivalent experience. She worked in administration at a law firm to fund her football career, and received a message from some former co-workers during the Women's World Cup asking if this was the team she used to play for. 'Yes,' she responded, 'but not in front of nearly so many people.')

Powell's playing career involved mind-bogglingly long commutes. Every Friday afternoon for a year, she drove six hours from Grafton to Newcastle to play football, stopping to pick up other players on the way. At the time she thought nothing of it: 'I would finish work at 4.30 p.m., jump in my car, and head straight to Newcastle and pick the players up.' The return trip was equally arduous: 'If we played in Sydney on a Sunday, I wouldn't get back to Grafton until after 2 a.m. Then I'd kick off work at eight o'clock on Monday morning and do it all again every week.'

The years prior to that involved less distance but just as much complexity. The absence of a girls' team meant Powell played with the boys in both primary and secondary school. The teams had to write to their football federation to obtain permission for Powell to play in the boys' competition, and each and every game the coach had to advise the opposition that there was a girl playing. The lack of visibility of women's football also meant Powell was entirely unaware there was a women's national football team: 'No idea whatsoever. So it's great. Now at least we can move forward at a faster rate, because people are very aware of who the team is and what they're about.'

That's something Beaumont comments on, too. She was invited to speak at a FIFA fan site during the tournament: 'I am glad it was dark, because the park in Sydney was full of thousands of people. But speaking on behalf of the Matildas was an especially proud moment for me, because I could see how much we've grown as a profession and become a household name.' She contrasts the team's anonymity when she played with its contemporary brand recognition and ubiquity: 'Matildas posters are on bus stops now.'

★ ★ ★

Of course there is, as always, room for improvement. Alumni communication and involvement over time has been patchy, including for players from the smaller states, which have fewer alumni and therefore fewer opportunities and networks with which to connect. While social media has no doubt made things easier, being able to locate and connect with players from the early years due to changed addresses or changed names has posed challenges. South Australian Carla Grims, for example, found out late about alumni inclusion in the World Cup and was only able to attend the final in Sydney. (Equally saddening is that the alumni ticketing and events does not, at the time of writing, extend to key coaches and administrators. Without their integral logistical and advocacy contributions, none of the Matildas' success to date would have been possible. This oversight is hurtful and needs to be rectified.)

Grims is typical of the alumni experience. She came to the game courtesy of a father who was a referee and a boys' team that was short of players and needed her to fill in to complete it. She progressed from that under-13s entrance all the way through to the squad that played the Matildas' first A International match in 1979, but only received her cap a few years ago. That cap is so meaningful that Grims has had it framed and her granddaughter has asked if she might inherit it one day. Grims' entire family is incredibly proud of her football achievements. That includes her father. 'I didn't find out until he passed away,' she says, 'but he had all these newspaper clippings of me. He never showed emotion, but it turns out he kept all these clippings. He would have been so proud when I got my cap.' (At the same time, Grims is acutely aware that players such as Fiona McKenzie passed away before receiving theirs.)

Grims' home contains photos and other mementos of her playing time, and she has had her name and her cap number embroidered on the alumni hoodie she was given during the tournament. That identifying hoodie contributed to one of her favourite moments: a young girl, aged about twelve, recognised it and raced up to her with her *Encyclopedia of Matildas*. Grims and her peers signed the book next to their names, cap numbers and stats.

Although she notes that it was disappointing for the alumni to not have been introduced to the current and emerging Matildas generations (that's not a misplaced sentiment—if Football Australia could invite Cathy Freeman in for an inspiring meet-and-greet with the team, they could invite alumni for an equivalent), Grims made the most of her trip to Sydney. While there, she participated in a five-on-five alumni match in her characteristic goalkeeping position. 'I can't remember who kicked the ball, but I actually dived for it. I don't know how I did that. I'm sixty-three years old!' she says. Three-day post-match soreness aside, Grims was impressed at her instinctive reaction. She's come full circle, too, having been asked to attend the South Australian grassroots club where it all started for her to present the emerging generation with their new jerseys.

'We held a combination of pre-match functions, five-versus-five matches, and a past-player health day over the World Cup period. I had no idea if the five-versus-five would be of interest to anyone, but it turned out to be a hit. One thing is for sure, the players still have talent,' Mankowska says. (The alumni facilitated a BBC reporter filming taking a penalty in that game to emulate the experience for viewers at home. Thinking the reporter was filming segments for later editing, Beaumont's impromptu idea was to have the alumni rush over and embrace her in the celebration afterwards. It was only later that they realised that the match and their actions had been live-streamed to millions.)

Entwined with the reconnection, the tournament involved a fair amount of debriefing. It was ultimately a 'massively positive experience', Read says. But she also acknowledges that if Tracey Holmes hadn't investigated and pursued the exclusion story and if the alumni hadn't gathered as a group, it could have been very different.

★ ★ ★

Analogous to many of her peers and predecessors, Read recalls the fundraising efforts they had to undertake to pay for their representative careers. One that will make your heart ache involved players having to wash car windscreens in their sports bras at traffic lights. Something Read acutely appreciates is that her parents worked multiple jobs to fund her sporting endeavours. There were also bake sales, raffles and fundraising chocolates. 'My family must have eaten 8000 chocolates,' she recalls with a laugh. (Tangentially related, in 2024 Sue Monteath, for whom fundraising was similarly fundamental to her career in the 1980s, helped out selling raffle tickets for a local charity. Muscle memory kicked in. The person she was selling tickets with assumed it was her first time and complimented her on her proclivity for it. She thought to herself, *Oh, mate, you have no idea.*)

Read is cognisant of the extended impact when a player's career doesn't materialise in the way they hope it will: it affects the entire family, who have usually also been contributing, investing and making sacrifices. One example is involuntary retirement through injury: 'Many of us had major injuries, and it felt like there was no support. Once an injury happened back then, it felt like, "OK, bye", and you felt totally alone. There really wasn't any support.' As she notes:

> You're part of everything one day, and the next day you haven't heard from anyone. There wasn't the wraparound support of physios and ongoing medical treatment that might exist today. It was just left to your family or yourself to try to work and pay for all the ongoing medical expenses.

The lack of closure many experienced with their careers ending suddenly through omission or injury left its mark. Unsurprisingly, such elements surfaced as the tournament progressed. Read says:

> By the second time we caught up I was thinking, *I feel like my new specialty is sports trauma counselling*. There was so much debriefing and sharing of our collective experiences. It was sad, but also really connecting to know that it wasn't just me, or any one of us. There was some comfort that came through our shared experiences.

She notes, too, that:

> [perhaps] the ones who had the most pain were those who may have been involved for so long, and did all the training and national camps, but didn't always get the opportunity to perform in the tournaments that we felt we should have, either from injury or not being selected. Often, the way things ended was also particularly painful—for example, not being selected but having absolutely no further contact or explanation from the coach.

Speaking only for herself, Powell sums up the swirl of bittersweet pride the tournament prompted. Her playing experience involved being selected for the squad to train for the 2000 Olympics. The issue was that there were a limited number of full scholarships, and she wasn't one of the recipients. 'I'd already relocated to Newcastle [from Grafton], so I had a rental property and a job and everything there.' She would have had to relocate a second time and incur additional expenses. 'I couldn't afford to do it. For me, that was the ending point, which, I mean, it was my decision ...' Well, it was and it wasn't. 'I feel a bit disappointed,' she concedes, but immediately points out the upside: current and future generations are better remunerated and less likely to face such difficult choices.

So was the tournament healing for the alumni? Read thinks and hopes mostly so:

> I thought a lot of my bad experiences were very personal to me, but then other people were going 'I didn't make the Olympics either' or 'I got cut from the team with no explanation' or 'I snapped my knee and my shin and never heard from anyone again'. I think having the chance to connect on all those similar experiences really validated the emotions and challenges we had gone through. It feels healing, it takes away some of that isolation. It's a key part of trauma recovery, reconnection.
>
> I know for me, part of the damage had been thinking and ruminating over *What was wrong with me? What if I should have been there, but I wasn't?* Or those regretful thoughts of 'if only': *If this hadn't happened, that could have been.* But then you're like, *Oh my god, you have the same story.* And another person and another person has the same story. There were also some really high-profile players that I didn't know had had similarly challenging experiences. I think that was really, really healing.
>
> It's not good that we all had those experiences, but it stopped it feeling so personal. If we hadn't had a connected alumni group that was recognised and had regular pre- and post-functions, then it would have been a vastly different experience. Further to this, the fact that this current crop of Matildas have done so

> well, and did so well at the World Cup, has reflected so positively on the whole alumni and elevated our profile and connection immensely. That has been powerfully healing, so we have a lot to thank the current group for as well.

★ ★ ★

That restorative, regenerative element, that Matilda connection, and that galvanising aspect of football is perhaps no more evident than in Sally Shipard's story.

After her 2014 retirement, Shipard stepped back from football. 'I had to detach myself from the game to figure out who I was beyond it,' she explains. It wasn't deliberate distancing—more a necessary exploration of her next life and career phase. About the time Australia was announced as Women's World Cup bid co-host, she felt pulled back to the game. But life threw her a curveball: while undergoing IVF, she was diagnosed with a mucinous adenocarcinoma, a rare type of ovarian cancer.

Post-diagnosis and mid-treatment were full of uncertainty, but the football community rallied around Shipard. 'The support was huge,' she says. Former Matildas teammate Alicia Ferguson, with Shipard's permission, set up a GoFundMe campaign to provide a financial buffer while Shipard was recuperating after surgery. 'I'm lost for words. Every time I think back … I was in ICU following the surgery and the amount of pain I was in … but [I had] just the tiniest glint of a smile every time someone read out the name of someone having made [a donation]. It didn't have to be a big donation. It wasn't about the money. It felt much bigger than that.'

Shipard's partner, April Davis, had never known her as a footballer, so this purview was touching and new. The Women's World Cup timing in some ways also proved propitious. Shipard and Davis were housesitting Davis's parents' house in Geelong while Shipard's body knitted itself back together. Unlike their home, that house contained a TV, so Shipard rested in front of it and tried to take in as many games as she could. She also attended a couple of the Matildas matches and the alumni events held before them. She found the intergenerational catch-ups compelling, and gained new appreciation for the hallowed history of which she is part:

> I was just as happy to sit down with a Matilda who made her debut back in the 90s and only played once as I would have been Sam Kerr. I think everyone's got such an interesting story. By getting together with the Matildas Alumni group, you have that opportunity. Gosh, you'd almost need an hour with every single individual to truly get your fix. But even just being able to glance at someone or acknowledge them in some way and have everyone in the same room was pretty special.

She says she knows the current generation recognises that there's a history before them: 'To be a part of that history is a pretty incredible feeling.'

There were additional unexpected aspects that were equally powerful. 'Since finishing football, I've been surrounded by people who aren't elite athletes, who show little to no interest in elite sport,' Shipard says. What impressed her most during the World Cup was the Matildas' capacity to reach and inspire people for whom football would not normally have been on their bingo card. She gives an example close to her: her partner's sister Bree has never had much confidence in moving her body on a football field; nor is she comfortable running. Witnessing the Matildas play so confidently against Canada prompted important discussions around sport, body image and self-esteem. Neither April nor Bree had ever played football, so Shipard gently suggested they go to the park for a kick—low stakes, purely to move and feel good. That kick, buoyed by the wider motivating tournament conditions, was so metamorphic that the three have set up a walking football group[1] called Get Your Kicks in their small town, Candelo, on the New South Wales south coast. (They're in good historic company. Through later research, Shipard realised that the town was one of the first to field a women's football team, as far back as 1908.[2])

Get Your Kicks has a dual meaning: it's an invitation to people both to grab their shoes and to come kick with other members for pure pleasure. The group meets every second Sunday and its low-speed, low-fi mode is perfect for beginners and former pros alike. Alluding to the fact that walking is the great leveller, the group's motto is 'There's strength in restraint'.

Get Your Kicks' unofficial ambassadors are Katrina Gorry and Michelle Heyman. Recognising the importance of such a grass-roots initiative, the two took time out of their training and playing schedules to record videos introducing themselves. 'It's been a hoot. Everyone's just head over heels for them,' Shipard laughs. The group members were, for instance, completely invested in Gorry's pre–2024 Olympics ankle injury. It continues. The set-up is informal, with water bottles doubling as demarcations for goals. The goalie's nickname is Rae 'Foam Wall' Kennedy, a nod to Mackenzie Arnold's 'Brick Wall' moniker. 'She spends the entire time standing between the drink bottles, which are our goals, calling everyone after all the famous players she can remember from the World Cup,' Shipard says.

Such levity belies the group's serious mission: prioritising enjoyment over competition to help counter the unsupportive environments and negative outcomes many women and gender-diverse people have experienced in and around sport—the kinds of experiences that have led to reduced engagement in physical activity. The group itself, which encompasses one of the greats of the contemporary women's game and women who have found new or renewed pathways to the game, is representative of the grassroots-to-elite effect the Matildas have had Australia-wide.

⋆ ⋆ ⋆

Sports administrator Eugénie Buckley elected to take her young daughters to the Australia v England semi-final—as in the sold-out game that represented the most sought-after tickets in the country at the time. 'I thought that would be life-changing for them because it was life-changing for me. Like, [75,000] people ...' Buckley explains, adding, 'My wife's English, so I made sure they had the Australian kit on.' The match didn't go Australia's way, of course, but the experience itself was seminal. Wholly expecting responses that referenced the record crowd numbers, the players' athleticism and the euphoria around Sam Kerr's goal, Buckley later asked her daughters to nominate their favourite part of the experience. 'The seven-year-old was like: "Oh, the hot chips",' says Buckley. Having spent decades trying to carve out space for women athletes and administrators in male-dominated sporting environments with baked-in, men-centric inequity, Buckley could scarcely believe what she'd heard. 'Like, what?! You don't understand how many people wanted those tickets!' she recounts, laughing. 'Then I was reflecting: You know what, it's a good thing that my daughter didn't notice how amazing it was—because for her, it's just what happened. They're used to watching women's sports [in full stadiums]. She's lucky, right?'

Those deep-fried potato snacks are certainly indicative of the focus-flipping masterstroke the tournament provided. That marrying of the expected with the normalisation of the unexpected is what made it so awe-inspiring. Pair that with the ability to bridge the age and gender divide everywhere you looked, and there was a stunning confluence of past, future and patriarchy.

At first glance, there was the expected: parents took their young daughters to the games to show them wholesome, athletic role models, to ignite an idea of what was possible, and to enable them to be part of history. Sarah Styles was one of those parents: 'I had a ticket for my daughter and I, but when I bought them, I didn't appreciate that the game started at 8 p.m. She had just turned four.' Still, it was a one-time chance to create core memories, and well worth her daughter staying up past bedtime.

Girls likewise got the supporter memo and turned up to matches throughout the tournament with homemade, thoughtfully composed and decorated signs: Superheroes are real; Cortnee Divine; I'm going to be the next Sam Kerr; We are Kerr-ageous; Slaytildas; (later) Our Eras Tour: Tillies Version; I quit my job to be here.[3] Those alone would have been impressive, but the impact went deeper, wider—as McPhee identified, it got into people's DNA. Primary-school students of all genders dressed up as Matildas for the day of the semi-final. Matildas jerseys and Sam Kerr, Lydia Williams and

Hayley Raso books and jerseys later dotted Book Week parades. There were mischievous calls for a petition to rename the men's team 'ManTildas'.[4] Men bought black gloves to emulate Mary Fowler. Suburban street signs were temporarily amended to Caitlin Foord Avenue and Mackenzie Arnold Court. On Caxton Street, a normally hypermasculine environment during men's sporting events, a six-foot-tall cisgendered man navigated the crowd while wearing Raso ribbons affixed to tiny pigtails gathered from his short-back-and-sides hair. Older men gambolled over to chat to Tracey Holmes outside the stadiums. Holmes believes they sought her out 'because I've been around for so long, and they felt like I was as old as them,' she laughs. Regardless, 'So many of them said, "I prefer watching women's football now."'

Kim Anderson, too, points to how that inter-gender shift was genuine:

> I think for me personally having a lot of my male friends who are in their forties call and ask me for tickets or access to tickets to go with their male mates—not just their daughters because that was the right thing to do—I think that felt like a real step-change for me, someone who's had an on-and-off twenty-year career in sport. That is a very different conversation to be having when probably the last time they asked me for tickets was to an Ashes [men's game] or whatnot. They were hungry for those tickets.

Converting grown men is fantastic. There's no doubt that 'as the fathers of daughters' their conversion will go some way to improving attitudes towards girls and women trying to enter or operate in the otherwise built-by-men-for-men sporting space. Putting aside for a moment the nagging sense of wondering why our centre of gravity and value-determination always has to come back to boys and men, it's that perception-shifting next-generation normalisation that is most stunning. That's what is inspiring some seriously expansive thinking.

Ann Odong anticipated early the budding patriarchy-nudging potential the team and tournament represented:

> When I first said it to people I said, 'I'm aware that it sounds lofty, but stay with me. We can change society, we can transform society. Because if little boys can see the Matildas and their strength and their athleticism and their humanity and them displaying love and emotion in a sporting context and they become their heroes, that's going to change how they see their little sister, their aunty, their grandmother, the little girl next to them at school. That's going to change how they see women in their lives, and that's going to change society, eventually.'

'Eventually' is coming sooner than expected. Odong references a mum showing her images of her ten-year-old son's bedroom: 'It [had] Matildas posters all through it and he was reading *What Makes a Matilda?*' She had seen similar signs earlier. Activity in the digital realm had been steadily, organically building in the tournament lead-up through fans repurposing and reimagining Matildas images and videos to create TikTok and Instagram content. They were digital versions of what Odong recalls making as a fan of boy bands when she was in her early teens: 'I used to cut out photos of the Backstreet Boys from *TV Hits* magazine, or photos of NSYNC from *Smash Hits*.' Witnessing this, she thought, *Oh, OK, I see what's happening here.*

The interest has sustained. At a press conference for the 2024 China friendlies, boys aged 10–12 crept closer and closer to the gathered media. 'Is that Charli [Grant]?' they eventually asked Odong. Once they'd excitedly obtained Grant's autograph—having volunteered their school uniforms, no less, given the impromptu nature of the encounter and having nothing else at hand—they literally skipped away down the hill.

Sarah Walsh says:

> The times when I get a bit emotional is when I receive what is probably the most common feedback I or the players hear. It's from a mum who will find out what I do, or I'm at an event speaking, and they literally come up—I've heard the players say this [too]—and thank you for showing their son that women can

> play. Their sons are now wearing Raso jerseys—they don't know the difference. This is our future generation of male leaders. Or the mums are saying, 'My girls can now connect with something, and I can connect with my family through sport for the first time.' So probably the biggest thing I'm touched by is what we've done to that next generation of kids, and that boys just won't see anything different. I do wonder how that will shape a young girl's experience now in a community football club.

Anderson echoes this society-shifting aspect: 'I think the next generation see things through less of a gender lens, which is fantastic.'

Journalist Eleni Psaltis is helping raise that next generation. Her son Alexis is two years old. Next door to the swimming pool she takes him to is a football pitch where a regular men's club football match was playing one day. 'It was a bunch of older men, and he pointed to them and yelled out "Matildas". I thought, *The myth's become true ... We joked about the Female Socceroos and the Soccerettes and the Soccertoos, but are we now getting close to the Male Matildas?*'

Two of Walsh's individual highlights involve her young daughter Tully. The day of the Harbour Bridge walk Tully was running up and down the car-free lanes, oblivious to both the auspicious occasion and the whipping winter wind. 'I remember she was only just getting her sea legs running, and she's running up the bridge. It's like, *It's never going to happen again*. I don't think she appreciates it yet,' Walsh says. But Tully in that moment and beyond is representative of what will be standard for the next generation. 'She thinks everyone who plays sport is a 'Tilda. So watching other sports after that, she's like, "'Tilda?" and we're like, "Ah, yeah. Men's rugby? Yeah, 'Tilda."'

It's not just the really young kids, either. Beaumont visited the school at which inaugural Matildas captain Julie Dolan works. A boy who was about eight years old approached her and said without context: 'It's not fair.' Beaumont asked him what he meant, and he said, 'I want to be a Matilda.' 'I paused, had a chuckle to myself, and said, "Well, you have the Socceroos." But yeah, how the tables have turned. I did think, *Sucked in*, but I wasn't going to say that to a kid.'

Former Matilda Sonia Gegenhuber, now a primary school physical education teacher, is witnessing this intersectional adjustment in person in real time, too. Students had known she was a Matilda prior to the tournament but never made much of a connection to it. Girls in years 2 and 3 are now seeking her out to ask, 'Miss G, can you teach me to be a Matilda?' Boys also race up to her, saying, 'They're playing tonight. They're playing tonight.' These are the same girls who little more than a year ago would not have considered playing football; they're the same boys who dismissed girls' interest in the game and would only speak about and wear the jerseys of male footballers such as Messi.

One parent told Gegenhuber how her daughter had been inspired to switch from hockey to football: '[This wouldn't have happened] without incredible people like yourself, who paved the way. I know you may get this a lot—well, I hope you do. So thank you from one very out-of-my-depth new soccer mum and her very, very excited daughter.'

Indeed, the message of aspiring to be a professional footballer is landing for girls in ways it didn't prior to the tournament. Gegenhuber explains: 'I say to the girls all the time, "You can be one of these players." In the past, they were like, "Oh, yeah." Now, they're saying it back, and definitively: "I want to be a Matilda."'

Even better, they're focused on the team as a whole: 'They don't say they want to be Sam Kerr,' Gegenhuber notes. 'They want to be a Matilda.'

ACKNOWLEDGEMENTS

INFINITE THANKS MUST go to my parents, Jill and Alan, and my siblings, Weesie (Louise) and BC (Bryan), who are, as always, moral and tech support and the first and last readers of everything. As my father said on the day this content was commissioned, 'Congratulations. Now the stress begins.'

Michelle Gillett, Geoff Wilson, Claire Smiddy, Lise Schreiber, Ainslie Blunck, Clare Murphy, Julie Dalling, Elizabeth Livingstone, Grace Donaldson and Victoria McCreanor—as always, thank you. Your supportive pebbles, thoughtful suggestions and catch-ups are the absolute best.

Thank you to Melbourne University Publishing, especially Foong Ling Kong, Cathy Smith, Duncan Fardon, Daniel Chelchowski and Jackie Money, who were entirely on board with this project and the slightly impossible plan to complete it in record time. Thank you to my copyeditor, Katie Purvis, who again whipped my overlong but enthusiastic sentences into shape.

And, of course, my sincerest, deepest gratitude to every person who was interviewed for and/or gave feedback on this book, especially Heather Reid, Moya Dodd and Maria Berry, as well as other Matildas Alumni, administrators, fans, academics and media who make the wheels of the women's football world turn. Yours is, indeed, a history and a contribution that should never, ever be forgotten.

NOTES

Preface

1 John Lohn, 'When the backstroke went rogue: How underwater power changed the event', *Swimming World*, 16 May 2023.

2 Aimee Edwards, 'From Barbie to Taylor Swift: These were the top six cultural moments that shaped 2023', *B&T*, 23 November 2023.

3 See Isabel Allende, 'Foreword to the first edition', in John Roddan (ed.), *Conversations with Isabel Allende*, rev. edn, University of Texas Press, Austin, 2004.

1 Introduction: Something's Shifted

1 During the Women's World Cup, Heather Reid AM donated two historic items to the FIFA Museum: blazers that had been owned and worn by inaugural administrative matriarch Elaine Watson, one each from the Australian Women's Soccer Association and the Oceania Women's Football Confederation. Watson narrowly missed out on witnessing the tournament as she passed away just a month before it started. In addition, IDA Sports, a women-specific football-boot company founded in 2020 by Australians frustrated at the lack of women-specific sporting equipment, was invited to submit a pair of boots to the museum.

2 Gilbert Siahaan, Ashley Fell & Mark McCrindle, *Baby Names Australia Report 2023*, McCrindle Research, Norwest, NSW, 2023, pp. 8, 13; Laura Jackel, 'In the year 2028, kindergarteners will all be named Sam, Cortnee or Matilda', *Mamamia*, 18 August 2023.

2 100 Days, 25 Days, 20 Penalties

1 Zoe Samios, 'How women saved Australian soccer', *Australian Financial Review*, 20 June 2023.

2 Martin McKenzie-Murray, 'The Matildas' moment of truth', *Saturday Paper*, 29 July – 4 August 2023.

3 The use of 'alumni', rather than the feminine Latin form 'alumnae', is deliberate. It reflects increasingly common and more gender-neutral usage, is a term and a spelling people understand and are familiar with, and reflects language evolution. As was flagged, contemporary usage of the terms 'waiter' and 'host' encompass all genders now, and are more common and more appropriate than 'waitress' or 'hostess'.

4 *Women's Performance Gap: Building and Sustaining an Elite Matildas Team for 2023 and Beyond*, Football Australia, Sydney, 2020, pp. 7–11.

5 At the time of writing, contention remained about which team and which players comprised the first Matildas. While acknowledging that many women have made important contributions to the development of women's football in Australia, this book adheres to the original and established historical record that the first nationally selected team was the 1979 Matildas team. Further information about the issue can be found in such articles as Samantha Lewis's 'The "First Matildas"? Football Australia rewrites history with official caps for 1975 team', *ABC Sport*, 1 July 2024 and Kieran Yap's 'The Best of the Best: Matildas selection in the 70s', *Impetus Football*, 24 July 2024.

6 Ibid.

7 Isobel Cootes, '"We are not going to accept those offers": FIFA president Gianni Infantino rejects lowball Women's World Cup 2023 broadcast bids', *Optus Sport*, 25 October 2022; Tracey Holmes, 'FIFA condemns broadcasters and sponsors for not investing equivalent funds on Women's World Cup as men's event in Qatar', *ABC News*, 1 April 2023.

8 Suzanne Wrack, 'Fifa blocks rainbow armband and unveils Women's World Cup alternatives', *The Guardian*, 30 June 2023; Kieran Pender, 'Football Australia boss criticises Fifa ban on rainbow armbands at Women's World Cup', *The Guardian*, 17 July 2023.

9 Meg Linehan, 'Megan Rapinoe talks business of women's sports, the Caitlin Clark Effect, USWNT and more', *The Athletic*, 27 April 2024.

10 Emma Hruby, 'Ali Riley's World Cup Pride nails inspired mental health patient', *Just Women's Sports*, 17 August 2023.

11 Reuters/SBS, 'Brazil football team arrived in Australia with a tribute to Iran protesters', *SBS News*, 6 July 2023.

12 Kyra Sethna-McIntosh, 'Women's World Cup players launch football's biggest climate campaign', *The Guardian*, 12 July 2023.

13 Vince Rugari, 'Nike vs Puma: The ambush marketing campaign dividing the Matildas', *Sydney Morning Herald*, 19 July 2023. The 1975 team discussed in Rugari's article is the team Football Australia renamed as the First Matildas in 2024—a decision that was being contested at the time of writing. See note 5 above for further information about the history and controversy.

14 'Football Australia recognises achievements of former Australian Women's Representative players', Football Australia website, 18 May 2023.

3 The Calf That Stopped the Nation

1 For example, see Optus Sport [@OptusSport], '70% of the world is covered by water, the rest is Katrina Gorry …' [tweet], Twitter/X, 14 August 2023.

2 Amanda Meade, 'Channel Seven commentator under fire for comments on Matilda Katrina Gorry being a mother', *The Guardian*, 21 July 2023.

3 The Finkbeiner test is a tool for detecting and addressing gender bias when writing about women—for example, ensuring someone does not arbitrarily mention the subject's gender if it is not relevant. Or, in this context, not referencing tired tropes about motherhood.
4 re—inc [@re__inc], 'Almost late to the World Cup? Ali Riley, captain of the New Zealand national team and Angel City FC, told us a story …' [video], TikTok, 15 August 2023.
5 Jack Snape, 'Women's World Cup ticket sales break record with close to 1.4m sold on eve of 2023 tournament', *The Guardian*, 19 July 2023.

4 The Second Act

1 Sam Mewis, 'World Cup is an opportunity for exposure, but does it help in fight for fair treatment?', *The Athletic*, 23 July 2023.
2 The Big Bash [@bigbash], '"Nah stuff it, I'll still hit it" Grace Harris is pure comedy' [video], TikTok, 22 October 2023.
3 Joey Lynch, 'Gustavsson defends lack of rotations, Simon selection at WWC', *ESPN*, 19 August 2023.

5 The Comeback

1 Vince Rugari, 'Helicopter view: Gustavsson fears tactical leak as Matildas' interest goes sky-high', *Sydney Morning Herald*, 6 August 2023. Note that this is different from the drone spying scandal that would unfold during the 2024 Paris Olympics.
2 See also Fiona Crawford, 'From handing out their own flyers, to sell-out games: How the Matildas won over a nation', *The Conversation*, 11 August 2023.
3 See, for example, Dylan Caporn, 'Sam Kerr: Over five editions of *The West*, readers can piece together life sized portrait of Matildas superstar', *West Australian*, 26 October 2023.
4 Kieran Pender, 'Sam Kerr primed for World Cup clash with Denmark as Matildas play down "spying" on training', *The Guardian*, 7 August 2023.
5 Jonathan Yerushalmy, 'Commonwealth Games 2026: Why has Victoria pulled out and what happens now?', *The Guardian*, 18 July 2023.
6 'Matildas forced to wait as typhoon hits games', *The Age*, 20 September 2007.
7 Joey Lynch, 'Inside the furore over Melbourne's FIFA Women's World Cup 202 involvement', *Optus Sport*, 17 July 2023.
8 Emma Hruby, 'Canadian soccer players file $40 million lawsuit against Canada Soccer', *Just Women's Sports*, 22 February 2024.
9 At a panel discussion at Manly Writers' Festival, 16 March 2024. See 'Australia's Matildas: Their 50-year "overnight success" and what it means for the Australian sporting landscape', Manly Writers' Festival website, 2024.
10 US Women's National Soccer Team [@USWNT], 'Hope she unblocks us to see this' [tweet], Twitter/X, 21 October 2023.
11 Dan Colasimone, 'FIFA Women's World Cup updates: Brazil and Italy eliminated in day of upsets as France and Sweden show their class', *ABC News*, 2 August 2023.
12 Quoted in Isobel Cootes, '"Marta was who Sam Kerr is to the young girls and boys today"', *Optus Sport*, 3 August 2023.

6 More Than the Matildas

1 Australia's anti-siphoning media laws were designed to ensure events of national significance are available to all and not locked behind paywalls. For further information, see, for example, Daanyal Saeed, 'What are anti-siphoning laws? A Crikey clarifier', *Crikey*, 26 February 2024; Duncan Mackay, 'Anger in Australia as FIFA Women's World Cup set to disappear behind paywall', *Inside the Games*, 31 July 2023.

2 Madeleine Wedesweiler, 'Linda thought cancer ended her football dreams. Now she's a star of the Women's World Cup', *SBS News*, 31 July 2023.

3 See, for example, Fiona Crawford, 'From handing out their own flyers, to sell-out games: How the Matildas won over a nation', *The Conversation*, 11 August 2023.

4 '"Unity Beat" launched as FIFA Women's World Cup 2023™ celebrates 100 days to go', FIFA website, 11 April 2023.

5 Nick Perry & Jenna Fryer, 'Fatal shooting hours before the Women's World Cup began in New Zealand appears to be an isolated act', *AP News*, 20 July 2023.

6 Neil Johnston, 'Women's World Cup 2023: New Zealand players evacuate hotel after fire', *BBC Sport*, 23 July 2023.

7 Joshua Thomas, 'New Zealand city's hilarious "breakup" response after claims Spain team relocated due to boredom', *Optus Sport*, 30 July 2023.

8 Ibid.

9 Abby Halpin, 'Jamaica uses crowdfunding, focus to hit Women's World Cup high point against France', *AP News*, 24 July 2024.

10 Issy Ronald, Antonio Jarne & Krystina Shveda, 'Female soccer players earn 25 cents to the dollar of men at World Cup, new CNN analysis finds', *CNN Sports*, 20 July 2023.

11 Housnia Shams, 'Afghanistan women's national soccer team left to sit on the sidelines of World Cup', *ABC News*, 18 August 2023.

12 Ibid.

13 Joe Sommerlad, 'Meet Canada midfielder Quinn: The first trans player to feature at a World Cup', *The Independent*, 28 July 2024.

14 Brad Nash, '30-yard screamer gets Panama v France off to an incredible start', *Optus Sport*, 2 August 2023.

15 Amanda Shalala, Kate O'Halloran & Jon Healy, 'Five quick hits from Women's World Cup: Marta Cox scores a stunner, Brazil's Marta bows out, and South Africa rolls on', *ABC News*, 3 August 2023.

16 Samantha Lewis, 'Matildas to face world number 5 France in final friendly in Melbourne before 2023 Women's World Cup', *ABC News*, 28 February 2023.

17 Chloe Hart, 'Brazil's government changes work hours so fans can watch Women's World Cup in Australia', *ABC News*, 24 July 2023; Krysyan Edler, 'Brazil to host FIFA Women's World Cup nearly 50 years after repealing ban on women's sports', *Yahoo Sports*, 18 March 2024.

18 Courtney Hill, 'Nouhaila Benzina makes history in Morocco's first ever win at a Women's World Cup', Olympic Games website, 30 July 2023.

19 A safety hijab is affixed with velcro strips that come apart in the event the hijab is pulled. This prevents choking or garrotting or other injury. For more information, see, for example, Angelica Silva, 'Nouhaila Benzina is the first player to wear a hijab

at the Women's World Cup. Why were they once banned by FIFA?', *ABC News*, 25 July 2023.

20 Shireen Ahmed, 'Nouhaila Benzina and Morocco blazing a path of inclusion at Women's World Cup', *CBC Sports*, 24 July 2023.

21 Geneva Abdul, 'BBC apologises for LGBTQ+ question to Morocco's football captain', *The Guardian*, 26 July 2023.

22 Lucy Slade, 'Matildas create $7.6 billion economic boost for retail and travel industries', *9News*, 12 August 2023.

23 Brianna Boecker, 'Corporate partners should invest in women's elite sport: Research', *Women's Agenda*, 15 August 2023; *Change Our Game: The Value of You Can Be What You Can See: Addressing the Sponsorship Gap for Women's Elite Sport*, Victorian Government Office for Women in Sport and Recreation, Melbourne, 2023, p. 7.

24 'FIFA Fan Festival a first for FIFA Women's World Cup', FIFA website, n.d.

7 A Millimetre Matters

1 Isobel Cootes, 'Sam Kerr's slip against Denmark made Matildas coach Tony Gustavsson "very nervous"', *Optus Sport*, 8 August 2023.

2 Emily Keogh, 'USWNT drops to 5th in latest FIFA ranking, lowest place ever', *ESPN*, 14 June 2024.

3 Seth Vertelney, 'USWNT causes international incident by calling Melbourne "Melby"', *Pro Soccer Wire*, 5 August 2023.

4 Isobel Cootes, 'Alyssa Naeher "will go to her grave" claiming she saved Sweden's penalty', *Optus Sport*, 1 September 2023.

5 Fiona Crawford, *The Matilda Effect*, Melbourne University Press, Carlton, Vic., 2023, p. 2.

6 The Croissants [@croissants_on_tour], 'Melbourne' [story], Instagram, July 2023.

7 Meg Linehan, 'Megan Rapinoe's injury during NWSL Championship robs her of "perfect ending" with OL Reign', *The Athletic*, 12 November 2023.

8 Hunter Fujak, *Code Wars: The Battle for Fans, Dollars and Survival*, Fair Play Publishing, Balgowlah Heights, NSW, 2021, pp. 90–1.

9 Sarah Carrick, Alex Culvin & Ali Bowes, 'The butterfly effect? Title IX and the USWNT as catalysts for global equal pay', *Journal of Legal Aspects of Sport*, 31, 2021, pp. 289–311 (esp. pp. 289–90).

10 He said this at a panel discussion at Manly Writers' Festival, 16 March 2024. See 'Australia's Matildas: Their 50-year "overnight success" and what it means for the Australian sporting landscape', Manly Writers' Festival website, 2024.

8 17 Minutes Under Saturday Night Lights

1 'Socceroos goalkeeper Andrew Redmayne wins penalty shootout with dancing antics', *ABC News*, 14 June 2022.

2 Cheek Media [@cheekmedia.co], 'I'm at the pub …' [post], Instagram, 31 July 2023.

3 Marissa Lordanic, 'The Matildas' moment: Each penalty had its own story to tell', *ESPN*, 14 August 2023; Stav Davidson, Abby Coleman & Matty Acton [hosts], 'The Scoop' [podcast], *Stav, Abby & Matt—B105 Brisbane*, 14 August 2023.

4 Cheek Media [@cheekmedia.co], 'no baguettes tonight slayers' [post], Instagram, 12 August 2023.

5 James Cooney, 'Eye-opening charts show how the Matildas completely changed the way Aussies perform one everyday task during their dream run at the World Cup', *Daily Mail Australia*, 21 August 2023.

6 'Aloisi "happy to be relegated" as epic moment in Aussie football history has Matildas legend in "tears"', *Fox Sports*, 12 August 2023.

7 Kieran Pender, 'Mackenzie Arnold: Australia's World Cup hero stays grounded amid Matildas hype', *The Guardian*, 16 August 2023; Bryant Hevesi, 'Richard Marles "resigns" as minister, hands over defence responsibilities to Mackenzie Arnold for Matildas World Cup match', *Sky News*, 16 August 2023.

8 Taryn Heddo, 'Vine Time: Beyond the person who scored that history-making penalty', Matildas website, 24 January 2024.

9 Lordanic, 'The Matildas' moment'; Davidson, Coleman & Acton [hosts], 'The Scoop' [podcast], 14 August 2023.

10 National Library of Australia, 'Book event: The Matilda Effect with Fiona Crawford and Grace Gill' [video], *YouTube*, 30 August 2023.

11 Quoted in Joanna Tweedie, 'The Matildas' 2023 legacy: A line in the sand', *BroadAgenda*, 29 August 2023.

12 Many fans kindly shared their stories with me via social media; I have included as many as I could within the word limit. Those that weren't included were only due to word limit or because I already had a similar story. But a huge thankyou to everyone who so generously shared their stories. I'm hoping there will be many more opportunities for them to come to light in other books, articles, musicals, movies …

13 Full disclosure: they are my brother and sister-in-law.

14 See endnotes 5 and 13 in Chapter 2 for information about about the contention around the First Matildas.

15 Mostafa Rachwani, 'Barnaby Joyce admits watching wrong Matildas game after pub showed July friendly', *The Guardian*, 14 August 2023.

16 Ellen van Neerven, 'Murri fan's Matildas diary', *Siren Sport*, 20 July – 19 August 2023 (12 August entry).

17 Tony Magee, 'Orchestral concert goes nuts over the (Matildas') score', *CBR City News*, 13 August 2023.

18 Joshua Thomas, 'Matildas make their way across Australian stadiums in an unprecedented cross-code collaboration', *Optus Sport*, 11 August 2023.

19 Triple M, 'The Triple M box erupts as the Matildas beat France: Triple M Footy' [video], *YouTube*, 12 August 2023.

20 Dylan Alcott [@dylanalcott], 'My god closest I've ever been to standing up!!!' [post], Instagram, 12 August 2023.

21 'Football Australia celebrates landmark FIFA Women's World Cup and record-breaking success', Football Australia website, 4 August 2023.

22 Jimmy Rees [@jimmyrees], 'Everyone in Australia rn!!! What a bunch of LEGENDS!!!' [video], TikTok, 15 August 2023.

23 See 'Champions of change: Mackenzie Arnold and Tony Gustavsson' (Sydney Opera House, 10 June 2024), Vivid Sydney website, 2024.

24 ABC iView, 'Such amazing soccer pioneers' [Facebook post and video], 13 June 2024; see also Samantha Lewis, '"A bunch of ratbag, lesbian feminists": The coming-out

story of the Adelaide Armpits, Australia's first LGBTQIA+ football club', *ABC News*, 19 June 2022.

25 Anika Wells MP [@anikawellsmp], 'Mission Impossible: finding a @matildas goalkeeper jersey …' [post], Instagram, 28 February 2024.

26 Pre-wrap is medical gauze that goes under tape. Players such as Carpenter wear it in the absence of being allowed other types of headbands. For more information about the origins of Raso's ribbons and Carpenter's pre-wrap headband, see, for example, Charlotte Begg, '"I never knew that." The hidden meaning behind the Matildas' hair accessories', *Mamamia*, 14 August 2023.

27 Oli. [@oliclothing], 'One of the busiest weeks ever …' [post], Instagram, 25 August 2023; David Adams, '"So many of you on the website that it crashed": Perth clothing label scores big with tribute tee for Matildas goalie Mackenzie Arnold', *Women's Agenda*, 25 August 2023.

28 Samantha Rogers, 'Matildas captain Sam Kerr wears Perth brand Oli Clothing's t-shirt honouring Mackenzie Arnold', *Perth Now*, 24 October 2023.

9 We'll Always Have That Sam Kerr Goal

1 'Cultural Panel's success highlighted amid NAIDOC Week and Matariki celebrations', Inside FIFA website, 7 July 2023.

2 'Four images that defined 2023', *Australian Photography*, 13 December 2023.

3 Cheek Media [@cheekmedia.co], 'oh and someone check on Barnaby Joyce …' [post], Instagram, 16 August 2023.

4 ABC iView, 'Such amazing soccer pioneers' [Facebook post and video], 13 June 2024; see also Samantha Lewis, '"A bunch of ratbag, lesbian feminists": The coming-out story of the Adelaide Armpits, Australia's first LGBTQIA+ football club', *ABC News*, 19 June 2022.

5 'Football Australia celebrates hosting the most successful FIFA Women's World Cup ever', Football Australia website, 22 August 2023.

6 KEEPUP [@keepupau], 'We'll always have that Sam Kerr goal [tweet], Twitter/X, 16 August 2023.

7 National Library of Australia, 'Book event: The Matilda Effect with Fiona Crawford and Grace Gill' [video], *YouTube*, 30 August 2023.

8 Alexis Ohanian [@alexisohanion], 'I've been saying it since 2019. Facts don't care about your feelings: people want to watch women's sports …' [tweet], Twitter/X, 15 July 2022.

9 Wendell Hussey, 'Sydney Matildas fan's heartbreak soothed by unexpected 3 hour catch up with 100,000 closest mates', *Betoota Advocate*, n.d.

10 Third or Fourth Is Actually Very Good

1 Chloe Dalton [host], 'Managing the Matildas: General Manager Gina Rees' [podcast], *The [Female] Athlete Project*, 16 July 2024.

2 Joey Lynch, 'Gustavsson defends lack of rotations, Simon selection at WWC', *ESPN*, 19 August 2023.

3 Billie Eder, 'The Matilda who ran almost two marathons at the World Cup', *Sydney Morning Herald*, 22 August 2023.

4 Lynch, 'Gustavsson defends lack of rotations'; Isobel Cootes, 'Kyah Simon still isn't "ready to play many minutes" 7 days out from the Women's World Cup', *Optus Sport*, 13 July 2023.
5 Ibid.
6 Saleem Al-Fahad, 'Matildas re-ignite World Cup hopes with miracle in Montpelier', *SBS Arabic24*, 14 June 2023; 'Chloe Logarzo reflects on the Miracle in Montpellier' [video], Matildas website, 16 June 2019.
7 Samantha Lewis, 'Matildas beat stubborn Uzbekistan 3–0 in first leg of Olympic qualifying play-off', *ABC News*, 24 February 2024; Joey Lynch, 'Michelle Heyman hits four as Matildas thrash Uzbekistan 10–0 to reach Paris Olympics', *The Guardian*, 29 February 2024.
8 Michelle K Ryan & S Alexander Haslam, 'The Glass Cliff: Evidence that women are over-represented in precarious leadership positions', *British Journal of Management*, 16(2), 2005, pp. 81–90.
9 'AIS pursues gender equality in High Performance Coaching', Australian Institute of Sport website, 1 November 2023.
10 Kieran Pender, 'Not a pinnacle but a preview as Matildas reboot for Olympic gold', *The Guardian*, 21 August 2023.
11 Kieran Pender, 'Matildas' loss to Sweden falls short in a World Cup that surpassed expectations', *The Guardian*, 20 August 2023.
12 Threat Matrix & FIFA/FIFPRO, *Social Media Protection Service: FIFA Women's World Cup Australia and New Zealand 2023: Full Tournament Analysis*, FIFA/FIFPRO, Zurich, 2023, pp. 6, 14, 16.
13 Kim Toffoletti, Caitlin McGrane & Sarah Reddan, *Addressing Online Harm in Australian Women's Sport: Project Report*, Deakin University, Burwood, Vic., 2024, pp. 4, 5, 10, 16.
14 Ibid., p. 15.
15 Vita Pilkingron, 'It's not just retiring athletes who need mental health support—young sportspeople need it, too', *The Conversation*, 23 May 2024.
16 Marnie Vinall, 'There is a word this former Matilda's wife has banned her from using', *Sydney Morning Herald*, 21 July 2023.
17 'Matildas drop one spot in FIFA rankings after finishing fourth at Women's World Cup', *ABC News*, 25 August 2023.
18 Joey Lynch, 'Tony Gustavsson: Matildas would have failed if knocked out in group stage', *ESPN*, 30 July 2023.
19 Taryn Heddo, 'Gustavsson: "It makes you feel alive ... This is what life is about"', Football Australia website, 13 August 2023.
20 Joshua Thomas, 'Matildas miss out on a medal, but Tony Gustavsson believes they've won "something bigger" after Women's World Cup heroics', *Optus Sport*, 19 August 2023.
21 Vince Rugari, '"We're winners, no matter what": Sam Kerr reflects on the best month of her life', *Sydney Morning Herald*, 18 August 2023.
22 Samuel Leighton-Dore [@samleightondore], 'Third or fourth is actually very good!! ...' [post], Instagram, 19 August 2023.

23 Isobel Cootes, 'Matildas surprised by Nikki Webster singing their Women's World Cup song "Strawberry Kisses"', *Optus Sport*, 20 August 2023.

24 Gemma Ferguson, 'Matildas gifted keys to the city after FIFA Women's World Cup third-place playoff in Brisbane', *ABC News*, 20 August 2023.

25 Tory Shepherd, 'Albanese government to pledge $200m for women's sport after Matildas inspire Australia', *The Guardian*, 19 August 2023.

26 Mike Meehall Wood, 'Queensland to celebrate Matildas' legacy with funding boost—but most of it is already going to Rugby and AFL', *The Roar*, 22 August 2023.

27 'Football Australia celebrates vibrant CommBank Matildas mural at iconic Bondi Beach', Football Australia website, 7 August 2023; 'Giant mural to celebrate the Matildas at Accor Stadium', Austadiums website, 21 August 2023.

28 Alana Schetzer, 'Pearson snubbed as newspaper names horse as Sportswoman of the Year', *Sydney Morning Herald*, 23 December 2012.

29 James Vyver, 'Women are under-represented among public statues across Australia, but the tide is turning', *ABC News*, 22 September 2023.

30 Ibid.

31 Quoted in Dan Colasimone, 'If you don't think the Matildas deserve a statue for their World Cup exploits, you haven't been paying attention', *ABC News*, 1 September 2023.

32 Tanja Kovac, '"Our equal state": No-one does gender equity like Victoria', *Women's Agenda*, 31 August 2023; Vyver, 'Women are under-represented among public statues across Australia'.

11 The Final (Straw)

1 Victor Sojo [@victorsojo], 'Choosing between two colonist nations ...' [tweet], Twitter/X, 16 August 2023.

2 Ellen van Neerven, 'Murri fan's Matildas diary', *Siren Sport*, 20 July – 19 August 2023 (20 July entry).

3 Joshua Thomas, 'Why history beckons for whichever team can win the FIFA Women's World Cup 2023', *Optus Sport*, 12 August 2023.

4 'Prince William is president of England's Football Association. So why didn't he go to the final?', *SBS News*, 21 August 2023.

5 'Spain captain and Women's World Cup hero Olga Carmona learns of father's death after final victory', *ABC News*, 21 August 2023.

6 Laia Cervelló Herrero, 'Inside Spain's turbulent Women's World Cup build-up: Protest, peace talks and now an uneasy truce', *The Athletic*, 20 July 2023.

7 Sid Lowe, 'Women's World Cup: Spain pick three of 15 players who quit national side in 2022', *The Guardian*, 13 June 2023.

8 'Aitana Bonmati: "The recognition of fellow players is the most beautiful thing in football"', FIFPRO website, 16 January 2024.

9 Lucia Garcia, 'I stood up for our rights. This is my story', *Players' Tribune*, 14 December 2023.

10 GQ Spain [@gqspain], 'Jenni Hermoso es Mujer del Año GQ 2023 ...' [post], Instagram, 28 November 2023.

11 Sam Mewis, 'World Cup is an opportunity for exposure, but does it help in fight for fair treatment?', *The Athletic*, 23 July 2023.
12 Suzanne Wrack, 'Luis Rubiales' actions are not abnormal, they are symptomatic of the system', *The Guardian*, 26 August 2023.
13 Annabel Crabb, 'An infamous Spanish kiss overshadowed meritorious women doing their job—can you believe it?', *ABC News*, 29 August 2023.
14 Ibid.
15 Alex Kirkland, 'Rubiales' mother goes on hunger strike in church over FA row', *ESPN*, 28 August 2023.
16 Suzanne Wrack, 'Piers Morgan's weak line of questioning allowed Rubiales to appear reasonable', *The Guardian*, 13 September 2023.
17 Wrack, 'Luis Rubiales' actions are not abnormal, they are symptomatic of the system'; 'Spanish soccer president refuses to resign after kissing player', *Just Women's Sports*, 25 August 2023.
18 Ashifa Kassam, '"It's over": World Cup kiss becomes Spanish football's #MeToo moment', *The Guardian*, 28 August 2023.
19 PA Sports Staff, 'Spanish football in civil war as 81 players go on strike over president's explosive U-turn', *Optus Sport*, 26 August 2023.
20 Charlotte Harpur & Ben Burrows, 'Luis Rubiales three-year football ban confirmed by FIFA after appeal dismissed', *The Athletic*, 26 January 2024.
21 'UEFA takes note of Luis Rubiales' resignation', UEFA website, 11 September 2023.
22 Michelle K Ryan & S Alexander Haslam, 'The Glass Cliff: Evidence that women are over-represented in precarious leadership positions', *British Journal of Management*, 16(2), 2005, pp. 81–90.
23 PA Media, 'Jenni Hermoso "received threats"' after Luis Rubiales World Cup controversy', *The Guardian*, 7 November 2023.
24 'Gianni Infantino hails transformational FIFA Women's World Cup', Inside FIFA website, 18 August 2023.
25 Spencer Nusbaum, 'FIFA's Gianni Infantino instructs women to "pick the right battles"', *Washington Post*, 19 August 2023.
26 Lindsay Gibbs, 'You first, Gianni Infantino', *Power Plays*, 18 August 2023.
27 Sean Ingle, '"I feel gay, disabled … like a woman too!": Infantino makes bizarre attack on critics', *The Guardian*, 19 November 2022.
28 Marina Hyde, 'Lionesses, feeling let down by men? Don't worry, Gianni Infantino will explain how to fight those battles', *The Guardian*, 18 August 2023.
29 Meg Linehan, 'Luis Rubiales is latest father to hide behind his daughters: The excuses must stop', *The Athletic*, 2 September 2023.
30 'FIFA president praises Australia and New Zealand for Women's World Cup' [video], *ABC News*, 21 August 2023.
31 'Australia will not bid for 2034 World Cup, with Saudi Arabia set to win hosting rights', *ABC News*, 31 October 2023.
32 'PFA Post: Women's World Cup prize money explained', Professional Footballers Australia website, 22 June 2023; Brianna Boecker, 'The Matildas call out FIFA's unequal World Cup prize money in unifying video', *Women's Agenda*, 17 July 2023; 'Gianni

Infantino announces significant investment increase for FIFA Women's World Cup', Inside FIFA website, 17 March 2023.

33 Josh Sim, 'Fifa president: "World Cup equal pay would not solve anything"', SportsPro Media website, 18 August 2023.

34 Asif Burhan, 'Men and women split over equal prize money in women's soccer', *Forbes*, 26 September 2023.

35 'New payment model guarantees support for every FIFA Women's World Cup 2023 team and player', Inside FIFA website, 9 June 2023.

36 'FIFPRO statement: Nigeria women's national team', FIFPRO website, 8 August 2023.

12 The Olympics (and the Knee That Stopped the Nation)

1 Jordan Bakhsh, 'What was the true nature of the "Matildas Effect"? New research shows it was profound, but uneven', *The Conversation*, 22 November 2023.

2 Blake Kagi, 'Matildas coach Tony Gustavsson speaks of pride at team's role in growing soccer in Australia', *ABC News*, 25 October 2023; Jack Snape, 'Matildas sell out 12th-straight stadium for Olympics qualifier', *The Guardian*, 21 December 2023; A-Leagues, 'Matildas' boss Tony Gustavsson reacts to 100,000 Matildas tickets being sold!' [video], *YouTube*, 26 October 2023.

3 Mel Buttle [@melbuttle], 'Good idea? #football #soccer #samkerr' [video], TikTok, 15 January 2024; FW (Future Women), 'Do the Matildas accept ACL donations? We volunteer as a tribute' [post], LinkedIn, 9 January 2024.

4 Jordyn Beazley, 'Oversimplifying a serious matter or a fair cop—were Sam Kerr's alleged words really racist?', *The Guardian*, 9 March 2024.

5 Michael Lynch, '"Suck on that": Kerr's blunt message after Matildas' stunning win', *Sydney Morning Herald*, 14 June 2019.

6 Missing Perspectives [@missingperspectives], 'Overnight it was revealed that Sam Kerr allegedly …' [post], Instagram, 7 March 2023; TEDx Talks, 'Reverse discrimination? It doesn't exist … but "tokenism" does: Antoinette Lattouf, TEDxSydney' (video), *YouTube*, 19 October 2022. Missing Perspectives is a media company that aims to provide coverage and storytelling to fill gaps in media coverage of women.

7 Tiffany Turnbull, 'How retired Australian striker earned Olympic comeback', *BBC News*, 24 July 2024.

8 Sacha Pisani, 'Michelle Heyman's beautiful reaction to Matildas recall as "weird" Sam Kerr déjà vu emerges', A-Leagues website, 24 February 2024.

9 Matildas [@matildas], 'We asked a special friend to help us announce our #Paris2024 Round 3 Olympic Qualifiers squad …' [video], TikTok, 7 February 2024.

10 Fran Kelly [host], 'Katrina Gorry + Michelle Heyman: Football is just the start' [podcast], *Yours Queerly*, 26 February 2024.

11 'Paris 2024: The first games to achieve full gender parity', International Olympic Committee, 9 March 2023.

12 Graham Dunbar, 'Paris Olympic competition nears total gender parity. Take a look at the athlete gender breakdown', *AP News*, 18 July 2024.

13 Gregory Quin, Elodie Wipf & Fabien Ohl, 'Media coverage of the Athens Olympic Games by the French press: The Olympic Games Effect in *L'Équipe* and *Le Monde*',

in Jorid Hovden, Toni Bruce & Pirrko Markula (eds), *Sportswomen at the Olympics: A Global Content Analysis of Newspaper Coverage*, Sense, Leiden, 2010, pp. 103–14 (p. 106).

14 See, for example, 'The women's medal tally following Day 7 of the 2024 Paris Olympics', *Women's Agenda*, 3 August 2024.

15 Missing Perspectives [@missingperspectives], 'Thoughts and prayers to Australia's female athletes who are really carrying the load xx' [post], Instagram, 30 July 2024.

16 Missing Perspectives [@missingperspec], 'BREAKING: Cam McEvoy swims like a girl to win gold for Australia' [tweet], Twitter/X, 3 August 2024.

17 Wendell Hussey, 'Gender medal gap blows out to an unprecedented 800% disparity', *Betoota Advocate*, 3 August 2024.

18 Mel Browne [@melbrowne.money], 'POV: if we addressed the Gold Medal Gender Gap like we address the Gender Wage Gap …' [post], Instagram, 1 August 2024.

19 Shireen Ahmed, 'When women were forced to choose between faith and football', *Global Sport Matters*, 21 May 2018.

20 Samantha Lewis, 'Lydia Williams's emotional Matildas farewell showed the indelible mark she has left on Australian sport', *ABC News*, 4 June 2024.

21 Lydia Williams, 'Dear Matildas', *Player's Tribune*, 30 July 2024.

22 The Croissants [@croissants_on_tour], 'TBC' [story], Instagram, 3 August 2024 (no longer available but viewed by the author).

23 Emily Keogh, 'USWNT drops to 5th in latest FIFA ranking, lowest place ever', *ESPN*, 14 June 2024.

24 Samantha Lewis, 'FIFA deducts Canada six points and bans coaches after Paris Olympics drone spying scandal', *ABC News*, 28 July 2024.

25 Kieran Pender, 'Matildas to again call on "never say die" spirit after nightmare start to Olympic campaign', *The Guardian*, 26 July 2024.

26 James Hilsum, 'Barbra Banda becomes second-most expensive women's player ever after joining Orlando Pride on four-year contract', Eurosport website, 8 March 2024.

27 Wendell Hussey, 'Matildas secure easy victory that was never in doubt after cruising past Zambia in group stage', *Betoota Advocate*, 29 July 2024.

28 Isobel Cootes, '"Obviously, that was s***": Tony Gustavsson apologises for Matildas drama', *Optus Sport*, 29 July 2024.

29 Samantha Lewis, 'Miraculous Matildas escape death against Zambia, but can they escape their Paris Olympics group?', *ABC News*, 29 July 2024.

30 See The Roar [@theroarsports], 'Robbie Slater has again LAUNCHED at the Matildas—and Football Australia—as the fallout continues from their Olympic disaster …' [post], Instagram, 2 August 2023.

31 The Women's Game [@womensgamemib], 'A stream of Sam Kerr and Kristie Mewis watching the Australia vs. USWNT game would be epic' [post], Instagram, 30 July 2024.

32 Just Women's Sports [@justwomenssports], 'Missed this sportsmanship in today's USA vs. Australia match' [post], Instagram, 1 August 2024.

33 Isobel Cootes, 'Matildas suffer 2–1 loss to the United States to end their Olympic campaign in Paris 2024', *Optus Sport*, 1 August 2024.

34 AAP, 'Tony Gustavsson departs as Matildas coach after early exit at Paris Olympics', *The Guardian*, 1 August 2024.

35 Emily Keogh, 'Marta shown red card in potential Brazil Olympics farewell', *ESPN*, 1 August 2024; 'Brazil beats France to keep Marta's Olympic dream alive', *ESPN*, 4 August 2024.
36 Samantha Lewis, 'Obrigado, Marta—Brazilian legend makes way for the future after Paris Olympics final', ABC Sport, 11 August 2024.
37 Samantha Lewis, 'Matildas' Paris Olympics exit is the reality check Australian football has been bracing for', *ABC Sport*, 1 August 2024.
38 'Australia announced as host country for 2026 Women's Asian Cup', *ABC News*, 16 May 2024.

13 Our Roman Empire

1 Tim Biggs, 'Matildas, Barbenheimer top Australians' Google searches for 2023', *Brisbane Times*, 12 December 2023.
2 'The Matildas waltz in as Australia's Word of the Year', Australian National University website, 15 November 2023.
3 Lisa Murray, 'The 10 most culturally powerful people in Australia in 2023', *Australian Financial Review Magazine*, 28 September 2023.
4 Tangentially, Barbie made an additional appearance around the 2023 Women's World Cup. Meshelle Ryan's niece's favourite player is Sam Kerr, so she named her Barbie 'Sam'. That Barbie, coincidentally, looks quite a bit like Kerr, further aided by the fact that Ryan's mother sewed the doll a matching yellow shirt. Ryan's niece once took the Barbie to a game and had a photo with Kerr with it, which Kerr later posted to her own social media. It was fascinatingly meta.
5 Vince Rugari, '$4 million in four days: Why the "Matildas effect" isn't slowing down', *Sydney Morning Herald*, 28 May 2024; Matildas, 'A history-making night ...' [Facebook post], 4 June 2024.
6 See Her Way [@abbieherway], 'It's just the beginning' [post], Instagram, 4 June 2024.
7 This relates to a recent TikTok trend in which women asked men how often they thought of the Roman Empire. The answer: men think about the Roman Empire surprisingly frequently. For more information, see, for example, 'The Roman empire: Why men just can't stop thinking about it', *The Guardian*, 19 September 2023; Lia Walsh, 'What fascinates men about the Roman Empire? We asked experts about the TikTok trend', *ABC News*, 1 October 2023.
8 Marion Stell & Heather Reid, *Women in Boots: Football and Feminism in the 1970s*, Australian Scholarly Publishing, Melbourne, 2020.
9 Full disclosure: Louise is my sister.
10 Isobel Cootes, 'West Ham goalkeeper Mackenzie Arnold shares her hearing loss journey with the world', *Optus Sport*, 17 April 2023.
11 Australian Community Media, 'Amy Poehler and Seth Meyers react to Matildas tearful video' [video], *YouTube*, 7 June 2024.
12 Nicholas Jordan, 'Australian supermarket sliced cheese taste test: "Like eating a reconstituted swamp of plastic and milk"', *The Guardian*, 22 May 2024.
13 'Audio Descriptive Commentary training kicks off ahead of FIFA Women's World Cup 2023', Inside FIFA website, 29 March 2023.
14 Susan Harris Rimmer, *Independent Human Rights Context Assessment: Australia & New Zealand*, Griffith University, Nathan, Qld, 2019.

15 The Project [@theprojecttv], 'The Matildas [*sic*] secret weapon has been revealed …' [video], TikTok, 21 August 2023.
16 Isobel Cootes, 'Why Matildas striker Mary Fowler plays in gloves', *Optus Sport*, 5 August 2023.
17 Fiona Crawford, *The Matilda Effect*, Melbourne University Press, Carlton, Vic., 2023, pp. 98–9.
18 Samantha Lewis, 'Meet the Indigenous artist who helped design the 2023 Women's World Cup branding', *ABC News*, 6 November 2021; 'Chern'ee's artwork adorns the FIFA 2023 Women's World Cup', Chern'ee Sutton website, n.d.
19 Jack Snape, 'Women's World Cup ticket sales break record with close to 1.4m sold on eve of 2023 tournament', *The Guardian*, 19 July 2023.
20 'Staggering statistics demonstrate FIFA Women's World Cup growth', Inside FIFA website, 4 August 2023.
21 Mel Buttle [@melindabuttle], 'In light of Hayley Raso not replying to my numerous DM's, I married my partner instead …' [post], Instagram, 18 March 2024.
22 Mel Buttle, 'You can't glance a screen this week without seeing Sam Kerr's face pop up …' [Facebook post], 11 August 2023.
23 Samantha Lewis, 'Lydia Williams's emotional Matildas farewell showed the indelible mark she has left on Australian sport', *ABC News*, 4 June 2024.
24 Joshua Thomas, 'Former Matilda Michelle Heyman reveals how little players were paid for quarter-final run at Women's World Cup in 2015', *Optus Sport*, 12 August 2023; Isobel Cootes, 'What players at the FIFA Women's World Cup 2023 will be paid', *Optus Sport*, 20 August 2023.
25 Caitlin Murray, 'USWNT–US Soccer pay dispute settlement: What the decision means, what happens next', *ESPN*, 24 February 2022.
26 'MAS chants', Matildas Active Support website, n.d.
27 See Henry Hanson, 'How the Matildas effect has inspired Australia's next generation of women's blind and deaf footballers', *ABC Sport*, 29 June 2024.
28 Basket carriers accompany the athletes to the lanes and collect and remove their personal effects from the track; Montague's recollection is that she was on Lane 5.
29 Chloe Mac Donnell, '"Sport has infiltrated all of fashion": Anna Wintour on Vogue World, sport and UK arts', *The Guardian*, 11 June 2024.
30 For example, see Jessica Montague, 'The secret weapon that spurs on Sam Kerr and the Matildas', *Vogue Australia*, 18 July 2023; Vogue Australia, 'Go behind-the-scene[s] of the Matilda[s'] Vogue shoot with Nike' [video], *YouTube*, 17 August 2023.
31 See, for example, 'Vogue's guide to styling a jersey', Vogue Australia website, 18 May 2023; 'Vogue's guide to styling 5 of our favourite Women's World Cup jerseys', Vogue Australia website, 16 August 2023.
32 One can't help but wonder if this had something to do with it being one of the first times girls and women could obtain flattering, women's-cut kit. Technically, the first women's-cut option was in 2019, but the pattern it featured was the intense 'Spew 2.0' print. While it was out of the Matildas' hands—brands make the call on these—it seemed like a contemporary nod to previous Matildas' kits; even incorporating First Nations artists' designs or important historical and cultural references would have been a better way to go. Instead, we got a jersey similar to all other Nike-sponsored countries,

most of which looked like they'd been generated by AI. To be fair, it didn't hamper sales, and the teal away jersey is a stunning colour.

33 Fiona Crawford, '7 of the most important moments in Matildas history', *Vogue*, 7 August 2023.

34 Kris Marano [host], *Game Changers: Trailblazing Stories from WA Women in Soccer* [podcast series], 13 July 2023.

35 ABC News In-depth, 'Matildas, motherhood and making it big with footballer Katrina Gorry | Australian Story' [video], *YouTube*, 19 February 2024.

36 'Football Australia launch the Our Game Women & Non-Binary Persons in Media Program', Football Australia website, 31 May 2023.

37 Chloe Dalton [host], 'Managing the Matildas: General Manager Gina Rees' [podcast], *The [Female] Athlete Project*, 16 July 2024; Chloe Dalton [host], 'Managing the Matildas: Sports scientist Georgia Brown' [podcast], *The [Female] Athlete Project*, 8 July 2024.

38 'The 2024 TDA x Nike Training Squad', The Daily Aus website, n.d.

39 Ibid.; *Change Our Game: Representation of Women in Sports News Coverage 2022–23*, Victorian Government Office for Women in Sport and Recreation, Melbourne, 2023, pp. 16–17.

40 Janine Mikosza, ed. Heather Reid, *Inching Forward: Newspaper Coverage and Portrayal of Women's Sport in Australia*, Womensport Australia, O'Connor, ACT, 1997.

41 Kieran Pender, 'Progress but a long way from parity', *News & Reviews Magazine*, 2 August 2023.

42 Ibid.

43 Cache, 'Tobin Heath: "Women's sports is the future of sports"' [video], *YouTube*, 21 June 2024.

44 'Secretary General speaks at Gender Equality Symposium', Inside FIFA website, 28 July 2024.

45 'Celebrating the Beyond Greatness Speaker Series: Empowering women's voices', Inside FIFA website, 8 August 2023.

46 *Legacy '23: Post-Tournament Report, February 2024*, Football Australia, Sydney, 2024, p. 75.

47 'The Sports Bra Project', WomenSport Australia website, n.d.

48 See, for example, ABC News (Australia), 'The evolution of women's football in Australia: Ticket to the Cup' [video], *YouTube*, 21 June 2023.

14 The Matilda (After) Effect

1 St Catherine's School Sydney [@stcatherinessyd], 'It was such an incredible honour to have @Matildas and @sydneyfootballclub player Cortnee Vine join us this morning …' [post], Instagram, 19 September 2023.

2 Catherine Ordway, 'Reflections on the FIFA Women's World Cup' [post], LinkedIn, 24 August 2023.

3 Fiona Crawford, *The Matilda Effect*, Melbourne University Press, Carlton, Vic., 2023, p. 6.

4 Catie Powers, 'How the Matildas have changed women's sport in Australia forever', *Australian Women's Weekly*, 22 August 2023.

5 See Oriol Gasquez, 'Why you need to learn the basic principles of Futures studies', *Medium*, 13 December 2016.
6 Samantha Lewis, 'The Matildas are entering their Taylor Swift era, so what does that mean for them and for us?', *ABC News*, 4 November 2023.
7 'The Overton window', Mackinac Center for Public Policy website, 2019.
8 Patricia Karvelas, 'The rise and rise of the Matildas is about more than one team. It's a feminist cultural reckoning for our daughters', *ABC News*, 16 August 2023.
9 See, for example, '"Backflip incoming": Sam Kerr delivers again as relentless goalscoring continues', *The Guardian*, 15 May 2023.
10 Rebecca Shaw, 'Old blokes at the pub and teenage boys on the train—Matildas fans are now everywhere, and I couldn't be happier', *The Guardian*, 11 August 2023.
11 See, for example, Sarah Tillot & Diarmuid Hurley, 'Connection, camaraderie and belonging: Why the Matildas could be making you a sports fan for the very first time', *The Conversation*, 16 August 2023.
12 Dani Maher, 'A psychologist explains why the Matildas have suddenly awoken your inner sports fan', *Harper's Bazaar*, n.d.
13 See Kasey Symons & Paul Bowell, '"Felt alienated by the men's game": How the culture of women's sport has driven record Matildas viewership', *The Conversation*, 17 August 2023.
14 M Livingston, *The Association Between State of Origin and Assaults in Two Australian States*, Centre for Alcohol Policy Research, La Trobe University, Bundoora, Vic., 2018, p. 6.
15 Mary Dulwich, 'Women's Aid: "He's coming home"', MHP Group website, 13 December 2022.
16 Georgia Roberts, 'Seventeen more women killed by men than at this same time last year, government launches intimate partner homicide counter', *ABC News*, 1 July 2024. Note that figures continued to climb throughout the year and the number of women killed will likely be even higher by the time this book is published.
17 Lisa Sugiura, 'Why women would prefer to be alone in the woods with a bear than a man', *The Conversation*, 3 May 2024.
18 Lucy Small [@saltwaterpilgrim] & Equal Pay for Equal Play [@equalpayforequalplay_], 'This has to fkn end' [post], Instagram, 28 April 2023.
19 Used widely in films and books, the MacGuffin is a goal, object, concept or event crucial to the characters' motivation and that triggers plot advancement. See, for example, '7 common plot devices and how to use them in your writing', MasterClass website, 11 September 2021.
20 Small & Equal Pay for Equal Play, 'This has to fkn end' [post], Instagram.
21 *Legacy '23: Post-Tournament Report, February 2024*, Football Australia, Sydney, 2024, p. 69.
22 'Global interest in women's sports is on the rise', Nielsen Sports website, 2018.
23 Cheek Media [@cheekmedia.co], 'Maybe I'm wrong, but I can't imagine an Australia three years ago …' [post], Instagram, 12 August 2023.
24 Symons & Bowell, '"Felt alienated by the men's game"'; see also Katherine W Jones, 'Female fandom: Identity, sexism, and men's professional football in England', *Sociology of Sport Journal*, 25(4), pp. 516–37 and 'Sexuality and gender perspectives on sports

ethics', Clearinghouse for Sport website, 2022; Catherine Ordway & Kasey Symons, 'It doesn't happen by magic: Creatively exploring the process of changemaking in sport through Moya Dodd and FIFA', in Lee McGowan & Kasey Symons (eds), *Intersections of Sport and Society in Creative Writing*, Springer Nature, Singapore, 2023, pp. 175–90.

25 Hunter Fujak & Heath McDonald, 'Dreading footy season? You're not alone—20% of Australians are self-described sport haters', *The Conversation*, 5 March 2024.

26 Carrie Dunn, 'No matter how glossy the top level of the women's game gets …' [post], LinkedIn, 10 June 2024.

27 Alison Schenk, 'Local woman actually enjoys watching sports now that messy buns and people being nice to each other on the field exists', *Betoota Advocate*, n.d.

28 Mike Hytner, 'Matildas break new ground as fans scramble for tickets on resale market', *The Guardian*, 12 September 2017.

29 Vince Rugari, 'Olympic send-off in Sydney shapes as Matildas' 14th straight sell-out', *Sydney Morning Herald*, 5 March 2024.

30 Her Way [@abbieherway], 'Symbolic, and personally, very relatable—The men's NSW State of Origin leave the team hotel …' [post], Instagram, 4 June 2024.

31 Missing Perspectives [@missperspectives], 'Former pro soccer player and sports commentator Robbie Slater has argued …' [post], Instagram, 12 June 2024.

32 See, for example, Madeline Hislop, 'Sam Kerr's career defining hat-trick for Chelsea in League Cup final', *Women's Agenda*, 15 March 2021.

33 See, for example, Ed Bourke, 'Salary bump for women's cricket in groundbreaking new pay deal', *Fox Sports*, 3 April 2023.

34 Matt Balmer, 'Katy Perry stuns MCG with "brilliant" WC final show', *Fox Sports*, 8 March 2020.

35 'Australian Cricketers Association confirms fighting fund to support netballers in pay dispute', *ABC News*, 18 October 2023.

36 ABC Sport [@abcsport], '"It makes me really sad" …' [tweet], Twitter/X, 15 October 2023.

37 Emily Patterson, 'Breathtaking injustice exposed by Matildas' potential $6m payday at FIFA Women's World Cup', *nine.com.au*, 9 August 2023.

38 Kasey Symons & Bess Schnioffsky, 'Australia just won the Netball World Cup. Why isn't there room for multiple women's world cups in our sports media?', *The Conversation*, 11 August 2023.

39 Quoted in Madeline Hislop, 'Wallaroos call out Rugby Australia's lip service on pay and conditions', *Women's Agenda*, 21 August 2023; see also 'Wallaroos unite to demand fair treatment from Rugby Australia', *ABC News*, 21 August 2023.

40 See, for example, Jack Snape, '"Real appetite" for women's rugby league with State of Origin set for latest record', *The Guardian*, 6 June 2024; 'Women's State of Origin opener breaks rugby league records', NRL website, 17 May 2024.

41 The [Female] Athlete Project, 'Huge numbers from the women's first ever 3-game State of Origin Series …' [Facebook post], 2 July 2024.

42 Sam Kerr [@samanthakerr20], 'LFG @caitlinclark22' [post], Instagram, 8 April 2024.

43 'The Seven Consulting Opals', Seven Consulting website, 12 March 2024.

44 Optus Sport, 'Patty Mills and his Boomers teammates repping Matildas kits on matchday …' [Facebook post], 15 August 2023.

45 'US rapper Macklemore rocking Aussie sports jerseys during tour down under' [video], *news.com.au*, 15 May 2024.

46 P!nk, 'Thank you, Lydia Williams, for presenting me and Willow with our very own Matildas goalkeeper jerseys …' [Facebook post], 27 February 2024.

47 Penelope Clifton, 'The Wiggles leave the Matildas in stitches with national anthem', *Kidspot*, 28 November 2021.

48 Brianna Boecker, 'Equal pay commitments set for women's sport in NSW, lead [*sic*] by female advocates', *Women's Agenda*, 27 October 2023; 'Balance the Board', Change Our Game website, n.d.

49 This relates to a meme about pointing to something that was established and obvious. More information can be found at Phillip Hamilton, 'Don't make me tap the sign', Know Your Meme website, 21 December 2020.

50 See, for example. 'International Women's Day 2024', UN Women Australia website, 1 March 2024.

51 '#CountHerIn (Oh, and [can] we just get on with it?)', Change Our Game website, 2024.

52 See 'Employer gender pay gaps published for the first time' [media release], Workplace Gender Equality Agency website, 27 February 2024.

53 Phoebe Saintilan, 'Our viral IWD campaign cheekily highlighted the gender pay gap', Missing Perspectives website, 11 March 2024.

54 The [Female] Athlete Project [@thefemaleathleteproject], 'Because sport should be for everyone' [post], Instagram, 1 April 2024.

55 Samantha Lock, 'Sydney's "absurd and wonderful" Progress Shark becomes WorldPride icon', *The Guardian*, 17 February 2023.

56 Lee Wallace & Victoria Rawlings, '"Wouldn't want to be on any other team": The queer joy of watching the Matildas at the "outest" World Cup ever', *The Conversation*, 18 August 2023; Frances Vinall, 'This is the gayest world cup ever and no one's batting an eyelid', *Washington Post*, 16 August 2023.

57 Marnie Vinall [@marnievinall], 'Taking a moment to appreciate the face of Australia this last month has been a gay woman of colour …' [tweet], Twitter/X, 18 August 2023.

58 *Where Will You Find Your Next Leader?*, EY, London, 2015, p. 9.

59 Jack Snape, 'Matildas Effect drives record football sign-ups but puts clubs under pressure', *The Guardian*, 8 February 2024.

60 Rochelle Eime et al., 'Longitudinal trends in sport participation and retention of women and girls', *Frontiers Sports Active Living*, 2, 2020, pp. 1–9; 'More than 1 million teenage girls fall "out of love" with sport' [media release], Women in Sport, 7 March 2022; *Suncorp Australian Youth & Confidence Research 2019*, Suncorp, Brisbane, 2019.

61 Ding Ding et al., 'The "Matildas Effect": Will the FIFA Women's World Cup generate a legacy in Australia?', *Journal of Physical Activity and Health*, 21(1), 2024, pp. 9–10.

15 Not Done—Never Done

1 ''Til It's Done', Matildas website, n.d.

2 Adam Burnett, 'A bedroom door in Qld holds the key to Australia's next football superstar', *Optus Sport*, 24 March 2023.

3 ''Til It's Done', Matildas website, n.d.
4 Olivia Cleal, '"Our work is far from done": Billie Jean King 50 years on From the Battle of the Sexes', *Women's Agenda*, 31 August 2023.
5 Fiona McLachlan, 'It's boom time! (again): Progress narratives and women's sport in Australia', *Journal of Australian Studies*, 43(1), 2019, pp. 7–21.
6 Kasey Symons et al., 'The (un)level playing field: Sport media during COVID-19', *European Sport Management Quarterly*, 22(1), 2021, pp. 55–71.
7 Samantha Lewis, 'Rain, hail or snow: AFC under fire for Young Matildas' snowy pitch at U20 Women's Asian Cup', *ABC News*, 4 March 2024.
8 Sophie Lawson, 'Women's Ballon d'Or mess shows soccer has a long way to go', *ESPN*, 1 November 2023.
9 Tom Garry, 'Manchester United women moved out of training building to accommodate men', *The Guardian*, 26 June 2024.
10 Kelly Burke, 'Mona hangs Picassos in women's toilet in response to court ruling', *The Guardian*, 24 June 2024.
11 Fiona McLachlan, 'It's boom time! (again): Progress narratives and women's sport in Australia', *Journal of Australian Studies*, 43(1), 2019, pp. 7–21.
12 See 'Julia Gillard: After office', National Archives of Australia website, n.d.
13 Ben Smee, 'As the Matildas chase glory in Brisbane, girls nearby are turned away from their overcrowded local club', *The Guardian*, 12 August 2023.
14 Madeline Hislop, 'Win or lose tonight, the Matildas have already achieved so much', *Women's Agenda*, 16 August 2023.
15 Ibid.
16 John Lyons, 'We're seeing women rise to the top and get respect they deserve, from the Matildas to the RBA and ASIS', *ABC News*, 13 August 2023.
17 Sam Buckingham-Jones, 'Matildas lifted Optus brand by almost $1b after cyberattack', *Financial Review*, 5 October 2023; John Lyons, 'We're seeing women rise to the top and get respect they deserve, from the Matildas to the RBA and ASIS', *ABC News*, 13 August 2023.
18 Tegan Jones, 'Matildas prove value of women's sport sponsorship, but what about local clubs and players?', SmartCompany website, 16 August 2023.
19 Asha Barbaschow, 'RIP Commonwealth Bank Dollarmites', *Gizmodo*, 26 October 2021. Please note that I'm not implying here that CommBank is trying to do anything untoward—I'm saying that its sponsorship of the Matildas is a savvy marketing strategy to persuade potential new customers to think well of the bank.
20 Bianca Hrovat, 'Australia's first women's only sports bar to open on Oxford Street', *Sydney Morning Herald*, 26 July 2024.
21 Will Evans, 'Record engagement—Optus Sport's mission to elevate women's football', Ministry of Sport website, 24 September 2023.
22 Ibid.
23 *Impact of the FIFA Women's World Cup 2023 on the Australian Community: Community Perceptions Monitor (CPM) Summary Report*, Australian Sports Commission, Canberra, 2023, pp. 2, 4.
24 Waleed Aly, 'Defend sport, our great unifier', *Sydney Morning Herald*, 1 December 2023.

25 Debi Enker, 'Free TV was considered a dinosaur. The Matildas have changed how we think about it', *Sydney Morning Herald*, 21 August 2023.

26 Cheek Media [@cheekmedia.co], 'Free to air will never be this relevant again' [image], Instagram, 12 August 2023.

27 Kate Allman, 'History-making all-female football commentary lineup is just the beginning', *The Guardian*, 1 March 2024.

28 Liam Mannix, 'A fascinating experiment in how sexism, and racism, affects the way we watch sport', *Sydney Morning Herald*, 9 November 2021.

29 Rebecca Sowden, 'Best women's sport campaigns of 2023: Top ten women's sport campaigns of the year', *Team Heroine*, 1 January 2024.

30 Suzanne Wrack, 'Meet the AI-created football expert aiming to teach Infantino a lesson', *The Guardian*, 22 November 2023.

31 Marcus Christenson, 'Lewes FC become first professional club to pay women and men equally', *The Guardian*, 12 July 2017.

32 Marcel Agency, 'Orange: La Compil des Bleues (English version)' [video], *YouTube*, 30 June 2023.

33 'The Drum Friday July 21' [video], *ABC News*, 21 July 2023.

34 The project is so named because it seeks out 'red links' (placeholder pages for entries not yet written) with the goal of converting them into 'blue links' (fully formed entries).

35 See Eduardo Graells-Garrido, Mounia Lalmas & Filippo Menczer, 'First women, second sex: Gender bias in Wikipedia', in *HT '15: Proceedings of the 26th ACM Conference on Hypertext & Social Media*, Association for Computing Machinery, New York, 2015, pp. 165–74.

36 'Wikipedia Edit-a-thon', Angel City FC website, n.d.; 'Wikipedia: Meetup/LA/Angel City FC WoSo Edit-a-thon 2024', *Wikipedia*, 26 March 2024.

37 'The Matildas hope this World Cup is "just the beginning" of investment in women's football', *SBS News*, 17 August 2023.

38 Isobel Cootes, 'Sam Kerr on her Women's World Cup: "If I hadn't played one minute, it still would have been the best moment of my career"', *Optus Sport*, 18 August 2023.

39 Rachel Allison, Alex Culvin & Stacey Pope, '"They are doing it because they love it": US and English fan perceptions of women footballers as "role models"', *Sport in Society*, 2024, pp. 1–18; Megan Maurice, '"Can I have your shirt?" Access to women athletes should be a privilege, not an entitlement', *The Guardian*, 3 November 2023; Isobel Cootes, 'Rock, paper, scissors for a jersey? The new trend that highlights impossible Matildas task as popularity soars', *Optus Sport*, 2 November 2023.

40 FIFA, FIFPRO & Edith Cowan University, *Multiple Job-Holding in Elite Women's Football*, FIFPRO, Hoofddorp, The Netherlands, 2024.

41 Vince Rugari, '$4 million in four days: Why the "Matildas effect" isn't slowing down', *Sydney Morning Herald*, 28 May 2024.

42 *Legacy '23: Post-Tournament Report, February 2024*, Football Australia, Sydney, 2024, pp. 7, 9.

43 Stephen Conroy, 'Open letter to A-Leagues fans', A-Leagues website, 12 February 2024.

44 Samantha Lewis, 'Did the A-League Women make the most of the Matildas' World Cup legacy?', *ABC News*, 10 May 2024.
45 Jack Snape, 'Kate Jenkins to push gender equality after taking top sports administration job', *The Guardian*, 21 May 2024.
46 Isobel Cootes, 'Canberra United's rare place in Australian football almost didn't happen', *Optus Sport*, 22 November 2022.
47 Jack Snape, 'Canberra United handed government lifeline for next A-League Women season', *The Guardian*, 18 April 2024.
48 Ibid.; see also Sue Read, 'Save Canberra United', Chuffed website, n.d.
49 See Fiona Crawford, *The Matilda Effect*, Melbourne University Press, Carlton, Vic., 2023, pp. 81–2.
50 Snape, 'Canberra United handed government lifeline'.
51 Melanie Anzidei, 'What San Diego Wave sale means for skyrocketing NWSL club valuations', *The Athletic*, 28 March 2024; Reuters, 'Angel City to become world's most valuable women's team with $250m sale', *The Guardian*, 17 July 2024.
52 Samantha Lewis, 'FIFPro to launch groundbreaking "Project ACL" to address knee injury epidemic in women's football', *ABC News*, 30 April 2024.
53 Caroline Criado Perez, *Invisible Women: Exposing Data Bias in a World Designed for Men*, Random House, New York, 2019; see also Emma Sherry et al., 'Researching women in sport development: An intersectional approach', *Sport in Society*, 27(5), 2023.
54 Paige Cockburn, 'Wearing the wrong bra could put you at a greater risk of a knee injury, study suggests', *ABC News*, 24 April 2024.
55 Criado Perez, *Invisible Women*; see also Emma Sherry et al., 'Researching women in sport development: An intersectional approach', *Sport in Society*, 27(5), 2023.
56 Caitlin Cassidy, 'Matildas unveil first period-conscious kit design for Women's World Cup', *The Guardian*, 4 April 2023.
57 Moya Dodd, 'New women's football calendar will stifle club game—FIFA must be open to dialogue', *The Guardian*, 3 June 2024; see also *Matildas 2023 Women's World Cup Report*, Professional Footballers Australia, West Melbourne, 2024, pp. 6, 7, 13 and Samantha Lewis, 'Will FIFA's new international match calendar help or hinder the growth of women's football?', *ABC News*, 7 June 2024.
58 Isobel Cootes, 'Teagan Micah's 6 month journey back to the pitch after Champions League concussion', *Optus Sport*, 9 June 2023.
59 Pub Nab, 'Noran Abaza retires', *Medium*, 29 July 2021.
60 Amy James-Turner, 'Women's football holds immense potential as a lever for climate action', *The Guardian*, 11 June 2024.
61 Shane Wright & Felicity Caldwell, 'Millions in Australia's east face natural disaster risk', *Sydney Morning Herald*, 1 January 2019.
62 Holly Thorpe et al., 'Journalists on a journey: Towards responsible media on transgender participation in sport', *Journalism Studies*, 24(9), 2023, pp. 1238–40.
63 Clint Wheeldon [host], 'Christina Matthews: 12 years is a long time in any job' [podcast], *Best of ABC Sport*, 17 December 2023.
64 Samantha Lewis, 'Moya Dodd: "Denying women in football is like trying to defy gravity"', *The Guardian*, 28 July 2020.

65 Angela Priestley, 'If small groups of women can lift economies, imagine what millions could do?', 21 December 2023.

66 '89% of women in football have experienced discrimination at work, but survey reveals surge of optimism about gender equality in the game', Women in Football website, 19 June 2024.

67 This scene from the *Beckham* documentary relates to David Beckham roasting Victoria Beckham on her efforts to portray herself as working class when her father in fact had a Rolls Royce. The light-hearted moment has inspired memes about saying one thing when the reality is another.

68 FW [@futurewomen], 'This post is for the bossy queens …' [post], Instagram, 12 December 2023.

69 *Gender Equality Action Plan 2019*, Football Federation Australia, Sydney, 2019, p. 10.

70 'ASC welcomes new Chair', Australian Sports Commission website, 20 May 2024.

16 The Past, Future and Patriarchy

1 Walking football is a low-impact, small-sided, accessible version of the game suitable for people returning to or just starting out in the game. For more information, see 'What is walking football?', Play Football website, n.d.

2 Lee McGowan, 'From banned to international glory, women's soccer has sown a rich field for the future', *The Conversation*, 9 February 2017; Fiona Crawford & Lee McGowan, *Never Say Die: The Hundred-Year Overnight Success of Australian Women's Football*, NewSouth Press, Sydney, 2019, p. 23.

3 I was conflicted because I had to be the person who told a little girl she needed to put her sign down. The middle-class white male boomer in front of me was pretty relieved that he didn't have to—that sign was a waving, glitter-covered banner that prohibited others from seeing the match while it was held aloft her tiny body. Sorry, future Matilda, and you're welcome, boomer—I really took one for the team crushing her tiny sign dreams.

4 See, for example, Australian Kitsch [@OzKitsch], 'Petition to rename these guys the Man Tildas' [tweet], Twitter/X, 8 August 2023.

INDEX